The Philosophy of Early Christianity in the Era of Digitalisation

The Philosophy of Early Christianity in the Era of Digitalisation

Edited by

Yip Mei Loh

Cambridge Scholars Publishing

The Philosophy of Early Christianity in the Era of Digitalisation

Edited by Yip Mei Loh

This book first published 2021

Cambridge Scholars Publishing

Lady Stephenson Library, Newcastle upon Tyne, NE6 2PA, UK

British Library Cataloguing in Publication Data
A catalogue record for this book is available from the British Library

Copyright © 2021 by Yip Mei Loh and contributors

All rights for this book reserved. No part of this book may be reproduced, stored in a retrieval system, or transmitted, in any form or by any means, electronic, mechanical, photocopying, recording or otherwise, without the prior permission of the copyright owner.

ISBN (10): 1-5275-6903-9
ISBN (13): 978-1-5275-6903-4

Contents

Acknowledgements vii

Preface viii
Maria John P. Selvamani

Introduction xi
Yip Mei Loh

Chapter One 1
The Process of Social Digitalisation in Russia: Expert Opinions and Developmental Features
Igor Pavlovich Ryazantsev, Maria Podlesnaya,
Vasiliy Pisarevskiy

Chapter Two 35
Taiwanese Contextual Theology in the Age of Digitalisation: Digital Storytelling as A Way of Doing Story Theology
Ya-Tang Chuang

Chapter Three 60
Mimesis, *Diegesis*, *Logos*: Re-Evaluating Greek Concepts toward an Audible Cinema
James Batcho

Chapter Four 85
Augustine and Internet Addiction: Augustine on Desire and Will in the Age of Digitalisation
Andrew Tsz Wan Hung

Chapter Five 116
Justification by Faith and Aristotle's Concepts of *Dunamis* and *Energeia*
Le-Chih Hsieh

CHAPTER SIX 133
ANCIENT PHILOSOPHERS IN THE AGE OF DIGITALISATION
YIP MEI LOH, BERNARD LI

CHAPTER SEVEN 152
NOTES ON TWENTIETH CENTURY TRANSLATION OF GREEK AND LATIN
PHILOSOPHY
MARK EDWARDS

CHAPTER EIGHT 176
THE NEOPLATONIC DEBATE ON EVIL IN LATE ANTIQUITY
CHRISTOPH HORN

Acknowledgements

I am indebted to the Cardinal Yu Pin Foundation for Catholic Studies and the Research Room of Philosophy and Theology, Department of Philosophy, Fu Jen Catholic University, for sponsoring the International Conference of 'The Philosophy of Early Christianity in the Era of Digitalisation', which was held on 6th -7th December, 2019 in Fu Jen Catholic University. I am also grateful to the organizers of the Department of Philosophy and Fu Jen Academia Catholica at Fu Jen Catholic University, who provided me with enormous support. I am much obliged to former President Bernard Li, current Vice President Leszek Niewdana, Chairman of Department of Philosophy Prof. Chien-Shuo Chiu and Prof. Chin Kenpa of Fu Jen Catholic University for the quiet efficiency through which they made this conference possible.

I especially would like to thank Prof. Christoph Horn of Bonn University and Prof. Mark Julian Edwards of Oxford University, who, as well as giving me immeasurable encouragement and assistance as editor of this book publication, stepped up at very late notice to provide excellent contributions of their own to the insights proffered therein. And finally, I must extend my sincere gratitude to Adam Rummens, of Cambridge Scholars Publishing, whose idea it was to bring these essays together, and publish.

Yip Mei Loh

Preface

Maria John P. Selvamani

One of the major impacts of the unprecedented Covid-19 pandemic is the rapid digitalization of many aspects of human society. As the cities were locked down to control the spread of the pandemic, digital platforms replaced the offices, schools, restaurants and even the places of worship. As the Churches were closed, the pastors turned to digital platforms to reach out to their faithful. Virtual worship, which was unthinkable a year ago, has become the norm as the pandemic continues to ravage many countries. This pandemic has forced upon us an era of digitalization which even religions could not resist. This conference, held just before the pandemic, focused on the impact of the digitalization on Christianity.

Early Christian philosophy, which was greatly influenced by the ancient Greek philosophers, plays an important role in understanding the theological development and the history of the nascent Church, and becomes the yardstick in maintaining the orthodoxy and tradition of Christian faith. The study of early Christianity is a much-neglected field in Taiwanese academia. To revive interest in the philosophy of early Christianity and to encourage Christian scholars to engage in the digitalization of modern society, this conference, titled "The Philosophy of Early Christianity in the Era of Digitalization", was held on December 6-7, 2019 at Fu Jen Catholic University, Taiwan and was organized by the Department of Philosophy and Academia Catholica, a research institute on Catholic Studies.

This book is the collection of the papers presented at the conference. The topics range from the philosophical basis of early Christian theology, especially the influence of ancient Greek philosophy, to the influence of digitalization on the society at large and on Christianity in particular. This collection of papers draws from the wisdom of early Christian theology and addresses the impact of digitalization on Christianity in modern times. Apart from providing an overview on this topic, this book, in a special way, focuses on the perspectives from Russia, Hong Kong and Taiwan.

This book first focuses on digitalization as a social process that influences all the spheres of modern human society and the way it affects Christians in understanding and interpreting their faith. Igor Pavlovich Ryazantsev describes the social digitalization process in Russia. He points out that there is a conflicting attitude towards various aspects of digitalization. Though most of the respondents are supportive of the process, there is also deep concern on the risks of digital technology to the economical, sociopolitical and educational institutions of the society.

The rest of the book deals with the philosophy and theology of early Christianity and the impact of digitalization. Ya-Tang Chuang attempts to contextualize the theological reflection for the digital age by proposing a theology of digital story telling. He contends that story telling is a way of theologizing and the digital technology makes this process more accessible and powerful. James Batcho re-evaluates the Greek concepts *Mimesis*, *Diegesis* and *Logos* as applied to audible cinema. The paper by Andrew Tsz Wan Hung explores Augustine's ethics in the light of internet addiction. From Augustine's theory of will, desire and concupiscence, he argues that these concepts and the Augustinian model of lust-habit-addictive necessity, are relevant in understanding the damage that internet addiction causes.

Le-Chih Hsieh argues that a better comprehension of Aristotle's concepts of *Dunamis* and *Energia* can help in understanding St. Paul's theology of justification by faith in his letter to the Galatians (2:16). The next paper by Bernard Li and Yip Mei Loh discusses the relationship between digitalization, the Bible and Philosophy. They affirm that the philosophy of ancient Greece, early Christianity and the modern technology are all intertwined. They conclude that human innovation in digitalization proceeds from the effluence of God's wisdom and assert that technical advances are meant to glorify God's wisdom.

Mark Edwards reviews the twentieth century translation of Greek and Latin Philosophy. His excellent survey of the translated works reveals that no translation can capture the original ingenuity and will always be a hedge between the reader and the original. The final chapter by Christoph Horn discusses the Neoplatonists' debate on the concept of evil. He provides insight into Plotinus' conception of matter as evil and how Proclus, after rejecting Plotinus' understanding, develops his own theory of evil. This paper concludes with an observation on the innovative employment of the Plotinian concept of evil by Augustine in ascribing the cause of evil to human free will.

As we continue to grapple with the impact of modern technology on the philosophical and theological foundations of Christianity, it is necessary to understand the way early Christianity responded to its socio-political environment. This collection of conference papers is a valuable resource for those who are interested in the theological and philosophical development of early Christianity and those who are concerned about the impact of digitalization on human society.

Author's Biography:

Maria John P. Selvamani is an associate professor in the Department of Medicine and the dean of Academia Catholica at Fu Jen Catholic University, Taiwan. He holds a doctorate in molecular biology and bachelor degrees in philosophy and theology. His research interests are science and religion and bioethics.

Introduction

Yip Mei Loh

Cicero gave up his political business after the death of his daughter, subsequently devoting himself to philosophical studies. While thus occupied he engaged in five philosophical conferences in a Tusculan villa, and in Bk 1 of his *Tusculan Disputations*, observed that 'living well depends on the study of wisdom, which is called philosophy'. It is clear that philosophy is a subject in which to search for wisdom by means of endeavouring to comprehend the truth of the cosmos and man. In other words, wonder is the beginning of philosophy, Plato says in the *Theaetetus* 155d; and philosophy, the *paideia* of mind, is the beginning of human speculation; and the Bible is the seed of the wisdom planted in our mind, 'of which office is to use its reason well'[1] as Cicero says. Reason (ratio) is number, and number is made clear to us by means of '*lux mentis*[2]', leading to the creation of the artificial mind, in imitation of our own mind, with the numbers 0 and 1.

Digitalisation is changing the methods of our learning, work and lifestyle, and more importantly, it is transforming our patterns of thinking. Being guided by the digital world in all aspects of our life is our inescapable fate. The controversial issue of Big Data becomes the most necessary lesson that we have to investigate and understand in order not to be manipulated and enslaved by it - to avoid censorship, to maintain our independence of thought and to publish freely, since the better we apprehend it, the more transparency we demand about it, to prevent us not only from being monitored unconsciously, but also from abusing it. As St. Augustine says, the knowledge of life (*vitae scientia*) is better and higher than life itself, since once we are living in a stage of understanding, our mind is more perfectly enlightened; [3] and our knowledge is deepened for us to

---

[1] Marcus Tullius Cicero. *Tusculan Disputations*, BK III, vii (New York: Harper & Brothers Publishers, 1877), 63.
[2] Augustinus. *De libero arbitrio*, Liber II, 21, 82 (Paderborn/Germany: Ferdinand Schöningh, 2006), 158.
[3] Augustinus. *De libero arbitrio*, Liber I, 17, 59, 96-97.

distinguish truth from falsity, and information from misinformation, by means of 'rational reflection and thought [4]' (*animadversione et cogitatione*). And the President of Harvard University, Drew Gipin Faust, quoted Jeremy Knowles, saying 'the most important goal of higher education is to ensure that graduates can recognize when "someone is talking rot"'.[5] It is thus clear that from the ancient days to these, we are challenged by the same issue - misinformation and falsehood. We all are immersed in a world of specious information. In these information-filled generations, training students to distinguish truth from falsehood is the key to a good education, along with independent thinking.

In Plato's *Protagoras* 314a-c Plato warns us that the risk of purchasing knowledge to be absorbed by learning is serious, since we have no way of knowing whether our soul may be either injured or benefited by it. We have to be very careful what kind of knowledge we have learned, since our soul can suffer drastic pain if we have bought false knowledge and fake information. He reminds Hippocrates not to be a parrot, but to be capable of distinguishing truth from falsity. Plato's famous Allegory of the Cave in his *Republic* VII described Socrates as a true philosopher telling his compatriots to think independently and not to be imprisoned by specious nonsense. For this his destiny is to forfeit his life.[6] His heroic sacrifice was witnessed by the Greeks, and served as an essential guide to justice and courage, demonstrating that universal values – truth and virtues - cannot be compromised. Thus Greek philosophy prepares the way for the Christian faith, as evinced by Titus Flavius Clement (c. 150-216). In his *Stromateis* he holds that 'philosophy is a preparatory science for Christianity, since it was a direct gift of God to the Greeks before the Lord extended his appeal to the Greeks'.[7] And Mark Edwards underscores the fact that Origen quoted Plato more often than any other philosopher for the purpose of 'availing himself of philosophy in the service of exegesis and

---

[4] Augustinus. *De libero arbitrio*, Liber II, 9, 29, 138.
[5] https://www.harvard.edu/president/speech/2017/freshman-convocation-address-to-class-2021 (accessed 11th December 2020).
[6] See Yip Mei Loh. 'The Allegory of Pistis and Eikasia in Plato's Divided Line and Social Media Bespoke Groups as Virtual "Ekklesia" in Taiwan' in *Цифровизация общества и будущее христианства*, (Материалы V Международной научной конференции 24.01.2019 / Отв. ред. И. П. Рязанцев, ред.-сост. Р. М. Плюснин. – М.: Изд-во ПСТГУ, 2019), 33-47.
[7] Clement of Alexandria. *Stromateis*, translated by John Ferguson, Bk I, 5, 28(1) (Washington, D.C.: The Catholic University of America Press), 41-42.

the defence of ecclesiastical tradition'[8]. Hence, philosophy is the means by which early apologists could rebuke the pagans for the vindication of the Christian faith. For example, St. Augustine, in his first philosophical encounters, reads Cicero's work, *Hortensius*, which leads him to turn to the Bible, and which he discovers can provide him with guidance in seeking for truth, happiness and salvation; thus replacing the role of Manichaeism in his life. [9] Furthermore, after he read the work of the Neoplatonists, he not only thinks that their philosophy is compatible with the Bible, but also depicts Plotinus as the 'resurrected Plato'.[10] Under the mentoring of Ambrose, whom he met in Milan, he converts to Christianity and deploys Greek philosophy to rebuke the quarrels of Donatism and of Pelagianism to defend the Bible.[11] Hence the important role of philosophy is to train us in independent thought, to sift through popular opinion, and to not be manipulated by fake information.

Nowadays we are bombarded with information overload and are facing a challenge in having our lives overseen by the digital world. Digitalisation is the invention of man, and a gift from God for us to possess a better life and a better view to comprehend Him. Transparency and truth are becoming more and more urgent. Therefore, individual independent thinking and judgment becomes necessary to avoid confusion and puzzlement, and philosophy is the best way to help people to achieve this. The very earliest apologists utilized Greek philosophy to defend the truth of the Bible, and in our own time we can likewise employ the core principles of the Bible and the same philosophy of early Christianity to protect our values from false information in the event that we are unknowingly drawn into a vortex of evil. As Immanuel Kant (1724-1804) says, in his *Grundlegung zur*

---

[8] Mark Julian Edwards. *Origen against Plato*, Introduction (Ashgate Publishing Company, 2002), 1. Cf. 馬克・愛德華斯。《歐利根駁斥柏拉圖》，羅月美譯，(台北：五南出版社，2020 年 5 月)，2 頁。

[9] Christoph Horn. *Augustinus* (München/Germany: Verlag C.H. Beck oHG, 1995), 14. Cf. 克里斯多夫・霍恩著。《奧古斯丁—哲學思想導論》，羅月美譯，(台北：五南出版社，2021 年 03 月)，26 頁。

[10] Christoph Horn. *Augustinus*, 29. Cf. 克里斯多夫・霍恩著。《奧古斯丁—哲學思想導論》，羅月美譯，40 頁

[11] Christoph Horn. *Augustinus*, 18-19. Cf. 克里斯多夫・霍恩著。《奧古斯丁—哲學思想導論》，羅月美譯，30-31 頁。

Metaphysik der Sitten, when we encounter difficulties with morality in practice, we need the help of philosophy to surmount these hurdles. [12]

Today digital technology has been managing our lives in various fields, and affecting our thoughts and behaviours, so we should appreciate Socrates in being the first philosopher to bring down philosophy from the heavens, to proclaim it in cities, to introduce it into families, and to oblige it to examine life and morals, and good and evil, as Cicero observed of him.[13] With the help of philosophy, I think that we are able to resist the bad temptations of digitalisation in our lives by rational thinking. The free choice of our will is faced with the two kingdoms of good and evil, also called the kingdom of Christ and of Satan, as determined by Augustine in his *De civitate dei*. In dealing with the conflict between these two kingdoms, correct and hard philosophical training, and the values of Christianity, can assist us to make correct decisions about values.

---

[12] Immanuel Kant. *Grundlegung zur Metaphysik der Sitten*, Herausgegeben von Karl Vorländer, 3 Auflage, Erster Abschnitt, 405 (Hamburg/Germany: Verlag von Felix Meiner, 1957), 24.

[13] Marcus Tullius Cicero. *Tusculan Disputations*, BK V, iv. (New York: Harper & Brothers Publishers, 1877), 107.

Chapter One

The Process of Social Digitalisation in Russia: Expert Opinions and Developmental Features

Igor Pavlovich Ryazantsev, Maria Podlesnaya, and Vasiliy Pisarevskiy

This article discusses research approaches to digitalisation as a modern social process. One point of view is associated with the Israeli sociologist Shmuel Eisenstadt (1923-2010) and his theory of "multiple modernities", while another lies with his critics and academic opponents: Volker Schmidt and Thomas Schwinn. According to Eisenstadt, the European path to modernization is not the only possible one and the project of modernity itself is ontologically rooted in the religious and spiritual sphere. Schmidt and Schwinn, on the contrary, point to the universal nature of modernity, noting that it is primarily a European project and its multivariant nature is nothing more than the result of the adaptation of individual elements of the value-institutional matrix of modernity by different civilizations. Describing the key features of the social process of digitalisation, the authors focus on the relationship between social action in the social space, both online and offline. The main characteristics of digitalisation are considered, including widespread robotization, labor market decentralization, and the desire for a "technological singularity" where machine intelligence surpasses human intelligence by several orders of magnitude. Special emphasis is placed on consideration of the spiritual risks of digitalisation, including "dehumanization", and the corresponding statements of Orthodox clergy on this issue are given.

The article shows the developmental features of the social process of digitalisation in Russia using examples of relevant sociological research, including research by the Information and Analytical Center of St. Tikhon's Orthodox University. This study assessed the local population's attitudes to digitalisation in the Kirillovsky District of Vologda Region, as well as in Belgorod Region. The article emphasizes the importance of interdisciplinary study of the social processes of digitalisation and the productive international exchange of results.

Introduction

We will start with a story about Russian realities; a story that has led us look at this topic from a particular angle. Russia, like many other European countries, has recently been actively developing industries in the fields of robotics, nanotechnology, and artificial intelligence. This was the subject of an international conference held at the highest level (with the participation of heads of government of the Russian Federation, major IT leaders, and 5,000 participants from 20 countries) in Moscow in early November 2019.

This conference was reported on in the final broadcast of "Weekly News" on the TV channel "Russia 1" and at the most accessible time for the majority of the Russian audience (Prime time). This event was presented as an undoubtedly high achievement of Russian business and government, with appropriate rhetoric and pathos.

The report that followed dealt with a flood in Irkutsk Region (Siberia) and the widespread flooding of residential areas there. Here, we can see two completely different realities: the so-called world of the elite, with its constant dreams of a digital future, the approach to which is so hurried that you might think that such a future already exists in the present; and the world of ordinary citizens living their usual lives and facing everyday problems, far from the world of big technology, artificial intelligence, and other things. In addition, as it turns out, this world will largely depend on both territorial and climatic factors, which, in turn, will determine that not every technology is suitable for Russia's geography.

This leads us to the problem addressed by this article and we ask the following question: what are we really dealing with when we talk about digitalisation? Is it the phantom of power and business? Is it a media construct? Is this future inevitable? Or are we dealing with necessity, as a continuation of everything preceding it (digitalisation)?

Once we had formulated these questions, it suddenly became quite clear that we were talking about digitalisation, on different planes and at different levels: 1. at the level of science fiction; 2. at the level of expert evaluation; and 3. at the level of direct practice.

Therefore, we must talk about digitalisation with an understanding of these epistemological differences, but not be limited to them. It turns out that, as a kind of new social phenomenon, digitalisation has the capacity to change society in one way or another. It affects not just different social spheres to variable extents, but also, moving from changes in the social structure of society to the consciousness of the individual, as a result, digitalisation is realized in different ways, with different effects and consequences that the ideologists of digitalisation and its practices cannot predict. However, let us proceed in an orderly fashion. Firstly, let us address the origins of digitalisation.

Section 1. The origins of digitalisation and the signs of a new society

1957 can be considered to mark the beginning of movement in this direction as the US Department of Defense first began to think about how to achieve the reliable transmission of digital information. In 1969, a group of talented scientists created a computer network called ARPANET, which united four universities (UCLA, UCSB, Stanford, and the University of Utah). In 1973, ARPANET became international, connecting to the NPL network in London. In 1991, after the standardization of World Wide Web (WWW) pages, the Internet became a public invention for the United States and then across the world. What important conclusions can we draw from this brief history of the emergence of the Internet and, as we now understand it, a new and globally encompassing reality?

Our first conclusion: the history of the development of the Internet and the digitalisation process seems to have been developing now for the past few years, or even over the past decade, but it has seen at least 63 years of active development and research, attracting some of the greatest minds of our time.

The second conclusion: the initiator of this research and development was the US government (Department of Defense), under the presidency of Dwight Eisenhower, indicating not only the main subject and customer of such technologies, but also the corresponding institution of interest.

The third conclusion: digital reality, which we may say concerns our everyday lives, has changed many aspects of our attitudes to work, rest, leisure, relationships, communications, and our way of life in general.

These changes have taken place over no more than 30 years—in comparison to other historical forms of social life, this is quite a short period—but the resulting consequences have been quite tangible. This thirty-year period not only marks the life and maturation of a whole generation of people, but also a change in consciousness and the very structure of society, which is worth talking about in more detail.

Section 2. The IT class and its friends

In this regard, we may ask ourselves the following questions: what is digitalisation as a social process today? Is this process global? And how much does it coincide with globalization in general? When you first attempt to generate answers, it is not difficult to notice both some similarities and significant differences between the processes of digitalisation and globalization, which lie primarily in the source and causes of these two processes.

Globalization is a phenomenon on a global scale. Its processes have emerged as a reaction to the growth and development of multinational companies and the relevant forms of economy, production, and capital (by analogy with the capitalism of the late 19th century resulting from the Industrial Revolution and the emergence of appropriate sites and classes, particularly the bourgeoisie).

Digitalisation was a process initiated, as noted above, by the military government elites of the USA and with the support (development) of leaders of the IT industry. They represented, on the one hand, the scientific-technical elite and, on the other, a new business segment of the economy, though only partially developed at the time and only beginning to gain momentum, as lobbying interest groups.

In connection to this, even today we can talk about the emergence of a new class, if not referring to the bourgeoisie (in the usual sense), then to modern intellectuals who were not only able to create technologies, but also to update and (continuously) manage them. This latter point is a serious factor in the emergence of a new form of power and new forms of its formation. Hence, we can ask the inevitable question about the relationship between democracy and technology in modern neoliberal societies, the answer to which will probably put us in the very near future in need of reviewing currently available ways of implementing democracy and its basic principles. Thus, we can draw a first conclusion: digitalisation is not just a sequential process of development from the two preceding stages of capitalism and globalization, associated with the emergence of new technologies and relevant classes or social groups, but also new forms of governance and power.

At the same time, we are witnessing the birth of a new class of IT workers, which, already today, has a visible structure with at least four elements: 1. developers (scientific and technical elite); 2. IT business personnel; 3. IT communications personnel; and 4. IT service personnel (the grassroots mass element of this class structure).

A closer examination of the origins of digitalisation indicates a very interesting feature, namely, that this process was originally formed from a set of social practices and not with individual actors (as was the case with the growth and development of transnational corporations), but multiple groups and networks of actors. As a result, although the process was initiated by the scientific and technical intellectual elite, there were a number of interested groups involved and the process itself was very fast in terms of the speed of its coverage and dissemination.

Concurrently, major players involved in the process of forming a new digital reality have managed to create their own business strategies (for example, Yandex-taxi, which has displaced the usual city taxi services that use centralized dispatchers from the market in recent years). As such, digitalisation itself can be considered a business strategy. In the case of the possibilities of digital technologies being taken advantage of by special services and other shadow structures of power, digitalisation can be considered as a mechanism of control. This is also true of the field of management. In the case of the geopolitical alignment of forces, it can be seen as a project of the future also. Thus, unlike globalization, the process of digitalisation, if I may say so, is more practice-oriented and structures life not "from above", but "from below"; not just changing our economy or culture, but all of everyday experience itself. Such a far reaching process could be compared to conversion, with a transition from one group to another and with a qualitatively new approach to each group.

At the same time, the process of digitalisation, from the point of view of its own development, needs certain conditions. In connection to this, the question arises in the present as to its geopolitical and ideological boundaries (benchmarks).

Section 3. Modernity as a world of "multiple realities": Departing from European unification

In this regard, it is worth remembering a few theoretical ideas about modernity as it exists at the moment. An important viewpoint was expressed by the Israeli sociologist Shmuel Eisenstadt (1923-2010) through his theory of "multiple modernities".[1] Another perspective, one critical of his position, is found in the work of his opponents: Volker Schmidt[2] and Thomas Schwinn.[3] According to Eisenstadt, the European path to modernization is not unique. The project of modernity is ontologically rooted in the religious-spiritual sphere of civilizations, in "axial time", and, therefore, every civilization's "axial age" sees the generation of its own project of "modernity" embedded in its spiritual potential and embodying that civilization's respective achievements in the fields of culture, social organization, and technology, etc.

According to Eisenstadt, there is no single and universal Art Nouveau; rather, we can only talk about the possibility of the existence of various projects of Western and Eastern types that have formed naturally or have arisen in the course of confrontation, copying, and partial reproduction of the achievements of Western civilization in conditions different to those of the context of its origin. In this latter case, the determining role is played by the civilizational and cultural specificity of a particular society. However, this does not prevent modern companies having a set of common features.

Schmidt and Schwinn, opponents of Eisenstadt and proponents of a globalist modernization paradigm, point to the universal character of modernity. They note that, in this primarily European project and its multivariance (*mnogovariantnost*), there is no difference in the outcomes

---

[1] Eisenstadt Sh. N. (2007) Multiple Modernities: der Streit um die Gegenwart, Berlin: Kulturverl. Kadmos (in German).
[2] Schmidt V. H. (2010) Die ostasiatische Moderne: eine Moderne, eigener Art? Berliner Journal für Soziologie, vol. 20, iss. 2, pp. 123-152 (in German).
[3] Schwinn T. (2018) From the Comparative Sociology of Religion to the Comparative Political Sociology. Max Weber and Multiple Modernities. Sotsiologicheskie issledovaniya = Sociological Studies, no 1, pp. 121-131 (in Russian).

of adaptation of individual elements of the value-institutional matrix of modernism in various civilizations, which are beginning to interpret modernization as a challenge to their own existence and create the axiological groundwork for its assimilation and traditionalist legitimation. Therefore, pluralism can only be discussed within the framework of the existence of a single substantive core in all of these "multiple modernities". This plurality itself is nothing but the selectivity of reactions of modernizing societies and the adaptation of individual components of the modernization project to the national context. That is, the various forms of modernity are forms of a single, dominant content. Speaking about the plurality of ideological constellations of the institutional configurations of modernity, it is necessary to take into account the presence of a common core or common features of the "cultural program of modernity". This core includes: "a new concept of human action—the Autonomous Self"; "intense reflexivity"; multiple roles beyond narrow, stable, cohesive communities (translocal communities); the blurring of differences between the center and the periphery; the inclusion in the cultural core of the themes and symbols of protest—"equality and freedom, justice and autonomy, solidarity and identity"; and finally, the idea of progress and understanding of history as a "project" (domination over nature).

By the way, the presence of common features of the "cultural program of modernity" was not denied by Eisenstadt himself, who emphasized pluralism as diverse configurations arising from differences in national, regional, and global patterns of modernity.

Today, we are witnessing the "blossoming complexity" of the global world, the coexistence of different types of democracy and political institutions, the diversity of models of capitalism and civil society, the emergence, for example, of a unique Eastern path of modernization (we recall the successes of the "East Asian tigers" of China, Japan, Korea, and Singapore, for example).

One of the properties of modernity, according to Wolfgang Knobl, a proponent of the ideas of Eisenstadt,[4] in addition to its plurality, is its contingent nature. It can be understood in terms of a set of random events acting as a catalyst for processes and phenomena and the multiplicity of

---

[4] Knobl W. (2007) Die Kontingenz der Moderne. Wege in Europa, Asien und Amerika. Frankfurt a.M. (u.a.): Campus. [Contingent of modernity. Ways in Europe, Asia and America].

random conditions necessary to change any situation, as well as equifinality (a plurality of ways to achieve a single goal) and multifinality (a multiplicity of evolutionary paths leading to qualitatively different states). Hence, as Knobl argues, the immanent process of self-development of Western civilization, assumed by all, is nothing more than the interaction of many socio-historical factors initiated in reality, some of which are natural, while others are random (contingent) in nature.

This is typical not only for European civilizations, but also for others around the world. Continuing the ideas of Knobl, supporters of the evolutionary approach find a combination of contingent processes in the conditions of systemic instability. There is a new "critical assemblage point" of the system (critical juncture), formed according to the configuration of random factors and guiding the development of society in a new direction, and institutions that further enhance the effect according to movement along the selected trajectory.

Based on the concept of contingency, Knobl emphasizes that, in the course of "a large-scale reconstruction of the history of world civilizations, Eisenstadt hardly touches on the problem of real empirical mechanisms of reproduction and self-preservation of cultural programs of our time". At the same time, the author identifies three main mechanisms of institutional stabilization in conditions of dependence on the previous path of development. This ensures the stability of the system through the maintenance of cultural traditions, the institutionalization of the religious sphere, reproduction through forced political mobilization, strengthening of the institutions of power and control, and examining in detail, first of all, the relevant political mechanisms.

As a result, Knobl rejects the extreme version of the theory of predetermined development, admitting to the development of social systems both following and abandoning a given trajectory. In his opinion, contingency arises not only at the moment of structuring the system at the point of bifurcation, but is immanently present at any point in the trajectory of evolutionary dynamics. In addition, the stability of the system is possible only in the period of development of the system from one critical phase of development to another. The critical points in the development of institutions and socio-historical systems can be spoken of only from the standpoint of retrospective analysis.

In the context of the globalization of modernity, a different situation arises. The environment of modern society is a fundamentally open (contingent) space of possibilities in which the results of past decisions, although they limit the options for behavior in the present and in the future, do not completely determine the choice. As a result, we can talk about another property of modernity—reflexive temporalization—through which modern society becomes a society of constantly increasing permanent transformation.

Modernity is a historical category that does not presuppose the possibility of definitively determining the diversity of its constitutive features; their variation can be updated, changed, and replaced by others in the course of subsequent stages of development, leaving and fixing the achievements of previous phases of modernization as traditions and values. Considering the process of digitalisation in the context of the theory of "multiple modernities", we can see that the conditions for the development of this process in different countries will be different.

The process itself involves some unification, at least this is how its ideologists position it, and here we are faced with a certain contradiction. The contradiction lies in how this process occurs in reality and what is assumed in theory. This is theoretically still the same scheme given by Wallerstein, which sees the world divided into core and peripheral countries: core countries are successful, developed, and in a state of modernity; the periphery is backward, underdeveloped, and difficult to integrate into modernization processes. As a rule, the latter belong to so-called traditional societies and are seen to have strongly archaic ways of life. It is believed that, because of their traditionalism and the restrictive weight of tradition, in such societies modernization and development are both extremely difficult.

As such, we see not only an expansion of the European ideals of how this should be, but also an attempt to unify these countries in terms of European ideas about development. In this sense, Eisenstadt's theory, to put it mildly, changes the global strategy of the so-called "core", pointing to a number of features around which a unified modernity is impossible. Reality turns out to be wider than the narrow framework of a convenient, but somewhat biased theoretical approach.

Section 4. The "Ideal" model of digitalisation: Utopia or the future?

We can only talk about the process of digitalisation and its development (speed, intensity) within the framework of "multiple modernities", although we note, once again, that attempts to unify this process exist today and their features are easily recognizable. First of all, it relies on: the maximum openness of all citizens to possible control; a departure from tradition; and the reformatting and erasure of historical memory. As a result, a constant orientation towards the future, with the eradication of archaism (as a certain communal, close, and interpersonal way of life) and the creation of the myth that archaism is bad, is something close to social infantilism.

The question of whether the "ideal" model of digitalisation is a utopia or that the future can be left open, relies on an understanding that any theory can become a plan of action and the ideology of the ruling elites has an interest in all of this. From the point of view of our understanding, reality still takes a toll and we agree with Knobl in his discussion of the importance of contingent processes in the context of development. In this sense, it is very timely to recall an example from everyday life, when two opposing examples of modernity were voiced in the same media space with only the difference of a few minutes—the popularization of the development of artificial intelligence in Russia and the flood in Irkutsk Region (broadcast on 10/11/2019).[5]

We may conclude that there is a significant gap between digitalisation as a kind of dream of power of business elites and the daily lives of ordinary citizens; it lies not so much in their antagonistic relations, but in the discrepancy between their realities in different scenarios of modernity. Therefore, modernity is plural, not only from the point of view of country and macro-sociological analysis, but also from the point of view of intra-country structures, groups, and classes. In this sense, digitalisation is a project that is being updated by the ruling groups of society.

At the same time, in order for the "ideal" model of digitalisation to work, serious efforts must be made on the part of these groups, since, in fact, changes must affect more than a single social structure and consciousness. Let us now think about the fact that society is not only a "sticky" reality, as Sigmund Bauman said, but also a multi-layered reality consisting of different structural levels. It can be imagined in terms of: the structural level of society, with its classes, groups, and networks (this is the very first outer layer of society); as a level of the structure of action, with its relations, connections, and iterations (the second layer); as a level of social

---

[5] Vesti nedeli (Weekly News on Russia 1)
https://russia.tv/video/show/brand_id/5206/episode_id/2218835/video_id/2240352/viewtype/picture/

consciousness (the third layer), filled with stereotypes and historical memory; and finally, as a structure of individual consciousness, with its complex matrix of the conscious and unconscious experiences of life. In other words, in order for the standardization of a certain pattern of life to be accepted, it is necessary that it cover all the represented layers.

In this sense, standardization "works" both at the level of the social structure of society and at the level of individual consciousness. However, the "multiple realities" that Eisenstadt writes about, and which we can still observe today, tells us that, if the first two layers of these standardization processes can occur painlessly, then at the 3rd and 4th layers, variations begin and standardization takes form depending on cultural differences (recall that Eisenstadt also spoke about this, agreeing that there is a "cultural program of modernity", the pluralism of which is born from diverse configurations arising from differences in national cultures, and regional and global patterns of modernity).

Section 5. Digitalisation and religion in the context of a globalized modernist scenario

It is important to note that digitalisation as a process initiated by the elites of society, already has visible and articulated features today that have been shaped by developers of the digital environment. Let us try to understand this in order to determine how the process of digitalisation in Russia is taking place and whether it has its own national characteristics, based on our assumption of the "plurality" of modernity. In this regard, we will use the statements of the most influential experts in this field and statistics from various research companies to make our analysis.

Currently, the process of digitalisation is most actively developing in the economic sphere of society—a trend that is typical mainly for developed countries. Today, even traditionally "offline" sectors of the national economy are increasingly using cloud computing, big data, and the Internet of things.[6] At the same time, the process of digitalisation cannot be reduced exclusively to the development of the "digital economy", since it affects all significant areas of society—the social, political, and cultural.

---

[6] Weill P., Woerner S. (2018) Digital business transformation. Harvard Business Review Press (USA).

One of the first sociologists to study the information society in the context of the impact of the Internet on social processes was Manuel Castells.[7] He highlighted the key characteristics of such a society. Let us look at them in more detail.

First, social reality on the Internet (online) is not opposed to the usual forms of social reality (offline), but rather closely related to it. Castells characterizes this as the phenomenon of "real virtuality". Second, simultaneously with the advent of computer technology and online reality, social and economic structures have changed: relatively rigid and vertically oriented institutions are being replaced by flexible horizontally oriented networks through which resources are exchanged. In this regard, Castells defines the information society as a network society. Third, the ability to change and reconfiguration Castells notes as "a crucial feature in society". At the same time, the generation, processing, and transmission of information all become fundamental sources of power and influence.

An intermediate place between the scientific theory of Manuel Castels, considering the network society, and the concepts of digitalisation is occupied by the theory of the "digital revolution" by Chris Skinner.[8] On the one hand, he, like D. Bell and E. Toffler—researchers of the information society—and others, introduces a historical periodization of significant "revolutions" in the history of mankind. The first revolution, as Skinner notes, is the emergence of shared beliefs that help different groups negotiate; the second is the invention of money; the third is the industrial revolution; and finally, the fourth is the network revolution, which chronologically belongs to our time. The essence of the network revolution is that time and space are beginning to shrink, radically reshaping social institutions and processes. For example, the social institution of the banking system is rapidly being pushed to the sidelines by P2P lending technologies ("person-to-person", when individuals lend to each other through specialized digital platforms), and the money itself is taking on a digital form based on blockchain technologies.

On the other hand, Skinner talks about the evolution of the Internet as a network of networks within the historical stage of the network revolution. He identifies the stages of WEB 1.0 (the birth of the Internet); WEB 2.0

---

[7] Castells M. (2000) The Information age: economy, society and culture. Moscow: Higher school of Economics. 458 p.
[8] Skinner C. (2018) Digital human. The fourth revolution of humanity includes everyone. Marshall Cavendish International (Asia) Pte Ltd.

(the birth and development of social networks); and WEB 3.0 (the "Internet of values" in which individuals provide each other with a certain value through digital platforms and exchange these values. Note that the concept of "value" is used here in an economic, not a sociological sense). WEB 4.0, Skinner presents as the "Internet of things", when the maximum share in the information exchange will be occupied by machines and robots, rather than people. Finally, the fifth version of the Internet, according to Skinner, will develop through artificial intelligence, with which it will be extremely difficult for people to compete.

One of the most famous researchers of digitalisation, Ray Kurzweil,[9] should not be overlooked either. He is both an inventor (creating the first reading machine for the blind and being the first to teach computers to recognize human speech), and a futurist who studies the process of digitalisation. In his book, *The Age of Spiritual Machines*, he formulated the "law of accelerating returns", according to which the development of technology occurs exponentially. In other words, the more powerful a particular technology becomes, the greater the acceleration of its development.

The law of accelerating returns, Ray Kurzweil suggests, has three sequential phases. The first is slow growth—the early phase of exponential growth; the second is rapid growth—the explosive phase, when the curve rapidly rises; and the third is the stabilization phase, when a fundamentally new technological paradigm is formed. At present, we are in the first of these phases. In the next stages, the digitalisation process, according to Kurzweil, will have the following characteristics:

- Ubiquitous robotics, focusing on the use of artificial intelligence and deep machine learning. This will lead to revolutionary changes in a number of industries, ranging from medicine to urban management (such as the emergence of driverless cars).
- The development of decentralisation of the labour market (the emergence of "remote professions"), the replacement of a number of existing professions with artificial intelligence, and the emergence of fundamentally new ones.
- Striving for a "technological singularity", when machine intelligence surpasses human intelligence by orders of magnitude, leading to unpredictable consequences in all spheres of human society.

---

[9] Kurzweil R. (2008) How to Create a Mind: The Secret of Human Thought Revealed. Viking.

- The development of a number of complementary technologies that will influence the reformatting of existing social processes and institutions.

First of all, this concerns big data, which can include huge samples of hundreds of millions of Internet users, while taking into account hundreds of criteria—not just socio-demographic, but also behavioral and economic values. Such volumes of data can be processed exclusively by machine and there is a risk of using personal data without the consent of their owners, consequently giving total control over the activities of people.

This is also about the technology of the "Internet of things", in which a variety of devices (ranging from smartphones to fridges at the scale of the individual and from the "smart factory" to "smart cities" across the whole of society) exchange information via the Internet. This technology will allow the rebuilding of economic and social processes in such a way as to eliminate the need for human intervention in standard actions and operations.

Among complementary technologies, we can also describe the technology that constructs virtual objects, which people perceive and give meaning to. As an example of augmented reality, we can cite the game Pokémon Go, which gained massive popularity some years ago. Much has been written about the deplorable results of such a "game" in the Orthodox Christian media, but it is interesting that representatives of other faiths, such as Roman Catholics, also gave a sharply negative assessment of this game and the technology of augmented reality in general.

We should also mention the technology of 3D printing and, as some researchers note, in the near future we may be talking about printing not only complex objects, but also human organs, which would present many contradictions with the Orthodox view of man. In the same field, we find artificial intelligence and autonomous robots. The advantages of these technologies are obvious, but the danger of them escaping human control certainly exists.

We can identify the main features of the process of digitalisation, which conditionally sees development within the framework of the globalization-modernist scenario. They are as follows:

1. The process of digitalisation covers all spheres of society, starting primarily with the economic;

2. Changes to the structure of society from vertically oriented institutions to horizontal networks;
3. The main source of power and influence becomes the generation, processing, and transmission of information;
4. Social reality itself becomes identical to the social reality of the Internet;
5. We also see changing notions of time and space, which can be compressed;
6. The process of digitalisation covers not just stages of a revolution, but the stage of its own evolution, one which sees the development of artificial intelligence and active robotics;
7. Significant changes to the set of technologies promoting digitalisation. For example, the technology for building virtual human objects and the introduction of axiological traits and meanings.

Thus, we are dealing with a process that is radically changing the social reality we are familiar with, including the transformation of traditional social institutions. The latter is particularly significant from the point of view of the topic of this report and requires consideration of the role of religion and religious social institutions, particularly in today's digital society. Let us look at this issue in more detail.

In this regard, it is worth mentioning the role and significance of such a process as the rationalization of the development of a European-centered modernity. It was rationalization that contributed not only to the development of a certain way of thinking, but also to the idea of progress that is being implemented today, including through the digital age/society we are considering.

Rationalization and digitalisation, obviously inseparable, are closely related to each other in this process. At present, we are seeing a serious rationalization of religion, which is clearly demonstrated by the growth of new religious movements. There is a change in the number and basic functions of religion, including the worldview presented. Instead of forming a certain picture of the world for the individual, new religious movements are engaged in the scientific adaptation of ideas. This is due to the weakening of the transmission of religious identity between generations. A result of this is that the formation of an individual's worldview begins to depend on other elements.

> One of the most common elements is pseudo-scientific ideas, which are most often associated with Eastern religious ideas, as well as various health

practices and near-scientific ideas. In itself, this borrowing is not due to the individual building a new "world picture", but the inclusion of these elements in the already established "world" of man ... the function of pseudo-scientific adaptation of religious ideas allows a person to remain in the framework of his scientific picture of the world, through its rationality, not demanding a faith in the transcendent to achieve salvation. It only suggests adding to the individual's "picture of the world" those elements of spirituality that are convenient, understandable, and acceptable to him.[10]

In other words, we see a kind of hybridity of beliefs and ideas that include elements of all possible traditional religions, supposedly scientific in nature, but at the same time not drawing on pure science. In Orthodox theology, the mixing of non-ordained worldview religious foundations has been called ecumenism. Even S. Huntington, speaking about the uniqueness of Western civilization and its culture, noted that Western universalism is an ideology adopted by the West to resist non-Western cultures.[11] The ecumenism or holism of new religious movements has been considered by some authors as

> ...the desire to overcome the "non-Western", the inclusion of "foreign" cultural code in Western society ... the Holistic function, expressed through new religious movements, acts as a mechanism for overcoming the negative consequences of the loss of an individual's identity, restoring them, but on the basis of religious universalism. Through the holistic function, the "foreign" cultural code changes, creating a variety of elements for the construction of personal spirituality. The individual becomes a bearer not only of, for example, Orthodox or Protestant identities that may no longer meet certain expectations, but also of a new identity—a universal one that may contain, for example, the combined ideas of Christianity, paganism, Eastern teachings, and scientific worldview.[12]

Why is it important for the elite to offer a project of digitalisation in the framework of a globalized modernist scenario to reduce the influence of traditional religions in society and the emergence of new ecumenical religious movements (such as New Age movements)? The answer lies in the very essence of digitalisation, which implies a single space and a world without national and state borders. In turn, this should affect the

---

[10] Zudov E. V. (2018) Functions of new religious movements // Ideas and ideals, no. 2 (36), vol. 2, p. 147.
[11] Huntington S. (2003) Clash of civilizations. Moscow: AST. P.35
[12] Zudov E. V. (2018) Functions of new religious movements // Ideas and ideals, no. 2 (36), vol. 2, p. 148.

transformation of religious institutions, eventually leading to a single, unified, global church and religion.

Another sign of digitalisation is the atomization of individuals and their distance from each other in terms of their actual proximity, including within individual families, such as migrants (migration is in itself a feature of the times), which are increasingly transnational in nature. In this sense, digital means of interpersonal communication are already being used very successfully today, and communication itself is designated by the concept of "polymedia", which

> ...allows us to describe a new network of social connections that arise around technology, and not just the technological development of increased convergence.[13]

Thus, we are faced with the fact that technologies give birth to new forms of social connections and relationships, becoming part of the emotional and spiritual spheres of individuals. On the one hand, there is the necessary individualization of consciousness, where the intermediary in the interaction between people is conditioned by a third actor—technology—which mediates communication in a certain way and distinguishes it from the point of view of moral responsibility of the individual. On the other hand, for such communication, it is necessary to see at least three conditions: physical access to technology; accessibility (including financial) that ensures digital communication; and the media literacy of participants. As a result,

> ...polymedia is not just a medium; this is how users use the capabilities of various communication tools to manage their emotions and relationships.[14]

Such communication does not just require certain efforts, costs, technological means of communication, and user skills.

In the sphere of traditional religions, especially Christian confessions where personal contact and community ties have always been particularly important, being part of the most important sacraments like the Eucharist, such transformations of interpersonal communication driven by digital

---

[13] Medianu M., Miller D. (2018) Polimedia: a new approach to understanding digital means of communication in interpersonal communication // Monitoring public opinion: Economic and social changes, no. 1, p. 338.

[14] Medianu M., Miller D. (2018) Polimedia: a new approach to understanding digital means of communication in interpersonal communication // Monitoring public opinion: Economic and social changes, no. 1, p. 339.

technologies, also raise a lot of questions; in particular, the question of adaptation to such conditions.

It is obvious that these issues cannot be equally solved by all traditional religions, which differ not only in the content of their faith, but also in the level of personal involvement of believers in the structures of their church institutions and sacraments. Hence, on the one hand, the supposed unification of religion and the church for the elites promoting the process of digitalisation seems to be the most preferable, while, on the other, it requires additional efforts. In particular, in the process of interpersonal communication already described, where one of the actors is technology, several other actors must somehow be embedded, such as the priest, without whom such communication is difficult in certain religions, and of course, God himself. Therefore, even today, individual authors raise the following questions:

> ...is it possible to interact with God in the information environment? Most theistic religions recognize God as a spiritual, ideal entity that can reside everywhere. From this point of view, there can be no obstacles to communicating with God in the non-material Internet space. However, it as the religious sphere that was most sensitive to the substitution of the man—man relationship for the human—machine relationship.[15]

So, the globalizing-modernist scenario of the development of digitalisation assumes ecumenism in the sphere of religion, since without this there is no formation of a global state. At the same time, there are already certain difficulties in building such a religion and all sorts of risks for humanity.

Section 6. Risks of the digitalisation process

A number of researchers of digitalisation, who describe it as a new social process, have highlighted several risk factors. These risks can be typologized as follows:

1) Technological risks;
2) Economic risks;
3) Socio-political risks;
4) Moral or spiritual risks.

---

[15] Bylieva D. Information and communication technology and religion: from communications to virtualization // Scientific and technical statements of Saint-Petersburg state university. Humanities and social Sciences. 2018. t. 9, no. 1. pp. 63-71.

Technological risks are primarily related to the fact that the development of artificial intelligence is uncontrolled. Russian digitalisation researcher Andrey Kurpatov says that improving technology may lead to the creation of such a powerful intelligence that it will have its own essence, which cannot be controlled.[16]

Ray Kurzweil defines this situation in terms of a "technological singularity". According to Kurzweil's definition, this is a social reality in which, on the one hand, technological progress will become exponential and inaccessible to human understanding and, on the other hand, artificial intelligence will reach a stage of development that will be beyond the control of people. In Kurzweil's estimation, this will happen by 2040.

Risks in the economic sphere are associated with increased unemployment, as new and easily controlled machines and robots replace human labor in production and manufacturing processes. This change may result in increased social tensions in society. However, a number of researchers believe that automation will also lead to the creation of new professions and fields of employment.

In the socio-political sphere, risks may include such phenomena as cyber wars between states and the manipulation of social groups using big data. In the sphere of internet use, we will see constant tracking of the interests of every individual user and the creation of social portraits using big data and artificial intelligence technologies.

Carl Frey, a professor at the University of Oxford and a well-known British researcher on the impact of digitalisation on the labor market, notes that the advent of digital technologies and artificial intelligence resembles previous industrial revolutions that have already occurred more than once in human history. He believes that 47 % of workers in the US are currently engaged in activities that are highly likely to be replaced by machines over the next decade or two.[17]

The Internet of things continues to grow exponentially. Data from Cisco suggests that the Internet of things currently accounts for 10 billion users. In 2020, the number of IP addresses associated with this technology had

---

[16] Kurpatov, A.V. (2019) The Fourth world war. The future is near! / A.V. Kurpatov. - Saint Petersburg: Publishing house of Bookselling "Capital", 400 p.
[17] Frey C.B., Osborne M.A. (2017) The Future of Employment: How Susceptible Are Jobs to Computerization? // Technological Forecasting and Social Change. Vol. 114, pp. 254-280.

already increased to at least 50 billion. According to the leading analytical company Nielsen, the Internet of things already accounts for more than 70 % of internet traffic.

The universal "internetization" of things surrounding a person, both at work and in everyday life, is exacerbating the problem of information security, since it multiplies the number of interacting networks. In an environment where even the largest state networks are almost monthly victims of hacking, it would be utopian to expect that all components of the Internet of things will be properly protected. According to Symantec, the manufacturer of the Norton line of programs, currently no more than 3 % of things that have access to the Internet have at least the minimum acceptable level of information security. For combat programs, the Internet of things is probably the most vulnerable segment of electronic communications.

The risks of cyber warfare, as noted by the Russian researchers Elena Larina and Vladimir Ovchinsky, are significant. Today, a number of countries are developing fundamentally new weapons, behavioral in nature, the purpose of which is to change the social behavior of individuals and groups.[18]

Let us note the main digital technologies of the fourth industrial revolution: 3D printing, big data, the Internet of things, virtual reality, distributed registries (blockchain), artificial intelligence, and autonomous robots. Andrey Kurpatov gives concrete examples of the future use of these technologies. In the sphere of internet use, we see every-second tracking of the interests of each individual user and the drawing up of social portraits based on big data and artificial intelligence technologies (for example, in China, a system is being actively tested that determines the degree of loyalty of an individual to the authorities based on his/her requests and publications on the network). In the field of medicine, we see the functioning of "personal robots" that can prescribe individual medications and the 3D printing of organs. Ray Kurzweil talks about the possibility of "digital immortality" and "the transposition of consciousness into the cloud", i.e., directly putting oneself in the place of God.

He sees human beings becoming cyborgs controlled by a virtual reality matrix:

---

[18] Ovchinsky V. S., Larina E. S. (2014) Cyber Wars of the XXI century. What did Edward Snowden omit: Book world; Moscow.

> We will not have biological bodies. We will be able to create bodies using nanotechnology, we will be able to create virtual bodies and virtual reality that will be completely realistic due to the fact that virtual bodies will be as detailed and convincing as real ones.
>
> It will become habitual for us to quickly change our bodies, as well as the environment in which we are in virtual reality, and this will be perceived very realistically.
>
> In the end, we will be able to do with real reality the same as with virtual reality, for example, a swarm of self-organizing nanorobots can form a virtual body. If we just extended our life, we would become very bored, we would be visited by a deep existential melancholy, we would have nothing to do, we would exhaust all ideas, but this is not what should happen.[19]

In the US, there is even a "digital church" in Silicon Valley, proclaimed by a certain Anthony Levandovsky—a former computer engineer at Google and Uber. He proposes that "God" is an artificial intelligence, or rather, a super-intelligence; more precisely, Kurzweil's "technological singularity" who will come into our world and "transform" it.

It seems that the category of moral risks should be expanded to the level of spiritual and moral risks with potential for serious impacts on individuals, social groups, and society as a whole. In a Christmas interview (January 7, 2019), Patriarch Kirill of Moscow and Russia noted the spiritual danger of total control over both the individual and entire social groups.

> When you use a gadget, whether you want it or not, whether you enable geolocation or not, someone can know exactly where you are, what you are interested in, what you are afraid of. And so the World Wide Web makes it possible to exercise universal control over the human race.
>
> This is today, and tomorrow there may be a methodology and technical means that will ensure not just access to classified information, but the use of this information. Control from one point is a harbinger of the coming of the Antichrist, if we talk about the Christian view.[20]

Archpriest Vsevolod Chaplin, a Russian Orthodox priest and public figure, considered biometric technology to be a serious spiritual risk.

---

[19] Kurzweil R. "Post human" [Electronic resource]. Access mode: https://vimeo.com/201810207 (date of visit: 01.10.2020).
[20] Patriarch Kirill spoke about the dangers of gadgets. [Electronic resource]. Access mode: https://ria.ru/20190107/1549084240.html (date of visit: 01.04.2019).

As you know, biometrics is a technology that identifies an individual by face and voice. The "digital economy", which is expected to attract our authorities with its fashionable slogans, cannot fail to include the individual in its deepest manifestations - Father Vsevolod warns - How will the "digitalisation of the soul" begin? Will it turn a person into an Android node of a tightly controlled system?

But such a system cannot live without totality and without absolute guarantees of identification of each "node" of a biological object. Otherwise, the creators and controllers of the system will not sleep well. And so they will probably "enrich" it with codes and chips—first voluntary, and then...[21]

Section 7. Digitalisation and religion in the world of "multiple" modernities: The Russian experience

We would like to start this section of our article with some trends noted by the Russian historian N. Popov when considering the now popular theory of generations and comparing the generations of American and Russian people since 1900. The author writes that the proposed typology of generations by the "founding fathers" of this theory, N. Howe and W. Strauss, not only offers a very imaginative idea of generations, but is also not transferable in its imagery to other countries that had quite different experiences of the same historical events (such as the Second World War).

There has also been criticism of the periodicity of seeing one generation as equal to 20 years; as the historian writes, individual generations are formed as a result of great social upheavals (for example, in America during the Great Depression, which lasted no more than 10 years). This critical approach allowed the author of the study to come to some interesting conclusions. He notes significant differences in the experience of historical events by generations of different countries throughout the twentieth century and speaks about the originality of not only the historical, but also the social context. This refers to the originality expressed by Eisenstadt in his theory of "multiple modernities". However, this pattern, as already noted, is typical mainly of the beginning and middle of the twentieth century. With the advent of the Internet, other

---

[21] Chaplin V, Archpriest. (2019) "What prevents putting the" electronic economy "under public control?" [Electronic resource]:
https://realnoevremya.ru/articles/69983-chaplin-o-nacionalnoy-biometrii-i-totalnom-kontrole (date of visit: 20.10.2020)

processes begin to occur, which Popov pays special attention to: "For these generations [the millennial generation, born between approx. 1982 and 2003] globalization acquires real features with the development of the 'World Wide Web', social networks, and the information revolution thanks to the Internet. For the first time, we can talk about the similarity of generations in the United States and Russia, which are becoming more common than different".

Thus, we can observe an interesting phenomenon: the equalization of generations (in terms of psychology and values) in the experience of distinct historical events from the emergence of new types of communication, i.e. the Internet. Before the advent of this global network, such commonalities were impossible and cultural diversity was better preserved. The data presented in "Spiritual and moral culture in Russian universities", conducted under the supervision of Professor Ryazantsev, also point to a certain unification of values among young people, including those in Russia.

It was conducted in capital and regional Russian universities in 2012 and 2018. The main conclusion was that, in talking about the stable maintenance of balance (in the sense of resilience) in society and the preservation of continued tradition, Russian University students showed a universalism in their values. They also showed an ability to be flexible in relation to the processes of modernization and the preservation of Russian-specific values.

It is evident that, with high significance of the values of self-affirmation (which, according to Inglehart, characterize post-materialist values), the university students affirmed the values of saving, the importance of leisure, and a trend towards active leisure. There was also a focus on volunteering and helping others (especially in the capital's universities).[22]

At present we are faced with a serious dilemma, which can be expressed through several questions: how much can we talk about the presence of "multiple modernities" in the global world today? To what extent is the theory of "multiple modernities" applicable to the study of modernity in various countries? How relevant is the digital age and do we not actually have (European-centered) universalism? This was previously mentioned

---

[22] Podlesnaya M. A. (2020) Development of Russian society from the point of view of student youth values // Sociology of religion in Late Modern society. Vol. 9, pp. 145-154.

by M. Weber and, later, his followers, who may be seen as representatives of the so-called global modernist trend. What are we really dealing with when we talk about the universal values of Russian youth, or the increasingly observed generational similarity of representatives of different peoples in the era of digitalisation? Finally, what place do the cultures and religions of people during this time occupy in all this?

There are several research centers in Russia studying the dynamics of digitalisation. First of all, there is the Moscow school of management "SKOLKOVO". Employees of this research center undertook the project "Digital Russia" to assess the level of digital development of the Russian regions. Seven sub-indexes were developed as follows:

1) Regulatory and administrative indicators of digitalisation;
2) Specialized personnel and training programs;
3) The availability and formation of research competencies and technological reserves, including the level of research and development;
4) Information infrastructure;
5) Information security;
6) Economic indicators of digitalisation;
7) The social effect of the implementation of digitalisation.

The sub-indexes, in turn, have been evaluated using sub-factors, which, in this study, were events, facts, and other information obtained from open sources.[23]

We should also mention the Higher School of Economics, which is actively working in this area. This research center undertook the project "Digitalisation in small and medium-sized cities of Russia".[24] The findings of the study indicate that, in small cities, the Internet is mainly used for communication: the share of social network users in the population is seen to increase as the size of the city decreases. Also, the difference in the use of digital services in small and large cities is well illustrated by purchases of goods and services via the Internet: 31 % of respondents used the

---

[23] Digital Russia index.
[Electronic resource]: https://finance.skolkovo.ru/ru/sfice/research-reports/1779-2019-04-22/ (date of visit: 25.10.2020)

[24] Digitalisation in small and medium-sized cities of Russia. Higher school of economics.
[Electronic resource]: https://www.hse.ru/data/2018/06/06/1149766040/2018-06-GSU-HSE_pres_v6.pdf (date of visit: 23.10.2020)

Internet in small cities to search for information about goods and services, compared to 52 % in cities with more than a million inhabitants. 60 % of residents had never bought goods or services over the Internet in small cities, compared to 40 % in those with more than a million people.

This feature cannot be explained by differences in the ability to use the World Wide Web, with difficulties in both small and large cities equally experienced by 6 to 8 % of respondents. The most likely reason is that more residents of small and medium-sized cities are not habituated to this kind of action—the most common explanation for a reluctance to make purchases over the Internet was "preference for personal purchases" (28 % of respondents in small cities answered in this way).

The patterns of use of state and municipal online services also differed significantly. The most significant differences are observed in the use of services related to interaction with local institutions, such as making an appointment with a doctor and resolving issues in the housing and utilities sector, as opposed to paying fines, taxes, paperwork, and other services that are standardized at the federal level and do not have a local link to the city.

We should also mention the Information and Analytical Center in the Faculty of Social Sciences of Orthodox St. Tikhon's University for the Humanities. This research center analyzes the process of digitalisation in terms of traditional spiritual and moral Christian values.

In June 2019, the Information and Analytical Center conducted a study in Kirillovsky District of Vologda Region, Russia. The uniqueness of the research site lies in the fact that four major monasteries, which have all played a significant role in the history of Russia, are located in a small territory: Kirillo-Belozersky; Ferapontov; Nilo-Sorskiy; and the Resurrection Goritsky Monastery. The study analyzed the socio-political attitudes of the population, their economic behavior, and their degree of readiness for the realities of the digital economy, as well as their religiosity. Residents of the city of Kirillov and respondents from various rural settlements of Kirillovsky District took part in the questionnaire survey.

Respondents were asked about their attitudes to the process of digitalisation in general, as well as their frequency of Internet use and purposes in using the World Wide Web. The vast majority of respondents (76 %) displayed a positive attitude to the process of digitalisation; 10 %

of respondents indicated a negative attitude; and 14 % found it difficult to answer. At the same time, a number of respondents expressed the concern that, due to the rapid development of digitalisation, robots could come to replace people in many professions, which can be attributed to the actualization of the economic risks of digitalisation in the minds of the population.

Despite positive attitudes to the process of digitalisation, frequent Internet use was seen in only 68 % of the respondents (according to a study by the All-Russia Center for Public Opinion Research, 81 % of Russian residents access the World Wide Web at some level of frequency).

56 % of respondents said they used the Internet every day (which is also less than the All-Russia indicator of 65 %). This group was dominated by respondents with secondary (24 %) or higher education (20 %) and the dominant age groups among respondents were 30 to 39 years (14 %), 40 to 49 years (12 %), and 50 to 59 years (11 %). 7 % of respondents said they used the Internet several times a week, and this group was dominated by respondents aged 50 to 69 years (5 %) with a specialized secondary level of education (4 %). 3 % of respondents used the Internet several times a month and 2 % used it less than several times a month. Among the respondents, 32 % did not use the Internet at all, of which the dominant age groups were aged 60 to 69 years (12 %), 70 to 79 years (8 %), and 50 to 59 years (5 %), with a specialized secondary education (13 %) or secondary education (10 %).

Thus, the most frequent use of the World Wide Web was among respondents living in a small city with secondary or higher education, and this trend was typical for all age groups. If we take both urban and rural respondents together, we can see that the older the respondent's age group, the less often they use the Internet.

Respondents were asked about their goals in using the Internet to identify their level of digital competence. It turned out that 50 % of respondents used the Internet to view websites and communicate on social networks; 39 % used e-mail; and 36 % used various Internet services (such as online stores and electronic banking and insurance services). At the same time, drawing attention to the dynamics of use of public services in Kirillov and the Kirillovka area, 53 % used online public services. The most popular services were: accessing a personal taxpayer account—31 % of respondents; marriage registration and use of maternity capital—10 %; and accessing various benefits, including sanatorium treatment—12 %.

On the one hand, we can say that, when comparing small/medium and large cities in Russia, small cities have not yet experienced "secondary digitalisation"—using the Internet not just for communication and entertainment, but also for work purposes on a permanent basis has not yet become a common habit. This can be explained by a number of infrastructural restrictions (for example, in a small city there may not be easily accessible Internet services and little use of online stores and delivery services).

At the same time, more than half of the respondents used public services. This means that, in small cities, digital competencies are being developed through the accessing of public services. The Russian Federation is constantly expanding the availability and range of public services, so we can assume that this type of access will only grow in the next few years.

In March 2020, the Information and Analytical Center of St. Tikhon's University completed a further study on the perception of digitalisation as a media construct in a small Russian city. The study was conducted in Stary Oskol (Belgorod Region) and included both church and non-church reference groups.

Residents of this small city, unlike residents of big cities, are less equipped with information on the subject of digitalisation, so it is important to investigate their attitudes and evaluations of digitalisation. We also wished to identify what they know about the subject (for example, have you heard about the risks of "digitalisation"? What future do you see in connection to this trend? And so on). It is also important to see if there are any differences in attitudes to digitalisation between the church and non-church population.

The sample for our study was 200 people, of which 100 respondents were ecclesiastical. These included clergymen, church workers, ordinary parishioners, teachers at the Orthodox gymnasium and Sunday schools, and people involved in the city's youth religious movements. The survey was also conducted with members of Orthodox communities through the social network Vkontakte in Stary Oskol (groups of churches, Orthodox movements in the city, and youth groups with religious themes). The second half of the respondents belonged to the non-church part of the population. Thanks to social networks, we found respondents who were members of various groups of the city, social movements, and news publications. We also asked respondents to rate their religious beliefs on a 10-point scale.

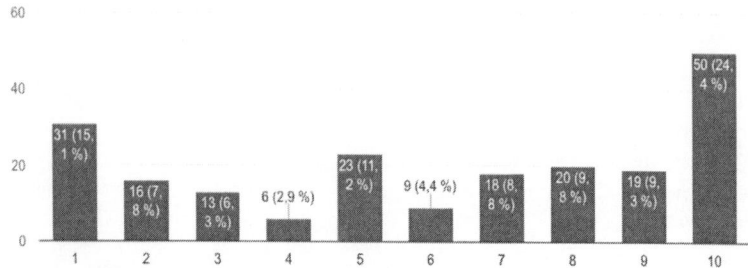

Figure 1. Respondent assessment of their degree of personal religiosity.

In percentage terms, the survey group was equally split by gender with 50 % women and 50 % men and an equal ratio of church and non-church respondents. The age of the respondents ranged from 20 to 70 years in approximately equal percentages by cohort. The average age of the respondents was 31.5 years. We interviewed people of different generations to understand the differences in their understanding of the process of digitalisation and their attitudes towards it. Most of the respondents have jobs and higher specialized education. The survey also included students who were getting an education, the unemployed, women on maternity leave, pensioners, and people associated with business activities.

In order to distinguish the church and non-church parts of the population, the survey questionnaire included a corresponding set of questions about the respondent's religiosity and involvement in church life (we investigated the degree of ecclesiasticism using a 10-point scale and introduced a question about attending services, which helped to show how important church membership and activity was to a person). It was found that 50 % of people interviewed were involved in church life and 50 % of people were not involved in church life or attend only on very large holidays.

All respondents actively use the Internet, mainly for viewing websites or for accessing the public services portal. In reference to our research tasks, we will highlight the main parameters for studying and assessing the population of an average city and what it tells us about the process of digitalisation.

The first parameter used to identify people's relationship to digitalisation was how people understood the concept of "digitalisation". The results of the study show that the majority of respondents, 70 %, know about digitalisation. This indicates that the population is aware of this topic and has its own opinions about the process.

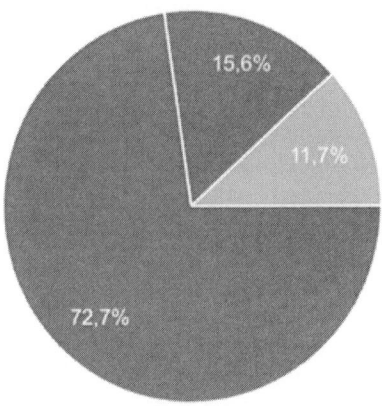

Figure 2. Respondent understanding of the term "digitalisation" (Blue "yes, I understand" (72.7 %); red "no, I do not understand" (15.6 %); orange "I can't answer" (11.7 %)).

Moreover, it is worth noting that more than 50 % of respondents were actively interested in the topic of digitalisation. This indicates that the topic is very popular among the research audience. In order to find out how interested people are in this topic, it was necessary to find out whether they talk to their relatives, friends, and colleagues about the process of digitalisation. Analysis revealed that 38 % of the respondents talk about digitalisation with their relatives, friends, and colleagues, amounting to 79 people out of the total.

We also asked respondents to define the term in their own words. Most people defined digitalisation in the following way:

1. Introduction of digital technologies, digital primacy;
2. Digitalisation in all areas of life;
3. Means for improving the life of the population.

According to the survey, more than half of the respondents (56 %) receive information and news about the digitalisation process from online publications. Internet portals are also popular, with 41 % of respondents using such sources. It should be said that, on the scale of accessing news media, more than half marked "3" on a five-point scale. From this we can conclude that information received from the media is a mechanism for forming public opinion. According to the level of trust, the most popular responses suggest that media related to the Internet, TV, and radio are no longer trusted, and perhaps not even used.

In addition, the majority (67 % of respondents) discuss news received from the media with their friends, colleagues, and relatives. It is also worth noting that 42 % of respondents want to get more information on the topic of digitalisation. Next, we would like to consider the answers related to the impact of digitalisation on the world. According to the respondents, digitalisation has had the greatest impact on such areas of life as the economy, science, and education. Culture, religion, and medicine are the least affected by digitalisation.

It follows that the population is not aware of how digitalisation can affect religion in our country, therefore, people do not think about the future of church life and the moral and spiritual risks. It should be noted that, even at the qualitative stage, experts, in their publications, have not touched much on the state and future of religious life within the framework of digitalisation. Most of their publications have focused on the impact of digitalisation on the economy, science, and education.

In the course of this quantitative study, it was found that the topic of digitalisation is not sufficiently covered in the media. The survey data show that the majority of respondents (40 %) receive news about digitalisation only "rarely", that is, several times a month. Only 6 % of respondents said that they hear such news every day and most likely these are people who are engaged in this topic or study it.

The second argument I would like to highlight concerns respondent attitudes to digitalisation. In the course of the research, we decided to find out from respondents how they feel about digitalisation, i.e. how they evaluated this process. For this purpose, the same ratings were introduced ("positive", "neutral", and "negative") as in the qualitative study in which we conducted a discourse analysis. The survey results show that the population of the city of Stary Oskol is neutral towards digitalisation (39 %); 35 % of the population was positive; but only 9 % gave a negative assessment (only 19 people). It should be noted that the city of Stary Oskol is seeing moderately rapid development of digitalisation (in terms of remote work, use of state services, and electronic libraries, etc.), creating benefits for a comfortable life and leading the population to evaluate this process either neutrally or positively.

Here we deal with the next parameter—the risks of the digitalisation process. The majority responded positively to the question, "have you thought about the risks of digitalisation?" Therefore, people are concerned about the future in the development of digitalisation. The most popular answers on the risks involved were: threats to individual freedom; global control; and artificial intelligence. Note that the options for a fall in morality and the deification of digital technologies were chosen least of all, suggesting that perhaps people are simply not aware of the moral and spiritual category of risks and do not yet see a close connection between digitalisation and a threat to spiritual life.

Conclusion

In today's dynamically changing world, digitalisation is not just a part of social reality. It is a new social process that is having a serious impact on how society develops. Digitalisation also affects other social processes in the economic, political, cultural, and technological spheres, as well as social institutions (for example, education, which is increasingly going online). Some researchers believe that the process of digitalisation affects not only the social, but also the personal sphere of the individual and affects changes in basic needs, where the need for information exchange becomes basic.[25]

Along with the opportunities offered by digitalisation, primarily in the economic sphere, this social process also carries significant risks. Russian digitalisation researcher Andrey Kurpatov identifies four risk areas—technological, economic, socio-political, and moral. The authors of this article separately identify the category of spiritual and moral risks, which are contrary to the foundations of the Christian religion.

Orthodox clergy—from his Holiness Patriarch Kirill to famous priests—have spoken out about the spiritual and moral risks of digitalisation today. The clergy point out that attempts to "transpose consciousness into the cloud" and "digitize the soul" contradict the anthropological purpose of man as an image and likeness of God. No less dangerous are attempts at

---

[25] Digital society Index 2019 from DENTSU-AEGIS [Electronic resource] https://www.dentsuaegisnetwork.com/reports/dsi_2019 (date of access: 24.10.2020)

total control over a person's personality, which are being carried out with the help of modern digital technologies.

Modern studies of digitalisation suggest that the digital development of various regions of Russia will gradually level out. In this sense, an empirical study of the population of the city of Kirillov and Kirillovsky District of Vologda Region, conducted by the Information and Analytical Center in the Faculty of Social Sciences and Law of St. Tikhon's University for the Humanities, is of interest.

The results of the study show that, although the level of "secondary digitalisation", i.e. the daily use of the Internet for more than entertainment and information purposes, is low, it has the potential for development. This potential will be realized through the increased use of online public services, the number and availability of which will increase within the framework of the state program on the digital economy. The social process of digitalisation needs to be studied in an interdisciplinary approach. It is very important that this study includes not only the traditional social sciences, such as sociology and economics, but also theology.

Bibliography

Bylieva D. *Information and communication technology and religion: from communications to virtualization* // Scientific and technical statements of Saint-Petersburg state university. Humanities and social Sciences, 2018. t. 9, no. 1.

Castells M. *The Information age: economy, society and culture.* Moscow: Higher school of Economics, 2000.

Chaplin V, Archpriest. *"What prevents putting the electronic economy under public control?"*, 2019. [Electronic resource]: https://realnoevremya.ru/articles/69983-chaplin-o-nacionalnoy-biometrii-i-totalnom-kontrole (date of visit: 20.10.2020)

Digital Russia index. [Electronic resource]: https://finance.skolkovo.ru/ru/sfice/research-reports/1779-2019-04-22/ (date of visit: 25.10.2020)

Digital society Index 2019 from DENTSU-AEGIS [Electronic resource] https://www.dentsuaegisnetwork.com/reports/dsi_2019 (date of access: 24.10.2020)

Digitalisation in small and medium-sized cities of Russia. Higher school of economics. [Electronic resource]: https://www.hse.ru/data/2018/06/06/1149766040/2018-06-GSU-HSE_pres_v6.pdf (date of visit: 23.10.2020)

Eisenstadt Sh. N. *Multiple Modernities: der Streit um die Gegenwart,* Berlin: Kulturverl. Kadmos (in German), 2007.

Frey C.B., Osborne M.A. *The Future of Employment: How Susceptible Are Jobs to Computerization?* // Technological Forecasting and Social Change. Vol. 114, 2017.

Huntington S. *Clash of civilizations.* Moscow: AST, 2003.

Knobl W. *Die Kontingenz der Moderne. Wege in Europa, Asien und Amerika.* Frankfurt a.M. (u.a.): Campus. [Contingent of modernity. Ways in Europe, Asia and America], 2007.

Kurpatov, A.V. *The Fourth world war. The future is near!* / A.V. Kurpatov. - Saint Petersburg: Publishing house of Bookselling "Capital", 2019.

Kurzweil R. *How to Create a Mind: The Secret of Human Thought Revealed.* Viking, 2008.

Kurzweil R. *Post human* [Electronic resource]. Access mode: https://vimeo.com/201810207 (date of visit: 1.10.2020).

Medianu M., Miller D. *Polimedia: a new approach to understanding digital means of communication in interpersonal communication* // Monitoring public opinion: Economic and social changes, no. 1, 2018.

Ovchinsky V. S., Larina E. S. *Cyber Wars of the XXI century. What did Edward Snowden omit: Bookworld.* Moscow, 2014.
Podlesnaya M. A. *Development of Russian society from the point of view of student youth values* // Sociology of religion in Late Modern society. Vol. 9, pp, 2020
Schmidt V. H. *Die ostasiatische Moderne—eine Moderne, eigener Art?* Berliner Journal für Soziologie, vol. 20, iss. 2 (in German), 2010.
Schwinn T. *Ot sravnitelnoj sociolog i ireligii k sravnitelnoj politicheskoj sociologii maks veber i mnozhestvennost modernov* [From the Comparative Sociology of Religion to the Comparative Political Sociology. Max Weber and Multiple Modernity]. Sotsiologicheskie issledovaniya = Sociological Studies, no. 1 (in Russian), 2018.
Skinner C. *Digital human. The fourth revolution of humanity includes everyone.* Marshall Cavendish International (Asia) Pte Ltd, 2018.
Weill P., Woerner S. *Digital business transformation.* Harvard Business Review Press (USA), 2018.
Zudov E. V. *Functions of new religious movements* // Ideas and ideals, no. 2 (36), vol. 2, 2018.

Author affiliation:
Ryazantsev Igor, doctor of economics
St. Tikhon's Orthodox University, Russia.

Podlesnaya Maria, candidate in sociological sciences
Federal Center of Theoretical and Applied Sociology of the Russian Academy of Sciences, Russia.

Pisarevskiy Vasiliy, candidate in sociological sciences
St. Tikhon's Orthodox University, Russia.

Chapter Two

Taiwanese Contextual Theology in the Age of Digitalisation: Digital Storytelling as a Way of Doing Story Theology[1]

Ya-Tang Chuang

Introduction

In this paper, the author uses the methodology of contextual theology to analyze the phenomenon and impact of digitalisation in contemporary Taiwan. The author also envisions a digitalized future Taiwan through the implementation of the Government of Taiwan's "DIGI+" program. Arguably, "digital theology" is called for in the age of digitalisation. It is clear that the trend of digitalisation brings threats as well as opportunities. Many thinkers have criticized the dangers and problems that digitalisation has created such as invasion of privacy, wholesale surveillance, and the dissemination of fake information, dangerous ideology, violent imagery, and pornography. While recognizing these potentially negative aspects of digitalisation, here the author will focus mainly upon the positive function of digitalisation for contextual theology. "Digital storytelling" is the art of storytelling using digital technology and is spreading widely and rapidly. Story theology, as proposed by Choan-Seng Song, is guiding the development of contextual theology in Taiwan. Pointing out the similarity between digital storytelling and story theology, the author

---

[1] This paper is based on the author's research project "The Challenges and Opportunities of Digitalisation for Taiwanese Contextual Theology" (109-2410-H-309-013-) with a grant from the Ministry of Science and Technology (MOST), Taiwan, Republic of China. Also, my thanks and gratitude for the editorial assistance of Mr. Marc Grenier, Director, MEG International English Center, Tainan, Taiwan.

argues that digital storytelling may have potential as a way of doing story theology within the digital context.

The Coming of the Digital Age to Taiwan

More than 20 years ago, Nicholas Negroponte, the founder of Massachusetts Institute of Technology's Media Lab, predicted the coming of the digital age. In *Being Digital*, he claimed: "Like a force of nature, the digital age cannot be denied or stopped. It has four very powerful qualities that will result in its ultimate triumph: decentralizing, globalizing, harmonizing, and empowering".[2] As he expected, the digital age is now sweeping the world; this is "not only about computers, but about a fundamental change of culture and our life experience".[3]

The digital age has also been called the age of information or the new media age. The introduction of the personal computers in the 1970s, driven by the development of transistor technology, promoted strongly the free and rapid transfer of information. The developmental shift was so rapid and radical that it can rightly be called a digital "revolution" since it radically transformed our world from an industry-based to an information-based one![4]

As Prensky points out, "digitalize or to die" is the crucial social issue today. If you were born after 1980, then you are a "digital native" and can adjust relatively painlessly to this new technologized reality. However, those not born digitally native, i.e. "digital immigrants", are not so lucky and their adjustment is not pain free, but a matter of social survival.[5]

The rate of Internet access and smartphone use in Taiwan indicates that the degree of digitalisation of society has resulted in it reaching a critical stage of development—one that makes daily life problematic without it.

The latest Taiwanese statistics (2018) underscored the high degree to which Taiwan society has been digitalized.[6] In 2018, Taiwan had a

---

[2] Nicholas Negroponte, *Being Digital* (New York: Alfred A. Knopf, 1995), 228.
[3] Negroponte, *Being Digital*, 7.
[4] Manuel Castells, *The Information Age: Economy, Society and Culture, Volume I The Rise of the Network Society* (Oxford: Blackwell, 2nd Edition, 2010), 28-76.
[5] Marc Prensky, *From Digital Natives to Digital Wisdom: Hopeful Essays for 21st Century Learning* (Thousand Oaks, CA: Corwin Press, 2012), 67-85.
[6] National Development Council, "Survey on 2018 Individual/Household Digital Opportunity Survey in Taiwan Executive Summary", *National Development*

personal Internet access rate of 86.5 % (male 88.2 %; female 84.7 %), representing a whopping increase of more than 23 percentage points in just 13 years! The mobile Internet access rate also reached a new milestone in 2018. It is now the case that up to 98.2 % of Internet users employ wireless or mobile Internet access. More than 97 % of Taiwanese (over 12 years old) are smartphone owners. More than 80 % "phub" (focusing on one's phone rather than the people around them) more than two hours every day, while 28 % spend more than 5 hours per day "phubbing".

These statistics reflect the fact that digital technology has deeply saturated the daily lives of Taiwanese people. In addition to Internet access and smartphone use, we can also observe other digitally-driven technologies used by the general public, including computers, digital cameras, digital video, e-mail, search engines, and software, to name just a few. For many of us, not having access to a smartphone or computer means living with a great deal of anxiety and panic.

The deep penetration of digital technology into every nook and cranny of Taiwanese society is projected to follow this trajectory in the future. In 2017, the Executive Yuan of the Taiwanese government started the grand DIGI+ Program (i.e., Digital Nation and Innovative Economic Development Program) as an administrative blueprint for continued digital development and innovation. In this blueprint, "digitalisation" is the key organizing principle and a "Digital Taiwan" is the intended end product:

> The goal of DIGI+ is to promote innovative digital development, improve quality of life, and hasten the transformation of Taiwan into a smart tech nation. This program will inject smart technologies like artificial intelligence, the Internet of things, and big data into industry and daily life.[7]

Council, accessed October 10, 2019. https://ws.ndc.gov.tw/001/administrator/11/relfile/5813/32110/078c2deb-b441-4c77-a033-d1543d40de2e.pdf.

[7] DIGI+ is an acronym derived from the fundamental concepts underlying the program. The "D" stands for "development" and a solid keystone to support it. "I" is for "innovation", a necessary component of an innovative digital economy. "G" stands for the "governance" of a smart tech nation. The final letter "I" of the acronym indicates "inclusion", embodied by Taiwan's welcoming and inclusive civil society. The "+" at the end of the acronym may be read as "plus" or "upgrade", in the sense that promotion of the DIGI+ program will deliver improvements in the nation's foundational digital infrastructure, and spur innovation at every institutional level of Taiwanese society. See Department of Information Services, Executive

The effectiveness of the DIGI+ program can be partly determined from statistics provided by the International Institute for Management Development (IMD). The IMD *World Digital Competitiveness Ranking 2019* raised Taiwan's ranking from 16th to 13th out of 63 major economies and ranked it 4th among Asia-Pacific economies.[8] It ranked 9th on the survey item "Overall context that enables the development of digital technologies",[9] and 12th on the survey item "Level of country preparedness to exploit digital transformation".[10] Taiwan also saw significant improvements in items related to "Executive perceptions about talent availability and access to capital", "Future readiness factor, particularly business agility",[11] and "Know-how necessary to discover, understand and build new technologies".[12]

The importance of new technology has clearly been understood by the executive political and administrative officials of Taiwan. For example, in an interview, Audrey Tang, the Digital Minister of Taiwan, noted that the government's strategy on technology was to bring it to "where people are", not leave it up to them to decide whether or not "to come to technology". For her, digital technology is the "foundation of liberal democracy". Linking technological development to fundamental democratic and human rights in order to promote economic growth is the stated political strategy emphasized throughout this interview.[13]

Given the positive political investment climate, private investment in the

---

Yuan, "DIGI+: Digital Nation and Innovative Economic Development Program", *Executive Yuan*, September 9, 2019, accessed October 20, 2018.
https://english.ey.gov.tw/News3/9E5540D592A5FECD/659df63b-dad4-47e3-80ab-c62cb40a62cd.

[8] The *World Competitiveness Yearbook* (WCY) is an annual report published by the Swiss-based International Institute for Management Development (IMD) on the competitiveness of nations. It has been published since 1989. The yearbook benchmarks the performance of 63 countries based on 340 criteria measuring different facets of competitiveness.

[9] IMD World Competitiveness Center, *IMD The World Competitiveness Ranking* 2019, digital version (PDF), 37. accessed November 21, 2019.
https://www.imd.org/wcc/world-competitiveness-center-rankings/world-digital-competitiveness-rankings-2019.

[10] IMD, *IMD The World Competitiveness Ranking* 2019, 38.

[11] IMD, *IMD The World Competitiveness Ranking* 2019, 18, 26.

[12] IMD, *IMD The World Competitiveness Ranking* 2019, 16.

[13] Keoni Everington, "Taiwan's breakaway from China was during the Neolithic Age: tech minister", *Taiwan News*, January 26, 2019, accessed November 20, 2019.
https://www.taiwannews.com.tw/en/news/3825048.

development of digital technology has also increased in Taiwan. Recently, Google Inc. received government approval to invest NT$26 billion (US$850 million).[14] Google had previously invested heavily in a data center in Changhua and expanded its investment several times until it had built the largest Google R&D center in the Asia Pacific region.[15] In addition to Google, other international digital high-tech companies are also investing heavily in Taiwan, including Facebook, Microsoft, Qualcomm, and Micron. Microsoft established an IoT Innovation Center (2016) and an AI R&D Center (2018).[16] Investment analysts cite many factors to account for the reasons why high-tech companies find Taiwan such an attractive place for investment. A welcoming political climate, Taiwan's geographical location, low operating expenses, and other factors have all been offered as explanations. However, the most important one is the size and quality of the available IT talent pool. Taiwan produces more than 10,000 graduates in computer science and information systems management every year.[17]

A Digital Theology is Called for

Though digital technology has proved its transformative power, it is unlikely to be capable of making a better world on its own. To understand the essence of this transformative power, while putting it in the service of creative and constructive work, is an urgent contemporary issue that remains open for discussion, debate, and critical analysis by theologians, as well as other thinkers from different fields.

Stephen Bevans rightly claimed: "All theology is contextual theology".[18]

---

[14] Focus Taiwan, "Google gets approval to invest NT$26 billion in Taiwan", *Focus Taiwan*, October 28,2019, accessed November 20, 2019. http://focustaiwan.tw/news/aeco/201910280020.
[15] Juvina Lai, "Taipei to house the largest R&D center for Google in Asia Pacific", *Taiwan News*, January 31, 2018, accessed November 20, 2019. https://www.taiwannews.com.tw/en/news/3352508.
[16] Microsoft Taiwan, "Taiwan AI R&D Center Expansion Lights up Microsoft 30th Anniversary", *CISION PR Newswire,* September 27, 2019, accessed October 30, 2019.https://www.prnewswire.com/news-releases/taiwan-ai-rd-center-expansion-lights-up-microsoft-30th-anniversary-300926997.html.
[17] Ralph Jennings, "Why Google is Expanding in Taiwan Again and Again", *Forbes,* accessed November 20, 2019. https://www.forbes.com/sites/ralphjennings/2019/04/10/why-google-is-expanding-in-taiwan-again-and-again/#47417c5f279d.
[18] Stephen B. Bevans, *Essays in Contextual Theology* (Boston: Brill, 2018), 30. See also Stephen B. Bevans, *Models of Contextual Theology, Revised and*

For him, any genuine theology must be *contextual* theology. Accordingly, theological reflection on digitalisation can definitely be viewed as a kind of contextual theology. As such, it will locate itself as a theological endeavor within human experience, rooted in the individual or community, through an explicit dialogue between the past (represented by the Bible and church tradition) and the present (represented particularly by digital experience).

In the context of digitalisation today, a "digital theology" is called for. Its main tasks include, but are not limited to: (1) using digital technology to enhance every aspect of the study of theology and religious beliefs and practices; (2) analyzing and critiquing the use of digital technology within the study of theology and religious beliefs and practices; (3) describing and contextualizing the impact of digital culture upon religious beliefs and practices; (4) determining digital trends in theology, specifically in terms of religious beliefs and practices; (5) working through multi-disciplinary research and with scholars from different disciplines.[19]

In the recent history of theological thinking and hermeneutics, there have been many scholars who have raised digitalisation as a highly significant theological issue. Po-Ho Huang may have been the first Taiwanese contextual theologian to raise the question of digitalisation, claiming it to be "an imperative issue for our theological exploration and reflection".[20] For him, Christian theology in the digital age must be intimately involved with and transformed by postmodern epistemological discourses and missiological approaches. He points out four urgent areas that need to be fully addressed in doing Christian theology relevant to the new digital age: (1) joining theological education with spiritual formation in order to address the felt need of people in the digital age to achieve a deep spiritual inspiration and affection that goes beyond the "rational supremacy" of the Enlightenment; (2) re-conceptualizing ecclesiology in the virtual society created by digitalisation in order to meet urgent human needs and to accommodate new forms of the church; (3) re-configuring the

---

Expanded Edition (Maryknoll, NY: Orbis Books, 2009), 3-16.

[19] Peter Phillips, Kyle Schiefelbein-Guerrero & Jonas Kurlberg, "Defining Digital Theology: Digital Humanities, Digital Religion and the Particular Work of the CODEC Research Centre and Network", *Open Theology* 5, no. 1 (January 2019): 29-43, 40.

[20] Po-Ho Huang, "The Impacts to Christian Theologies and Church's Mission from Digital Revolution", (Paper presented at the International Consultation—International Journal of Asian Christianity, November 2016, Chennai, India): 1-14, 1.

communication tools for missiological activities in the digital age, as well as formatting a new understanding of Gospel messages so that mission projects can maintain their relevance; and (4) re-formulating Christian ethics to take into account the rapid social changes sparked by the digital revolution, especially in terms of its impact on the structure of power relations in society.[21]

Viewed from Huang's perspective, the theological task is daunting in the digital age since there is scarcely an aspect of society that remains untouched by digitalisation. Complicating this is the fact that contextual theology itself deals with many different theological tasks and contains many different theological foci and methodological techniques. That being the case, then, I will confine my analysis and discussion to an exploration of the impacts of digitalisation upon the story theology proposed by Choan-Seng Song, a famous pioneer of Taiwanese contextual theology, in the digital culture today.

Story Theology and Taiwanese Contextual Theology

Huang's perspective on a uniquely Taiwanese contextual theology operates through Christian individuals and churches in Taiwan and draws upon cultural resources specific to Taiwan for theological reflection: "Any theology done by this pattern can be regarded as Taiwanese contextual theology".[22] In other words, the key elements of doing contextual theology in Taiwan are one's self-identification as a Taiwanese Christian and theological reflection based on Taiwanese experience.[23] So then, if we look at the widespread nature of digital technology in Taiwanese society today, it can easily be understood why digital experience has become a resource for doing contextual theology. It has become an essential part of the Taiwanese Christian religious experience and, as such, must be meaningfully incorporated into theological interpretations of that experience.

Contextual theology is closely related to the idea of "contextualization". Shoki Coe, a renowned Taiwanese theologian, coined this term to replace the concept of "indigenization" in the analysis and discussion of the sociopolitical context of 1970s in Taiwan. At that time, Coe worked as the

---

[21] Huang, "The Impacts to Christian Theologies and Church's Mission from Digital Revolution", 7-9.
[22] Po-Ho Huang, *No Longer a Stranger: Towards the Construction of Contextual Theologies* (Tiruvalla: CSS Books, 2007), 22.
[23] Huang, *No Longer a Stranger*, 22-23.

director of the Theological Education Fund of the World Council of Churches, where he promoted the use of contextualization as a theological methodology in the ecumenical movement.[24] Rather than being a fixed, static theological methodology, Coe envisioned this contextualization to be a constant process of de-contextualization and re-contextualization. He also considered that we should not be satisfied with the *status quo* as a contextualized theology. More to the point, contextual theology should always engage in the never-ending process of "contextualizing". In the age of digitalisation, it is imperative that we examine the role of digitalisation in this process.

Later, the theological spotlight in Taiwan shifted from Shoki Coe to Choan-Seng Song, affectionately known as C. S. Song. Partly due to his prolific corpus of highly creative theological writings, he has been very influential in the development of contextual theology in Taiwan. Song's works have greatly influenced the theological writings of numerous theologians in Taiwan and elsewhere. Taiwanese examples include the homeland theology of Hsieh-Chih Wang,[25] the *Chhu-thau-thi^n* theology of Po-Ho Huang, and the theology of identification of Nan-Jou Chen, all of whom have been strongly inspired by C. S. Song.[26]

In particular, Song's key concepts of "story theology" and "doing theology with cultural resources"[27] have played a dominant role in guiding the development of contextual theology in Taiwan. Lauded in Taiwan and Asia as a world-renowned native Taiwanese theologian,[28] he is affectionately

---

[24] M. P. Joseph pointed out there are four areas to which Shoki Coe contributed significantly: (1) theologizing in the context of colonization; (2) redefining the Christian mission; (3) political dimensions in faith; and (4) contextualization as theological and missional methodology. See M. P. Joseph, Po-Ho Huang and Victor Hsu eds., *Wrestling with God in Context: Revisiting the Theology and Social Vision of Shoki Coe* (Minneapolis: Augsburg Fortress, 2018), 1-18.

[25] Nan-Jou Chen ed., *A Testament to Taiwan Homeland Theology: The Essential Writings of Wang Hsieh-Chih* (Taipei: Yeong Wang, 2011), 1-4.

[26] In addition, story theology has been used as a methodology for doing aboriginal theology, feminist theology, ecological theology in the specific contexts of Taiwan.

[27] This guidance in doing theology was implemented by the *Programme for Theology and Cultures in Asia* (PTCA) and was founded on 1984; Choan-Seng Song was the first director.

[28] Choan-Seng Song is regarded as one of the most famous and influential Asian Christian thinkers. He dedicated himself to developing a new way of doing Asian theology that was attractive to many younger theologians. He was an associate director of the Faith and Order Commission of the World Council of Churches, Geneva, from 1973-1982. In 1996, he was awarded an Honorary Doctorate in

recognized as the "guru of story theology".[29] Song's perspective is that "stories" is prior to "doctrines" for "doing" theology. The Bible is the primary resource of theology and is full of stories rather than doctrines. This is the most important *raison d'être* for doing "story theology".

Clearly, then, Song agrees that the stories in the Bible are crucial for doing theology and shaping Christian identity. However, he is also quick to point out that the stories contained in the Bible do not exhaust all stories available from past and present daily lives and cultures. To do contextual theology in Taiwan is to access all of these "other" resources available in Taiwanese history and culture. In such stories, we come to better understand how Taiwanese people struggle for faith everyday as well as how they come to believe in and practice hope, love, freedom, justice, truth, goodness and beauty in the troubles and challenges of their everyday life experiences.

Furthermore, stories are not to be seen merely as narratives of characters in the Bible. For Song, they are the very fountain of theological thinking because they contain the elements that give rise to theological ideas, metaphors and symbols. This is the real reason why "theology" and "story" are symbiotic. "If this is what story does, it is already profoundly theological".[30] Wherever we find a "story", there we also find theology.

Given the well-established pivotal significance of Song's theoretical storytelling modality for the achievement of a deeper Scriptural understanding, theologians are obliged to closely examine the potential impact of technology upon the communication of those passages in terms of both form and content. In the age of digitalisation, the relevant theological questions become: how does digital technology influence the telling of Biblical narratives? Do digital media affect, in any way, the content of those stories? What are the theological meanings of stories we have experienced and are experiencing in our digital culture? What is the

---

Theology by New College, Edinburgh, Scotland. In 1997, he was awarded an Honorary Doctorate in Humanities by Cornell University. In the 23rd General Assembly of World Alliance of Reformed Churches (WARC), held at Debrecen, Hungry on August 18, 1997, he was elected as the chairperson for a 7-year term (1997-2004). C. S. Song was the first Asian to occupy this position.

[29] John C. England *et al*. eds., *Asian Christian Theologies, A Research Guide to Authors, Movements, Sources, Volume 3: Northeast Asia* (ISPCK/Claretian Publishers/Orbis Books, 2004), 688-691.

[30] Choan-Seng Song, *In the Beginning Were Stories, Not Texts: Story Theology*, (Eugene, Oregon: Cascade Books, 2011), 18.

relationship, if any, between institutional activities and trends occurring in the broader culture and the impact of digitalisation on the process of the Biblical interpretation? These are just a few of the many essential questions that need to be asked and answered comprehensively by theologians working in the pioneering field of digital theology.

The emergent and rapid development of "storytelling" in digital formats, and with varying kinds of digital instruments, has the potential to profoundly affect not only how stories are told, but also how they are received and the meanings that are attached to them. In addition to spoken words and written texts, digital storytelling employs several other powerful modes of communication that influence meaning. It may employ all or any combination of drawings, sketches, photographs, images and sound effects of various types in order to accomplish a visible transmission of stories and sound simultaneously. Among other things, digital technology prepares a storyteller to visualize, mobilize, and even dramatize a story. Digital story stimulates a large number of links in the sensory organs of our brains which, in turn, stimulate our power of imagination. It allows us to hear, vocalize, and read "stories" with all our senses and with transformative consequences for innovation, imagination, and creativity. This being the case, we may consider digital storytelling to offer a potentially new way of understanding theology in the age of digitalisation. Can we combine digital storytelling with story theology in developing a theology of digital storytelling? Can we conceive of digital theology as a newly emerging field of study? The answer appears to be resoundingly positive.

Digital Storytelling: Emergence, Development, and Application

The art of storytelling has been around for thousands of years in human culture. Due to technological advances, today it has given rise to a myriad of complex new forms of expression that can be described as digital storytelling" (DST).

In 1994, Dana Atchley[31] and Joe Lambert[32] co-founded the Center for Digital Storytelling at Berkeley, California, renaming it the StoryCenter in

---

[31] Dana Atchley was a producer and artist. He famously produced *NEXT EXIT*, a multimedia autobiography.
[32] Joe Lambert is a local theater producer/dramatic consultant and the executive director of StoryCenter.

2015. It is dedicated to assisting people in using digital media to tell meaningful stories from their own lives. To do this, it offers workshops to storytelling trainers and facilitators in the United States and other countries on appropriate DST methods to achieve the best results.[33] Since 1998, the StoryCenter has worked with many organizations around the world and trained a multitude of people in the art of digital storytelling.

The digital story, as guided and facilitated by the StoryCenter, focuses on personal experience. The recipe for an effective and efficient digital story is composed of seven elements, as revealed in the *Digital Storytelling Cookbook*. (1) *Point of view*: the general point or specific realization a student wishes to communicate with his/her story. (2) *Dramatic question*: the key question that a student will attempt to answer at the end of the story, drawing the greatest attention of the audience. (3) *Emotional content*: special forms of writing intended to keep audience attention. (4) *The gift of voice*: how to narrate the text including use of emotion, intonation, style, and inflection, so as to increase the meaning and relevance of the story and promote audience understanding. (5) *Soundtrack*: a great deal of attention is given to the selection of sounds and music in order to encourage further positive emotional responses and add embellishment. (6) *Economy*: the shorter the better, since most stories can be produced using a small number of words, sounds, images, and videos. (7) *Pacing*: refers to the rhythm of a story in terms of how slowly or quickly it moves on.[34]

To configure these seven elements into a digital story is the typical model of DST proposed by StoryCenter. Some other models add one or more elements, but these seven elements are viewed as essential for creating a digital story with maximum positive impact.[35]

Since the StoryCenter focuses on stories that are meaningful to people's personal lives, the modal DST story package highlights personal experience.

---

[33] John Hartley & Kelly McWilliam eds., *Story Circle: Digital Storytelling Around the World* (NY: John Wiley & Sons, 2009), 3.
[34] Joe Lambert, *Digital Storytelling Cookbook* (Center for Digital Storytelling, 2007), 1-19.
[35] For example, Robin and Pierson add three other elements to this model: "the Overall Purpose of the Story"; "Quality of the Images, Video & Other Multimedia Elements"; and "Good Grammar and Language Usage". See Educause Learning Initiative, "7 things you should know about digital storytelling", *Educause*, January 15, 2007, accessed November 20, 2019. https://library.educause.edu/resources/2007/1/7-things-you-should-know-about-digital-storytelling.

If a storyteller wants to keep audience attention, the StoryCenter believes it is important to be passionate about the themes and characters in the telling of the story. Some of the best stories begin with profound insights from one's own experience. "Economy" is strongly recommended since 2-3 minutes in length maximizes audience impact. Compared to the expense of making a film/video, DST encourages storytellers to employ widely available, low-cost digital technology.[36]

Atchley defined DST as "the short narrated film" (mini-film) told in the first person, using the creator's own voice, a definition later adapted and refined by Joe Lambert.[37] The most amazing thing about the approach of StoryCenter is that ordinary people are able to share their stories in a powerful fashion and a short period of time without spending a great deal of money. This makes a once extremely expensive media dominated by a closed community of individuals to be accessible to most people, thereby enhancing social democracy. The modal DST program of the StoryCenter has become very popular among activists, educators, health and human services agencies, business professionals, and artists looking for ways to innovate, raise awareness, and engage people.[38]

While the classical DST modal proposed by StoryCenter focuses heavily on the individual, with the narrating self and the process guided by facilitators, the new DST trend is moving increasingly towards more interactive, community-oriented, and participatory formats. The media ecosystem and culture seem drastically different today compared to when it was initially developed 20 years ago. Social media allows not only for the lifting and re-embedding of entire strings of text, but also for the indexing of new interpretations through photos, memes, and other kinds of semiotic resources.

Interactive DST emerges from interaction between individual authors and other people within a particular cultural setting and serves as an important resource for all of them to draw upon.[39] The community DST movement is another phase in the development of this innovative technology. This

---

[36] Lambert, *Digital Storytelling Cookbook*, 45-60.
[37] Julie D. Woletz, "Digital Storytelling from Artificial Intelligence to YouTube", in Sigrid Kelsey and Kirk St. Amant eds., *Handbook of Research on Computer Mediated Communication* (Hershey, PA: Information Science Reference, 2008), 587-601.
[38] Lambert, *Digital Storytelling Cookbook*, 45-60.
[39] Alan Davis, "Co-Authoring Identity: Digital Storytelling in an Urban Middle School", *THEN: Technology, Humanities, Education, & Narrative* 1 (2004): 1-12.

movement is a grassroots media phenomenon in which communities create their own short, 3-5 minute digital stories from material grounded in their personal lives (using digital videos, photographs, letters, and news clips, etc.). It has become an increasingly popular approach for development practitioners trying to help community members gain a deeper understanding of the multiple and complex ways in which people's lives are affected by social issues. The entire process is carried out with the firm intention of building new knowledge, as well as building up the skills, connections, and self-confidence of the storytellers themselves. In addition, community DST can provide multiple community perspectives on important life issues simultaneously. Clearly, then, it can be an important and powerful forum for communities to share their own experiences using their own voices.

In the context of the current participatory digital culture based on this sort of "bottom-up" mode of participation, the idea that ordinary people can share their views, experiences, and stories online does not seem to be as revolutionary as it was previously seen to be. Quite the contrary, posting status updates, photos, videos, blog posts, or podcasts online has become a rather mundane activity for many citizens in advanced information-based societies.[40] Of course, DST can be used to serve many purposes, as with the many other forms of participatory media. It has the potential to promote meaningful civic engagement and community development, and therefore have positive impacts beyond the lives of individual participants.[41]

The DST process invites participants to explore their own personal experiences through an effective, creative, and expressive lens, empowering them. The collective process of sharing honest emotions and working reflectively and creatively builds a solid bond between participants, which enables new sources of personal strength to be tapped into and collective challenges to be overcome. It is not surprising to find that some social activists employ DST to help marginalized groups discuss human rights issues that have typically been ignored by the mainstream media.

A growing body of literature has explored the ways in which increasingly diverse DST activities are being applied in various practical fields, such as public health, healthcare, social services, international development, therapy, museums, libraries etc., and, especially, education.[42] In many

---

[40] Pirita Juppi, "Engagement and Empowerment. Digital Storytelling as a Participatory Media Practice", *Nordicom Review* 39 no. 2 (2017): 31-41, 38.
[41] Juppi, "Engagement and Empowerment", 38.
[42] Hartley & McWilliam eds., *Story Circle*, 1-15.

significant ways, DST has truly become a powerful tool for the twenty-first century classroom.

Many researchers have claimed that DST can be used as a powerful tool in the classroom, covering grades K through 12, as well as in higher education to help students express themselves and come to view their lives differently. The ability to tell their stories in a variety of ways (through sounds, music, graphics, photographs, and original artwork) allows them to communicate their own perspectives and demonstrate their own understanding in a creative manner that engages their auditory, visual, and kinesthetic skills. When students are provided with tools that enable this kind of deep self-expression, they feel that they can contribute to the community around them in effective and meaningful ways. As such, they become more actively concerned and willing to change and respond to their realities. When they employ DST to create and envision their future, starting from the past and moving on to the present, greater empowerment becomes possible. They are empowered through confidently sharing their experiences and imagination.

In Taiwan, DST has been introduced into the educational system at all grades, including college and university. It has been used as an expressive medium within the classroom to integrate subject matter with knowledge and skills from across the curriculum. The Ministry of Education initiated a special project called "Talent Cultivation Project for Digital Humanities". At that time, several universities joined this project and applied DST in many different areas of their curricula: art, language, history, design, scientific knowledge, and so forth. A special "Digital Storytelling Competition" was held to promote its widespread application in pedagogy.

Not to be outdone by the Ministry of Education, in 2015 the Ministry of Culture of Taiwan initiated "The Island of Taiwan Story", a project aimed at encouraging the general public to share and collect folk stories using DST. Along the same lines, "I-Fun Learning"[43] was set up by the National Academy for Educational Research, Taiwan, offering many DST videos related to education. Arguably, then, DST has become quite popular in Taiwan and continues to develop at a rapid pace.

---

[43] See the website of *I-Fun Learning.* https://stv.moe.edu.tw/

Digital Storytelling within Religion

DST has not only been used in the above specified areas, but also in religious settings. For example, *I Am Second (IaS)*[44] became famous for using DST in the field of evangelism. *IaS* compiled an archive of highly professional short films, focusing on a particular style of glossy, celebrity-oriented faith narrative approach. These types of stories are shared through fan blogs, Facebook, YouTube, and other social media where subjects share life stories and renew their commitment to prioritize God/Christ in their lives. Unfortunately, a particular stereotypical narrative style commonly plagues this kind of story. The script reads something like this: the video subject overcomes struggles or achieves fulfillment only by surrendering his/her life to God and becoming 'Second'. This approach needs to be distinguished from other DST modal we mentioned earlier. Like modal DST, *IaS* formats pursue the transformative power of stories and rely heavily upon technological media. However, modal DST emphasizes the empowering potential of creating one's own narrative rather than inviting audience to identify with tales told by a few elite celebrities. There is a world of difference between the stories of famous celebrities and stories told by ordinary people about their own authentic life experiences.

After analyzing the design and circulation of and responses to these *IaS* films, Tim Hutchings claims that digital media are fostering significant shifts in the production and reception of religious storytelling.[45] From a theological point of view, *IaS* films tend to derive from the tradition of evangelical testimony. They present highly personalized narratives about a perceived need for divine intervention to require both full surrender to God and deep "suspicion of organized religion". Worldly success is viewed as a mixed blessing; as both a divine gift and a temptation away from God. Some *IaS* films provide roadmaps to salvation and references to the Bible. Altogether, these film stories cannot be viewed as a "single consistent theology". The most that can be said about them is that they "are united by their celebrity stars, traumatic real-life stories, slick presentation, and message of 'being Second'."[46]

---

[44] *I am Second* was founded by Norm Miller in collaboration with a small team from e3 Partners Ministry, on December 2, 2008.
[45] Tim Hutchings, "I Am Second: Evangelicals and digital storytelling", *Australian Journal of Communication*, 39 no. 1 (June 2012): 71-86.
[46] Hutchings, "I Am Second", 84.

IaS is not the only storytelling style being applied in religion. In 2005, the Lutheran Church of Norway initiated a project called "Digital Faith Stories", specifically aimed at helping youth experiencing crises of meaning in faith and life. [47] A careful study of this project in a congregation near Oslo concluded that the DST method could contribute to more systematic educational results by including the life expressions and worldviews of the young into religious training. There are many reasons that can account for this result. Personal narratives in a digital media format can touch viewers deeply and move them to reflect upon their own life experiences. In doing so, they can help to modify their behavior, treat others with greater compassion, speak out about injustice, and become involved in civic and political affairs and events. Sharing stories in this way can lead to positive, life-changing behavioral adjustments and the creation of meaningful support groups. Whether communicated online, in local communities, or at the institutional/policy level, sharing these stories has the potential to make a real difference at many levels of our existence. In sum, analysis of the design and circulation of and responses to these films quite clearly indicates that digital media are fostering significant shifts in the ways that religious stories are being told, produced, and received.

Recently, a novel genre of religious digital stories has emerged. This type of digital story, the so-called "Digital Faith Story", is used to establish initial contact with youth and attempts to integrate them into a religious community by having them construct stories about themselves—a process that implies both negotiation of self-experience and negotiation of authenticity in the narrative. They are produced in a religious setting under the supervision and guidance of the congregation. Birgit Hertzberg Kaare is perhaps right to say that, in these Digital Faith Stories, a transformation takes place "from an individualistic perspective to a more collective perspective—a shift from narrating selves to narrating communities". [48] These newer forms of modal seem to indicate that DST has developed towards the application of a more comprehensive institutional paradigm over the last decade or so. DST programs are hosted by educational systems, community centers, cultural institutions, and even religious congregations.

---

[47] Birgit Hertzberg Kaare, "Youth as Producers: Digital stories of faith and life", *Nordicom Review* 29 no. 2 (2008): 189-201, 193.
[48] Birgit Hertzberg Kaare, "The Self and the Institution: The Transformation of a Narrative Genre", *Nordicom Review*, 33 no. 22 (December 2012): 17-26, 17.

Towards a Theology of Digital Storytelling

Rossiter and Garcia have claimed that DST is "a dynamic and beautiful marriage of narrative and technology".[49] Whether it is wise to argue in favor of such a technology by appealing to the aesthetics of beauty is another question. After all, precious little empirical scientific work has been done on its potential adverse effects at both the social and individual levels of analysis. Without jumping wholeheartedly on the technology bandwagon, this much is relatively safe to say. Digital technology may not always promote social solidarity and stability. This new invention is empowering people, both digital natives and digital immigrants, to utilize digital media and create an audio-visual way of how we relate our lives to our world. Digital technology seems to serve the function of promoting a love of stories in and about human nature.

It should be remembered that DST is a method, as well as a genre, and its increasing diversity of applications and practices has turned it into a worldwide phenomenon.[50] It has become a new and popular cultural expression in our age of digitalisation. Today, DST is used both to express personal stories of the narrative self and to generate stories that promote community identity and the interests of an institution or organization. Working with digital stories tends to strengthen the connection between individuals and the surrounding communities and institutions within which they find themselves. This is why it is often argued that the very idea of DST itself means "capturing lives, creating community".[51]

Although DST uses advanced technology to deliver meanings and messages, this does not mean that good DST does not have a good story as its content. Communication technology is not the whole story, to be sure, and the content of the story still matters greatly. Many practitioners would agree, in fact, that it is the very soul of the DST. This is partly because everyone has a special story to tell and digital technology is a powerful instrument that can be used to frame such a story creatively and share it meaningfully with others in one's community and the world in which one lives.

At this point in our review of religious storytelling, it may be helpful to

---

[49] Marsha Rossiter and Penny A. Garcia, "Digital Storytelling: A New Player on the Narrative Field", *New Directions for Adult and Continuing Education 126* (2010): 37-48, 37.
[50] Hartley & McWilliam, eds., *Story Circle*, 129-217.
[51] Lambert, *Digital Storytelling Cookbook*, 87-89.

revisit story theology proposed by C. S. Song. We may expect DST to be a beneficial tool in doing story theology in the age of digitalisation if we apply it properly, mainly by configuring personal/community stories with the stories of the Bible, creating digital stories for the purpose of seeking self-understanding and knowledge about God.

Song's story theology affirms that we tell stories about God when we tell stories about Jesus Christ; and we tell the stories of Jesus Christ when we tell stories of the people with whom Jesus lived.[52] He claimed that story theology does not use the Biblical narratives to the exclusion of cultural stories existing outside of Biblical and church traditions. On the contrary, he encourages dialogue between the stories of the Bible and the stories of people located within larger cultural groups, either individually or communally. Based on his own plentiful and profound experiences, he proposes five approaches for doing story theology.[53]

(1) *To be aware of the theological nature of stories.* Here a story is not simply a story; it is already in a culture as story theology. This means that a story has theological meaning attributed to it. What a theologian needs to do is to immerse himself in the story by reading and listening to it over and over again, attentively and intentionally, until the meaning of it is disclosed to him. This means that theological doctrine and dogma are preceded by theological stories or story theology. This is why Song asserted that, in the beginning of theology were "stories", not "texts". He argues that, in the very beginning, the Word of God became stories that dwelt among them. The task of story theology, then, is to search for the revelation of God within those stories rather than to discuss the doctrines contained in "texts".

(2) *To do theology by storytelling.* Telling stories can be considered a way of "doing" theology. When stories about a long ago past are stored in our memories, it is the storyteller who turns those memories of the dead into stories that allow the dead to continue to tell their stories. In this way, the past regains life through storytelling. In storytelling, stories continue to live and the theological meanings they contain continue to spread out in time and space.

---

[52] Choan-Seng Song, *Jesus the Crucified People: The Cross in the Lotus World, Volume I* (Minneapolis: Fortress Press, 1996), 37.
[53] Choan-Seng Song, *In the Beginning Were Stories, Not Texts: Story Theology* (Eugene, Oregon: Cascade Books, 2011), 154-170. Here the author tries to summarize these five approaches briefly.

(3) *To respond to stories with empathy.* Stories are told for the significant purpose of soliciting empathy from listeners. Therefore, storytelling is not a storyteller's monologue, but, in fact, a dialogue between storyteller and story listener. There is both a telling "script" and a listening "script", so to speak. Empathy obtained this way makes dialogue possible. By the power of empathy in the actual act of "telling", a "story" materialized for both storyteller and listener: your story and my story becomes "our" story. Without empathy, in other words, the story loses its passion and soul. Without empathy, your story does not become my story and end in "our" story. Why is empathy so important? Perhaps the answer is that an empathetic response to a story effectively removes potent obstacles (ethnic, religious, cultural, etc.) that may exist between different persons, tribes, nations, religious groups, and all kinds of other human communities and organizations.

(4) *To reform and reunite a faithful community by sharing stories.* It stands to reason that every individual belongs to many different types of human community, as well as to humanity as a whole. In this very real sense, then, a story is not only a story belonging to individual people, but also a story of the communities to which they belong. More to the point, a story is a community event—a communion happening between the individual and the community. As such, a story can transform and reunite a community. It can create and recreate a common memory by awaking mutual trust and common faith. Therefore, an individual's story may stretch out horizontally to interweave with the stories of others hundreds of miles away; or it may stretch out vertically with stories told thousands of years before; or both. In this way, stories may have the capacity of crossing boundaries of time and space, connecting humanity scattered over all places and across all times. Stories appear to have amazing "time/space travel" powers of unity and solidarity.

(5) *To explore the multiple universes of meanings of stories through curiosity, association, and imagination.* In many ways, the story can be considered the very epitome of theological meaning. Indeed, stories invite us to explore the universe of meaning. On the one hand, they constitute the microcosm of meanings inviting us to explore meanings in terms of the vicissitudes of life for individuals, families, tribes, and nations. On the other hand, they constitute the macrocosm of meanings summoning us to discover the immense universe of meanings. The implication here, of course, is that the

exploration of the universe of meaning requires something more than simply logical reasoning, rational thinking, and doctrinal argumentation. Curiosity, association, and imagination are even more important than logic, reason, and argumentation in exploring this mysterious universe. With curiosity, we are pushed by a mysterious power to discover truth. With association, we connect God's reign to our world of ordinary life. God's reign is parabled by such things as mustard seeds, yeast, pearls, fishing nets, and so forth, and is understood through a panoply of metaphors and symbols. With imagination, we discard the old and worldly bondage of ideas and ways of thinking, and open ourselves up to new possibilities—to a new Heaven and a new Earth.

One of the most interesting things about the core ideas and values implied in Song's five approaches to story theology is their overlapping similarity with the seven essential elements of DST outlined earlier. Stories are theological by their very nature, since every story is related somehow to the meaning of "ultimate concern" and its relation to the fountain of existence. To be sure, the relationship between God and man continues to be the basic theological question. In terms of digital theology, then, the awareness of it is assumed to lead to a point of view (**element 1**) of a digital faith story s/he is going to share.

Actually, a theological question is a dramatic question (**element 2**); a monumentally significant key question that a storyteller will try to answer at the end of the story to draw audience attention. Storytelling is itself a kind of "doing" theology, since only by storytelling can the story be kept alive and theologically meaningful. Without storytelling, life would pass away and theology would fade away shortly after. DST is storytelling assisted by digital technology, which makes storytelling, among other things, much more colorful and polyphonic than it would otherwise be.

It emphasizes the gift of personal voice (**element 4**) in narration expressed with human emotions, intonations, and inflections. The positive effect is to magnify the meaning and relevance of the story and highly improved audience understanding. Additionally, it uses a soundtrack, which requires the selection of sounds and music intended to add further emotional response and embellishment. According to a Chinese proverb, this is what makes a good story a veritable "painting-in-poetry, poetry-in-painting". It almost goes without saying that DST makes this ideal possible by telling the story with pace and rhythm (**element 7**).

The use of pictures, images, and photos is helpful in making a story more "economical" (**element 6**) in terms of both spoken word and written text. DST asks for emotional content (**element 3**) to grab the attention of audience and generate a response. Interactive modal DST makes the dialogue between storyteller and listener possible and then expands it. In fact, as mentioned earlier, DST is a kind of art, imagination, spirituality, and life-sharing, functioning to enrich storyteller and audience empathy and build up community identity. DST, especially community DST connected through social media, is a great help in reforming and shaping a faith community. Finally, DST also creates a cyberspace, a universe of virtual reality full of meaning and mystery.

Deena Metzger, a famous American writer, once said:

> Stories move in circles. They don't move in straight lines. So it helps if you listen in circles. There are stories inside stories and stories between stories, and finding your way through them is as easy and as hard as finding your way home. And part of the finding is getting lost. And when you're lost, you start to look around and listen.[54]

The DST traits of non-straightness, circulation, inter-connection, mediation, and in-between are similar to the presuppositions of doing story theology proposed by C. S. Song. He claimed that, in seeking to understand God through stories, we find that:

> God moves in all directions: God moves forward, no doubt, but also sideways and even backwards. Perhaps God zigzags too. It does not seem God's interest to create neat and tidy landscapes in certain selected places. God goes anywhere a redeeming presence is called for.[55]

Here, he is at pains to point out that there are stories inside stories and stories between stories; stories linked with each other in a built up universe of meaning.[56]

In fact, DST is an art, and art usually relies heavily on imagination. It kindles creativity and innovation, releases imagination to travel beyond reality, and brings new and alternative connections in order to seek capacities that help us take action for change. By provoking imagination,

---

[54] Deena Metzger, "Writing for Your Life", *Deena Metzger,* accessed November 10, 2019. http://deenametzger.net/published-works-3/writing-for-your-life/
[55] Choan-Seng Song, *Tell Us Our Names, Story Theology from an Asian Perspective* (Eugene, Oregon: Wipf and Stock, 2005), 16.
[56] Song, *In the Beginning Were Stories*, 166-168.

DST provides a platform for social change and encourages us to think of new ways to see and envision the world.

Concluding Remarks

Dana Atchley, the pioneer of DST, once said "...digital storytelling combines the best of two worlds: the 'new world' of digitized video, photography and art, and the 'old world' of telling stories".[57] DST can be viewed as an effective way to help bridge the gap between the world of professional media and "everyday cultural practice".[58] For C. S. Song, story theology combines the best of two worlds: the world of the Bible and the world of our daily life in our own culture.

DST envisions a better world by digitalizing storytelling. Storytelling is powerful and digital technology makes storytelling a much more powerful medium than it would otherwise be. The digital story matters, but the content of that story matters much more. Story theology plays an important role in configuring the content of a digital story. To explore a theology of digital storytelling is a new and potentially powerful way to further the development of Taiwanese contextual theology as it is influenced by digital technology.

---

[57] Presentation Zen, "Dana Atchley (1941-2000): A Digital Storytelling Pioneer", *Presentation Zen*, accessed November 20, 2019.
https://www.presentationzen.com/presentationzen/2005/07/dana_atchley_19.html
[58] Hartley & McWilliam eds., *Story Circle*, 122.

Bibliography

Bevas, Stephen B. *Models of Contextual Theology, Revised and Expanded Edition*. Maryknoll, NY: Orbis Books, 2009.
—. *Essays in Contextual Theology*. Boston: Brill. 2018.
Castells, Manuel. *The Information Age: Economy, Society and Culture, Volume I The Rise of the Network Society*. Oxford: Blackwell, 2nd Edition, 2010.
Chen, Nan-Jou ed. *A Testament to Taiwan Homeland Theology: The Essential Writings of Wang Hsieh-Chih*. Taipei: Yeong Wang, 2011.
CISION PR Newswire. "Taiwan AI R&D Center Expansion Lights up Microsoft 30th Anniversary". *CISION PR Newswire,* September. 27, 2019. Accessed October 30, 2019.
https://www.prnewswire.com/news-releases/taiwan-ai-rd-center-expansion-lights-up-microsoft-30th-anniversary-300926997.html
Davis, Alan. "Co-authoring identity: Digital storytelling in an urban middle school". *THEN: Technology, Humanities, Education, & Narrative* 1 (January 2014): 1-12.
Department of Information Services, Executive Yuan. "DIGI+: Digital Nation and Innovative Economic Development Program". *Executive Yuan*. September 9, 2019. Accessed October 20, 2019.
https://english.ey.gov.tw/News3/9E5540D592A5FECD/659df63b-dad4-47e3-80ab-c62cb40a62cd.
Educause Learning Initiative. "7 things you should know about digital storytelling". *Educause,* January 15, 2007. Accessed November 20, 2019.
https://library.educause.edu/resources/2007/1/7-things-you-should-know-about-digital-storytelling
England, John C., Jose Kuttianimattathil, John Mansford, Lily A. Quintos, David Suh Kwang-sun, and Janice Wickeri eds. *Asian Christian Theologies, A Research Guide to Authors, Movements, Sources, Volume 3: Northeast Asia*, ISPCK/Claretian Publishers: Orbis Books, 2004.
Everington, Keoni. "Taiwan's breakaway from China was during Neolithic Age: tech minister". *Taiwan News,* January 26, 2019. Accessed November 20, 2019.
https://www.taiwannews.com.tw/en/news/3825048
Focus Taiwan. "Google gets approval to invest NT$26 billion in Taiwan". *Focus Taiwan*, October 28,2019. Accessed November 20, 2019.
http://focustaiwan.tw/news/aeco/201910280020

Hartley, John and Kelly McWilliam eds. *Story Circle*: *Digital Storytelling Around the World.* NY: John Wiley & Sons, 2009.
Huang, Po-Ho. *No Longer a Stranger*: *Towards the Construction of Contextual Theologies.* Tiruvalla: CSS Books, 2007.
—. "The Impacts to Christian Theologies and Church's Mission from Digital Revolution", 1-14. Paper presented at the International Consultation— *International Journal of Asian Christianity*, November 2016, Chennai, India.
Hutchings, Tim. "I Am Second: Evangelicals and digital storytelling". *Australian Journal of Communication* 39 no. 1 (June 2012): 71-86.
IMD World Competitiveness Center, *IMD The World Competitiveness Ranking* 2019, digital version (PDF). Accessed November 21, 2019. https://www.imd.org/wcc/world-competitiveness-center-rankings/world-digital-competitiveness-rankings-2019
Jennings, Ralph. "Why Google is Expanding in Taiwan Again and Again", *Forbes.* Accessed November 20, 2019. https://www.forbes.com/sites/ralphjennings/2019/04/10/why-google-is- expanding-in-taiwan-again-and-again/#47417c5f279d
Joseph, M. P., Po-Ho Huang and Victor Hsu eds. *Wrestling with God in Context: Revisiting the Theology and Social Vision of Shoki Coe.* Minneapolis: Augsburg Fortress, 2018.
Juppi, Pirita. "Engagement and Empowerment. Digital Storytelling as a Participatory Media Practice". *Nordicom Review* 39 no. 2 (2017): 31-41.
Kaare, Birgit Hertzberg. "Youth as Producers: Digital stories of faith and life". *Nordicom Review* 29 no. 2 (2008): 189-201.
—. "The Self and the Institution: The Transformation of a Narrative Genre", *Nordicom Review*, 33 no. 2 (December 2012): 17-26.
Lai, Juvina. "Taipei to house the largest R&D center for Google in Asia Pacific", *Taiwan News*, January 31, 2018. Accessed November 20, 2019.
Metzger, Deena. "Writing for Your Life". *Deena Metzger.* Accessed November 10, 2019. http://deenametzger.net/published-works-3/writing-for-your-life/
Microsoft Taiwan. "Taiwan AI R&D Center Expansion Lights up Microsoft 30th Anniversary". *CISION PR Newswire,* September 27, 2019. Accessed October 30, 2019. https://www.prnewswire.com/news-releases/taiwan-ai-rd-center-expansion-lights-up-microsoft-30th-anniversary-300926997.html

National Development Council. "Survey on 2018 Individual/Household Digital Opportunity Survey in Taiwan Executive Summary". Accessed October 10, 2019. https://ws.ndc.gov.tw/001/administrator/11/relfile/5813/32110/078c2deb-b441-4c77-a033-d1543d40de2e.pdf

Negroponte, Nicholas. *Being Digital.* New York: Alfred A. Knopf, 1995.

Phillips, Peter, Kyle Schiefelbein-Guerrero & Jonas Kurlberg. "Defining Digital Theology: Digital Humanities, Digital Religion and the Particular Work of the CODEC Research Centre and Network", *Open Theology* 5, no. 1 (January 2019): 29-43.

Prensky, Marc. *From Digital Natives to Digital Wisdom: Hopeful Essays for 21st Century Learning.* Thousand Oaks, CA: Corwin Press, 2012.

Presentation Zen. "Dana Atchley (1941-2000): A Digital Storytelling Pioneer". *Presentation Zen.* Accessed November 20, 2019. https://www.presentationzen.com/presentationzen/2005/07/dana_atchley_19.html

Rossiter, Marsha and Penny A. Garcia. "Digital Storytelling: A New Player on the Narrative Field". *New Directions for Adult and Continuing Education.* 126 (2010): 37-48.

Song, Choan-Seng. *In the Beginning Were Stories, Not Texts: Story Theology.* Eugene, Oregon: Cascade Books, 2011.

—. *Jesus the Crucified People: The Cross in the Lotus World, Volume I.* Minneapolis: Fortress Press, 1996.

—. *Tell Us Our Names: Story Theology from an Asian Perspective.* Eugene, Oregon: Wipf and Stock, 2005.

Woletz, Julie D. "Digital Storytelling from Artificial Intelligence to YouTube". In Sigrid Kelsey and Kirk St. Amant eds. *Handbook of Research on Computer Mediated Communication,* 587-601. Hershey, PA: Information Science Reference, 2008.

Ya-Tang Chuang,
Professor of Theology,
Department of Theology,
Chang Jung Christian University, Tainan, Taiwan.

CHAPTER THREE

MIMESIS, DIEGESIS, LOGOS: RE-EVALUATING GREEK CONCEPTS TOWARD AN AUDIBLE CINEMA

JAMES BATCHO

The narrative concepts *mimesis* and *diegesis* have a complex aesthetic and philosophical lineage that continues to be applied and argued today. While often framed as showing and telling, these translations belie the complexity of their regard in ancient Greek poetry and their subsequent aesthetic and religious applications. Scholars have devoted extensive written works to the interplay of these terms. With Aristotle's *Poetics* as the conceptual ground, *mimesis* became a key term for thinking through performed and written narrative methods. But it finds relevance in film theory as well, which frequently works through questions of representation and imitation. This also reveals film theory's analytical preoccupation with visuality—its *images*. Film theory rightly points out that the other half to images is the vitality of *sound*. But this study takes a further step to consider an *audible* approach to cinema in which sound gives way to hearing and listening. This invites a critical re-evaluation of *diegesis* and *mimesis* as applied to cinema studies and film philosophy.

Before focusing on the audible, we must address some key distinctions in form—on the one hand, oral/listened and on the other, written/read. In oral cultures, stories were heard. They were communicated through direct acts of speaking and listening. In written cultures, stories were read. The shift from one to the other finds Greek culture at less of a handover and more of an overlap between these traditions. Havelock (1986) describes this period as an "interlock" between forms: "the acoustic flow of language contrived by echo to hold the attention of the ear has been reshuffled into visual patterns created by the thoughtful attention of the eye" (13).

Yet reading does not happen in literal pictures. In reading, the eye functions as another form of listening. The processual unfolding is similar whether spoken/sung/heard or written/read in the following sense: The story, with all its imagery and events, is materially *unseen* and inwardly imagined. Cinema is different in that its unfolding happens visually and audibly. A film is not read; it is seen, heard and listened to.[1] Another way of thinking of this distinction is that prior to audiovisual forms, a story's images were *imagined* through listening and reading, while in audiovisual forms, the unfolding is *seen*.

Cinema's images are delivered as a line, in a stream of constructive montage.[2] In this, a single line of seeing unfolds. This does not mean that a single line of *thinking* unfolds, rather that the representation is singular. By contrast, film sound is plural.[3] Rather than a single montage, sound is able to function independently of the dominant image stream, and do so at multiple levels.[4] Film sound is commonly divided into three subcategories or disciplines: music, dialogue, and sound effects. *Music*, on its own, is included in Aristotle's *mimesis*. His discussion in *Poetics* is brief, but includes both the methods of singing and the use of instruments. *Dialogue*, at least as it is theorized, is closest to what Aristotle called mimetic *diegesis*, although there are various discursive aspects here as well, as we shall find. *Sound effects* as applied in today's cinematic practice has no relation to Greek poetic concepts.[5] It represents the sound of a natural world. Such sound has no place in the Greek aesthetic tradition because (1)

---

[1] This statement that a film is not "read" may seem obvious, but it runs counter to psychoanalytical and semiotic theories of film. This will be addressed over the course of this essay.

[2] The vast majority of the images seen on screen is "profilmic," or performed for the camera and arranged in sequence as montage. Images may be rendered via special effects such as CGI, but such effects all compose the imagery integral to the film world. Exceptions here would be any "reflexive" decisions, titles, the now largely abandoned intertitles of the silent film era, or the rare use of dissolves and superimposition, such as in early experimental French impressionist cinema. For more, see Bordwell and Thompson (2008) Chapter 12.

[3] For more see Batcho (2018) Chapter 4 and Chion (2009) Chapter 8.

[4] Claudia Gorbman writes that hearing is both more selective and lazier than vision (1987). To her, this means that one's audible capacity is more limited than seeing. With this, she de-emphasizes the key point that hearing is capable of separating, gaining independence, from the dogma of images.

[5] One may argue that sound effects fall into Aristotle's category of "spectacle," except that the term is distinctly visual ("spectatorship").

it had no moral or ethical value to Greek thought and (2) it is generally deemed as unnecessary to the plot. One could argue that it would, if need be, fall under the category of *mimesis*. Instead, it is identified in sound theory as "diegetic." Indeed, all three classes of film sound have now been contained in a diegetic conceptual framework, either by being part of "the *diegesis*" or separated from it as "non-diegetic."

This opens the question: How did sound effects—a door slam, the breaking of glass, the hum of machinery—become classed not as representation, not as "showing," but as *telling*? As I will argue, film scholarship's appropriation of *diegesis* is a fumbled step because it renders both sound and its hearing as rhetorically and visually analytical. However, my intent is not to move film sound toward its other, *mimesis*. To do so would be to grant hearing a representational or imitative status that limits sound to causal mimicry of visual objects. Indeed, too often the practice of sound design engages in such visual duplication. Instead, I aim to shift from what is falsely regarded as textual, material and representational toward expressions of audibility. The intent is to move what is named as "sound" away from textual and representational analysis and instead toward *expression*. To this end, I will argue that audible cinema is best conceived as *logos*. Such a move de-emphasizes transcendent readings and representations and instead grants audibility its own immanent expressions of hearing and listening.

We will begin by exploring why film theory has placed the sound of the world within the bubble of *diegesis* by tracing key movements in the migration of the term. Not only has *diegesis* stolen the audible expressiveness from sound, it also reinforces a visual and textual regard for an experience that has no language. The essay then explores different functions of *mimesis* and why this term also fails to capture immanent audible expressions. Finally, it argues that *logos* is a more expressive means of thinking through audible cinema. By shifting from the sonic to the audible, the hope is that a *logos* conceptual framework will resonate not only philosophically but in film practice, opening new paths of creativity and experimentation in cinematic arts.

Diegesis and *Mimesis* in Greek Poetry

Although often attributed in its origins to Plato, the word *diegesis* stretches back at least to Heraclitus. He used *diegesis* (διήγησις) as the means of explaining or narrating the truthful activity of nature, or genuine being (*phusis,* φύσις), in order to understand *logos* (λόγος) (Hülsz 2013). Plato and then Aristotle applied the word to Greek epic poetry, which in them denotes the narration of a story as presented orally by performers. Two points about Greek poetry and theater must be addressed for clarification: (1) "Poetry" in Greek times meant something other than how it is used today. Its root, *poiesis*, means "to make." It applied not only to fiction but also to creation theories about the cosmos, all of which was drawn into philosophical inquiry. (2) Greek poetry was *performed*; it was spoken for public listening. The purpose of the poem was social and civic: to *make* language and song in such a way that the hearer may retain the story being told, along with its moral purpose.[6] Before writing was widespread, stories were intended for attentive listening—to create imagery and ideas in the mind of the listener and to hold an audience's attention.

To elicit the complexity of ideas in the performance of poetry, different methods or voicings needed to be employed. An orator would either take on the role of an omniscient narrator—"the poet," as Aristotle writes (2006)—or a character within the play. The work of such a rhapsode was highly performative and artistic. His shifting vocal style and inflections would indicate which is being presented. In Book III of the *Republic* (Plato 2004), Socrates notes how in epic poetry an orator sometimes speaks as Homer, the poet-composer of the *Iliad*, and in other times as Chryses, the priest character within the *Iliad*. These were the two methods of a total *lexis* (λέξις). If the words were delivered as the poet himself, such delivery was termed *diegesis*, or "narration." If it was delivered "in character" it was *mimesis* (μίμησις), frequently translated in narrative theory as "imitation." The translation of *mimesis* more familiar to contemporary film and narrative arts is "representation." But imitation is an important way of thinking the term, since mimicry lay at its conceptual heart.

For Plato, *mimesis* is a style of *diegesis*. The distinction comes through a discursive presentation or method (*lexis*) regarding what is being said (*logos*) (Halliwell 2012). This is subdivided into *haple diegesis* (voice of the poet), *diegesis dia mimeseos* (mimetic narration, or the voices of characters in a story) and *diegesis di'amphoteron* (a mixture of the two). In practice, the variations in voice delivery (*lexis*) determine the nuanced complexities of image-making (*mimesis*) or story-telling (*diegesis*). *Diegesis* in the Platonic sense, unlike *mimesis*, can *only* tell; it cannot

---

[6] Havelock writes that "the purpose of oral poetry, including Homer's, was to contrive a memorized version of social and civic tradition and government..." (1986, 13).

show. The *dia-* of it and "dialogue" have the same origin: *through*. Dialogue then is a *dia-logos*, a means of channeling the unseen *logos* through speaking.[7] This speaker—or more accurately, this diegetic *speaking*—is only *as* the poet. *Diegesis*, according to Halliwell, means to give an account, to explain, or "verbal narration" (2012). In direct contrast to Plato, Aristotle in *Poetics* conceives of narrative as entirely mimetic, even in rare situations where he offers a diegetic *mimesis*, or "narrative imitation" (2006).

Diegesis in Sound Theory Part I: A Text and Its Reader

Prior to what we now name as "film theory," cinema was an experimental art of image production. Once it became arranged as montage, a change occurs. The associational and symbolic power of montage became ripe for the production of meaning, particularly through Russian practitioner-theorists.[8] Claudia Gorbman points to the Russian Formalists of the 1920s, who made a distinction between "fable," the narrated aspects of a film (the diegetic) and the "subject" (its "textual treatment" or "representation") (1987, p. 20).[9] She attributes French theorists Étienne Souriau and Gérard Genette for their renditions of the term "diegetic" in the 1950s.[10] In the former we have the *diegesis* as "'the world supposed or proposed by the film's fiction'" and in the latter a "'spatiotemporal universe referred to by

---

[7] All of this is a distinctly Platonic concept of *logos*, a word that in Heraclitus before him was more complex. For Plato, *logos* was engaged through speaking.

[8] Progenitors of what became film theory are Béla Balázs, Sergei Eisenstein and Vsevolod Pudovkin, among others. These were practitioners as much as theorists. It is also worth noting that "film theory" is methodologically and conceptually different from "film philosophy," although there are overlaps.

[9] See as well Sinnerbrink (2011) who points to David Bordwell's analysis of the Russian formalist distinction between plot and story. "The plot refers to the ordered structure of what is (visually or linguistically) narrated; it is literally what we see on screen, a selection of images composed in a certain sequential order. The story, on the other hand, is the narration (the telling or showing) of what happens chronologically, which viewers understand by reconstructing an account of events from the visual and narrative cues composing the plot. On Bordwell's view, viewers are therefore active participants in the construction of narrative, whereas plot and style are 'objective 'features that can be identified by historico-critical analysis" (Sinnerbrink 2011, 46-47).

[10] Anne Souriau also claims to have invented the term in 1950. See Taylor (2007) for more on this and for further accounts of the word's application during this period, generally supported by Gorbman (1987).

the primary narration'" (Gorbman 1987, 20-21).[11] She summarizes *diegesis* as "the *narratively implied spatiotemporal world of the actions and characters*" (21).

It is important to consider the changes underway in French philosophy during the 1950s and '60s coinciding with this concept of *diegesis*: a movement toward literary and narrative analysis on one hand and semiology and psychoanalysis on the other. François Dosse (1997) writes about how French philosophy had turned away from Sartrean existentialism and phenomenology in favor of structuralism. This movement, along with post-structuralism, was responding to a Saussurean emphasis on *ambiguity*, which functioned well with structuralism's linguistic/textual interpretations. Theory's emphasis shifted from ontology and its questions of *being* to Freudian analysis and its speaking of *language*. Dosse adds that in Jacques Lacan's synchronic and spoken emphasis, "Speech is forever cut off from all access to reality and only uses signifiers that refer to each other. Man only exists by his symbolic function and it is through this function that he must be grasped" (105). This leads to "textual readings" and a focus on language over representation. In a cinema-as-language approach, one endows film with a creative yet familiar constructive and referential component and a way of *thinking through* a film. Meaning and sight gave way to semiological interpretation and the film-as-*text*.

Through this change, the point of emphasis shifts from the *image* to the *camera*. A key writer working at this intersection of language, analysis and cinema was Christian Metz, still cited in contemporary film and film sound theory today. Metz (1974) writes in 1968 that cinema—in his conception, cinema *as language*—is denotative in its *shot* and connotative in its meaning. *Language*, as opposed to *langue*, was not only the selectivity of vision but its *ordering*, conceived as "syntagmatic" via the camera and delivered for an audience on behalf of the filmmaker. Metz picks up from Souriau and writes of a film *diegesis* as "the sum of a film's denotation, the narration itself, but also the fictional space and time dimensions implied in and by the narrative" (71). It thereby extends to characters, landscape, events—all narrative elements are thus considered

---

[11] Gorbman is citing Genette's "*D'un récit baroque*" from 1969 and Souriau's *L'Univers filmique* from 1953. See Gorbman, (1987) for full citations and references. Also, see Taylor (2007) who writes that this *use* of diegesis may not come from the Greek word but from the French words *diégèse* and *diégétique* (2007).

as *denoted*. Metz adds that cinema became "cinema" only after it stopped being a series of images and became a *narrative* art, in other words, a *diegesis*. Through Genette, Souriau, Metz and others, cinema is discursive, saying without speaking via the act of production and assembly. The apparatus is the element that narrates.

Genette's 1971 text *Narrative Discourse* (1980) was influential in this movement of cinema to a form to be *read*. He offers three definitions of the word *narrative*, emphasizing his third: narrative as a succession of events that are the subject of a discourse. This, he writes, involves "the study of a totality of actions and situations taken in themselves, without regard to the medium, linguistic or other, through which knowledge of that totality comes to us" (24). This he calls the "narrative *text*" (26). Narrative is different from *narrating*, which he defines as "the whole of the real or fictional situation in which the action takes place" (27). Narrating produces the narrative. The *act* exists only as the intermediary for producing the narrative, while the narrative exists to produce the story. Narrative can only be uttered by someone. For Genette, narrative discourse is the only method available to textual analysis, and therefore the only instrument available in thinking through narrative.

Diegesis in Sound Theory Part II: A Space and Its Viewer

When sound theory began to gain scholarly traction in the 1980s, this literary approach was folded into material and representational theories of film sound. Diegesis reduced sound to a dualist ontology. This has both stripped *diegesis* from its prior denotation as narration and rendered sound as either inside or outside a material world. "Diegetic sound" has little to do with listening and hearing that is immanent to a film's own world; instead it becomes a function, a linguistic signifier for visual and material veracity. Theories of film *sound diegesis* define the term as follows: if the sound exists in the space of the film world it is diegetic; if it is heard from the distance of audience only, it is nondiegetic. Michel Chion (2009) writes that diegetic sound is "Sound whose apparent source is in the space-time continuum of the scene onscreen. Diegetic sound is sound that the film leads us to believe the characters can (or could) hear" (474).[12] Diegetic sound as a concept denotes an average spatiotemporal condition—a link to normalcy by means of the character's ability to hear sound that is

---

[12] This is the glossary term from Chion's text, as translated by Gorbman.

extended in space from objects, seen or unseen, within that space. It is not an audible capacity, rather a law of material existence represented for an audience.

David Bordwell and Kristin Thompson (1985) offer the following definition for diegetic sound: "If the source of a sound is a character or object in the story space of the film, we call the sound *diegetic*. The voices of the characters, sounds made by objects in the story, or music coming from instruments in the story space are all diegetic sound" (191-192). Gorbman and Mary Anne Doane framed the term in relation to music (in the former) and the voice (in the latter). Gorbman (1987) writes that music as produced diegetically in film is "music that (apparently) issues from a source within the narrative" (22). The example often used to convey this idea is a radio or turntable that is evident (usually visually, but not necessarily) inside the world of the film, and heard by a character who shares its same space. Doane (1985) equates *diegesis* with world, describing the former as "the expansive area of the film world, seen or unseen, heard or unheard, the world itself" (166). Her arguments hinge on spatial thinking, which leads her to ask: Where in the film is the voice that speaks? For her the voice belongs to the "fantasmatic body" in the film, and in this way the film finds its subjectivity in the character. The voice is the means of anchoring the body in the space of the film in order to unify the technological difference between image and voice.[13] Diegetic sound thereby serves to maintain the ideology of synchronized unity at the level of verisimilitude—in other words, a universal hearing.[14]

Genette's literary application does not argue for such a hard binary and instead proposes *degrees* of diegesis. This is aligned with his distaste for common literary containers of first- and third-person perspectives. As Genette writes: "Absence is absolute, but presence has degrees" (245). Applying this to cinema, "nondiegetic" is absolutely outside, but "diegetic" involves a richer application of the various perspectives of characters and narrators within the *diegesis*. Genette marks off two sets of distinctions: extradiegetic and intradiegetic *narrative* levels, and heterodiegetic and

---

[13] Vinay Shrivastava critiques this notion of the fantasmatic body, arguing that Doane does not account for the role of the Imaginary, which is capable of establishing sound without needing a visual body to grant it unity (1996).

[14] Subjective versus objective "sound" are therefore commonly considered as subcategories of diegetic potentiality.

homodiegetic *story* levels.[15] The former pair composes the telling-of (degrees denoting within or outside the telling) while the latter composes the events underway (degrees of within or outside the events). What is interesting here in distinguishing literature from cinema is that the extra-narrative is considered as the primary level, while the intra-narrative is considered by Genette as secondary. In other words, the voice outside has higher status than the voice inside. Extradiegetic narrators are telling the story to the public. Extra-hetero is someone outside the action who tells, while extra-homo is someone who tells the story that one lives. Genette's diegetic levels aim to delineate narrative expressions occurring in its *textual* production *for the reader*. He writes that these levels designate "not individuals, but relative situations and functions" (229). Yet one may take note that in all such categories, a *telling* is underway.

While Genette is working at the level of the text, film sound theory analyzes at the level of the space. Other scholars following Genette have made efforts to extend his own extensive taxonomy of *diegesis* or to identify the degrees or levels of blending and overlapping between the transcendent apparatus and the immanent world.[16] Bordwell and Thompson (1985) propose their own diegetic split, reserving "internal diegetic" sound to what is "only from the mind of the character" and therefore "subjective" (193). Yet in doing so, they write of the *space* of this internality, which is, like Doane's, a curious move—opening the question of what this internal space is.

In film sound theory's application of *diegesis*, a reversal of Platonic-Aristotelian taxonomy has occurred.[17] Film sound's *diegesis* runs directly counter to Plato's claim that what is diegetic is not as or from characters but as or from the poet, the one who stands *outside* of the world, thus servicing the needs of exposition. Through such appropriation—*diegesis* as "film world"—all elements are legitimized *by the camera*, even when not presently visible. It is not simply a matter of what the camera reveals; it is what and how it constructs. Its *misé-en-scene* is entirely different from hearing and listening, which require no camera. No matter which conception

---

[15] See Genette (1980), the subsection titled "Narrative Levels."
[16] One of the strongest arguments in this regard is Robynn Stilwell's essay "The Fantastical Gap Between Diegetic and Non-diegetic" (2007), which develops nuanced accounts of subjectivity and empathy through music that occurs in the gaps within and outside the space of the story.
[17] See as well Taylor (2007).

or translation one adopts, *diegesis* must assume a process that is both linear and visual. The camera does this, as does literature. Such a syntagmatic structure—a word/shot following naturally from the one that proceeds it—is linguistic, oral, sequential and visual. This works well for the construction of images, which in cinema can only be syntagmatic because of the mandates of linear montage. But it is a poor model for sound and audibility for two conjoined reasons: hearing and listening do not require an eye and they involve more than voices. They are states that move outside of description, rhetoric and appearances because they are bound neither to image nor language. Therefore, while audible states can be experientially connotative, they defy denotation.

The Mimetic Voice

Before addressing such non-vocal audible relations, it is important to revisit what the voice is doing in Greek poetry and written literature, how this relates to poetic imagery, and how it applies to contemporary cinema. Greek poetry, as theater, was of course not cinema. Its voices in epic performance functioned to excite the imagination and invite future recollections within the listener.[18] Extending this to cinema, if any sonic or audible element of a film is diegetic, conceived from a Platonic-Aristotelian application of the adjective, it can only be that which is *actually* speaking: what film has named "voiceover." Voiceover is frequently employed as a device to fill in story gaps for what cannot be seen or discussed. In Genette's "Narrative of Words" section, he mentions "transposed speech," "inner dialogue," and "soliloquy" (1980, 170). While not directly correlative to voiceover, they are all hallmarks of its function. In this way of thinking, voiceover is "narratized," or "inner" speech, which performs cinema's greatest act of distancing from a story's immanent world.

Here, the question of narration (*diegesis*) versus representation (*mimesis*) depends on the *who* that speaks. Normally in a film, the character, not the director, speaks the voiceover.[19] By Genette's taxonomy, voiceover should

---

[18] Ong (2012) stresses that in Homer's day, knowledge had to be repeated or it would be lost. But even in the time of Plato and Aristotle, memory remained a critical aspect of the reproduction of ideas in the production of culture.

[19] There are exceptions, such as Ingmar Bergman's tendency to do his own voiceover in his films. In this case, the voice would be extra-heterodiegetic.

therefore be identified as extra-homodiegetic. This renders voiceover as a delivery distinctly more mimetic than in literature or in Greek poetry. In literature, the common third-person narrator is no one,[20] and in Greek theater it is the poet. In cinema, it is someone living the film's reality. Yet it is also a someone living outside of the time of its images, which is why the voice runs "over" cinema's images. It is a time presumably further into the future than the unfolding of cinema's image-events.[21] A voice *listened to* by the spectator through actual narration almost exclusively occupies a subsequent, or classic, time.[22]

Yet in film sound theory, "voiceover" is commonly categorized as nondiegetic. This is for spectatorial (audience) and spatial (in or outside) reasons, not poetic (in the Greek sense) or literary (in Genette's sense) reasons. Voiceover is deemed nondiegetic because it is for the audience's ears only, not heard by any character within the *space* of the film. Chion (2009) for example considers "voice-overs and pit music" as *son off*, or "nondiegetic sound." He defines nondiegetic as any sound that is "absent from the image but is also external to the story world…" (1994, 73). This is a common definition, one that extends as well to music. This exposes key problems with the diegetic binary: (1) the notion that if it is not materially inside it must be negated (*non*), and (2) the notion that if it is only for the audience it can only exist *outside* of the material world. This is what happens when cinema's ontology is imagined at the level of space: The character is not spatiotemporally "there," so that person must not *be* at all. In short, film theory conceives such a voice as a *device* transcendent to the story rather than a *person* who lives within an immanent world.

The voiceover classification issue also returns us to the problem of applying a vocal/textual concept to cinema sound. Recall Halliwell's distinction of *haple diegesis*, *diegesis dia mimeseos*, and *diegesis di'amphoteron*. The first is the voice of the poet, the second is the narration of the characters, the third is a mixture of the two. Genette concentrates on a division of

---

[20] One must grant that in literature, the third-person voice is often produced from someone's perspective even if there is no "I" written in the narration. This may also shift, often subtly from character to character over the course of the story. But without the "I," it is still written as the writer who is more inventor than recounter.
[21] For more on the "when" of a narrating voice in cinema, see Batcho (2018), Chapter 5, subheading "Narration: Layering Time, Speaking the Unspoken."
[22] Even the dead narrator of *Sunset Boulevard* (Wilder 1950) or *American Beauty* (Mendes 1999) voices a future act of narrating.

"*haplé diegesis*" and "*mimesis*." The former, he writes, is commonly translated as "simple narrative." But he takes issue with this translation, offering instead "pure narrative" because it better conveys that it is not mixed with *mimesis* in its delivery. In *haple diegesis*, the poet himself is speaking and does nothing to hide this fact. In Genette's *mimesis*, the poet speaks as if he were someone else (a character).

One might imagine that voiceover is thereby a form of *mimesis*. But by these definitions, it is dubious to claim that a cinematic *character* is speaking *as the poet* (or vice versa). Cinema is not literature. In cinema, a voice could be a subject thinking (recollection, rumination, reflection), a narrative speaking (exposition, description, representation), a moment displaced in time (past, present, or future), or any combination. These utterances are ambiguous and difficult to identify because (1) a plurality is underway in the audiovisual milieu, and (2) language does not, at least not necessarily, drive the content. Only three things are certain with the typical character-driven cinematic voiceover: (1) the character is *actually* speaking, (2) such a speaking is occurring at a time that is not necessarily fixed to image-events, (3) the voice is immanent to, rather than transcendent to, the story world. Through all of this, we can ascertain that the voice as a *capacity* is both independent of the image-time while inseparable from the story-reality. Concepts of inside and outside, text and representation are textual, visual and spatial concerns that impose divisions. *Diegesis* and *mimesis* both ignore the relational plurality that an audible cinema expresses.

There is another way of considering the image-time that unfolds, which draws us closer to a *logos* concept of audible cinema—that of the *inaudible* voice that *makes images*. In such a concept, one may speculate that the images we see are composed by the voice of Greek theater that is *muted*. Such a "non-voice" is then exclusively in the act of *creating* the imagery that unfolds as image-events. The images thereby stand in for or replace what a voice would otherwise describe but which a spectator does not actually hear. Overlapping this expression of time, a voiceover may then compose an *additional* time. Robert Bresson (1977) advises that what is seen and what is heard should never be duplicated. Voiceover has no purpose in saying what we already see in images. In this way, *diegesis* and *mimesis* do not mix, but rather overlap as a *coexistence* of time, a plurality. The voiceover speaks while another mute voice is making imagery within a listener, but whose actual sound is materially nonexistent. This is another way of saying that rather than the camera that narrates (*diegesis* as a concept), the mute voice produces the narrative images (a more *mimetic* concept). "A man walks down the road" of Greek poetry becomes the image (*a man walks down the road*) in cinema.

Consider again that in Greek theater, the performance of words as *mimesis* opens thought to an imagery that unfolds. This would be a Heideggerian approach to *logos*, the speaking that produces the image of truth (*aletheia*). Heidegger (2010) writes that language in our conscious engagement discloses a visual image to which we comport our thinking. This is his Aristotelian interpretation of *logos*, functioning as *deloun*, or to make visually manifest what is spoken of. Heidegger's *logos* is the speaking that discloses images to the mind. Such image-making from a muted voice would suggest that cinema is the *effect* without the cause—the images germinated from a poetic voice but whose words are inaudible and indeed unspoken. For who needs a poet to describe *mimesis* when a camera can provide images? But more to the point, the muted voice of imagery only happens through the one who listens. For this reason, *logos*, a listening relation, is a more apt way of conceiving audible cinema. What has been listened to is given its thought for all to see: the audibility that composes what now unfolds visually. This takes us back to the ancient traditions of storytelling in which, for example, the Homeric poems were told in such a way that in their listening images form.

Cinema conceived as a mute voice preserves a close connection between words and images, or more to the point, how words create not only images but the way in which such images are seen. Yet this still contains cinema under the authority of a voice (heard and unheard) that produces images. It also remains mimetic in how it *projects* a representation to the audience. Such a concept of *mimesis* thereby produces the same problem as *diegesis*: It limits cinema to what it is saying or representing what is being said. No poet speaks the *sound* of what is named in film practice as sound effects. Speaking may give rise to images, but it does not give rise to *hearing*.

Madness and Spectacle: *Mimesis* in Film Sound

This opens to the question of whether *mimesis* can relate to *non-vocal* audible content—what film practice calls "sound effects." Is *mimesis* a more useful description of such audible relations than *diegesis*? Genette writes that the term mimetic relates to information, while the term diegetic relates to the informer. *Mimesis* is a maximum of information, minimum of informer. *Diegesis* is the opposite: a maximum of informer, minimum of information. Yet Genette also reminds us that narration is regarded as an instance of writing. In fiction's particular form, the narrator is embedded in the fiction that is in its process: the story "telling."[23] A narrator of fiction, even in third-person voice, always has a point of view, a viewpoint, or a worldview. Cinema does not have this problem. Further, the arts of speaking and writing have a didactic element that is not as evident in the cinematic form. This aspect of *learning* is critical to Greek concepts of aesthetics. Socrates directly criticizes mimetic noise-making in the *Republic*. It is the reason Plato resisted *mimesis* and set it in contrast to *diegesis*. For him, as *praxis*, the performance of such sound theatrically imitates madness. Here is Socrates' exchange, in the context of what is virtuous in poetry, from the *Republic*:

> SOCRATES: And what about neighing horses, bellowing bulls, roaring rivers, the crashing sea, thunder, or the like—will they imitate them?
>
> ADEIMANTUS: No, they have already been forbidden to be mad or to imitate madmen. (Plato 2004, 77)

Socrates concurs, for it is his aim in this section of Plato's *Republic* to ascertain what values an imitator should promote. It is certainly not the sound of nature delivered through an inferior poet's mad vocalizations of roaring rivers and crashing seas. In a speaker,

> the more inferior he is, the more willing he will be to narrate anything and to consider nothing beneath him. Hence he will undertake to imitate, before a large audience and in a serious way, all the things we just mentioned: thunder and the sounds of winds, hail, axles, and pulleys; trumpets, flutes, pipes, and all the other instruments; and even the cries of dogs, sheep, and birds. (78)

Genette (1980) writes that Plato discounts Homer's "'shore of the loud-sounding sea'" because it is not "pure narrative" and is thus unnecessary (165). It is just *there* and does not demand to be *shown*. For Plato, showing can only be a way of telling. But Halliwell points to something more philosophical about the role of poetry. He argues that Plato is addressing the dangers of multiplicity over unity, for the former is a path to madness while the latter is needed to express virtue. This is why, unlike Aristotle after him, Plato wants to reject *mimesis* with the exception of vocalized imitations of *virtue*—his zenith of poetic arts. In the *Sophist*, Plato warns against speakers of imitation, who are "standing off at a distance" and who "enchant the young... through the ears" about "the affairs of truth" (1996,

---

[23] See Genette (1980), the section on "Voice," particularly on p. 213.

38). He warns of the sophists' "spoken images" and the way they "make it seem that they are spoken truly" in a display of apparent wisdom.

The problem with *mimesis* in Plato is that it encourages "the mind to step inside, and assimilate itself to, the character's viewpoint," which he finds seductive and dangerous (Halliwell, 2012).[24] *Mimesis* not only deceives, it "*aims* at deception concerning the identity of the speaker," which then invites us to do the same (Woodruff, 1992). In other words, one does not only imagine the character through oneself under the spell of performance, but one carries the spell of this *impersonator* into public discourse. The danger is that "we may be beguiled into becoming performers" and then we use such deception in daily life. *Diegesis* is fine, for it is the speaking that narrates; *mimesis* is harmful because it is speaking that deceives. The stranger in the *Sophist* thereby resolves to remove "likeness-making art" from speaking under threat of punishment.[25]

For Aristotle, a prime function of *mimesis* is to use a particular action to represent a general idea. *Mimesis* gives an idea of some object that says something about the concept of that object. This points again to pedagogy. Through a mimetic approach, one can experience an event from a safe distance without having to confront the actual thing. (Woodruff uses the example of a lion; it is best to learn from a mimetic one than an actual one.) Aristotle retains the emphasis of deception in its conception, although in him it is more positively didactic. Woodruff (1992) speculates that this "functional deception" of *mimesis* is necessary to make us respond to the universal because the truth itself of the universal is too general (88). In poetry, a universal takes on something of a conceptual persona; or as Woodruff writes, the universal is dressed up in clothing and character "to play the part" that particular people and events normally act out.

As with Plato's criticism, one may then wonder whether Aristotle would consider film sound design to be mimetic, since under his conception it acts out the particular activity of people and things to reveal a certain "side" or aspect of something more general and universal. Music is

---

[24] See also Genette on "Distance" (1980, 162-163).
[25] Here, Plato distinguishes a *mimêsis phantastikê* and a *mimêsis eikastikê*. The *eikastikê* tries to imitate reality (accurate copy); *phantastikê* gives a wider point of view, disregards reality and truth, and is therefore the art of sophistry—relativistic, simulacrum, illusion (Cassin, 2014, e-book chapter A, section Art).

mentioned as an example of *mimesis* because it has an emotional effect that is not directly causal to music itself, rather that the *to* is to some feeling (Woodruff 1992). Sound design is different. Although it can function symbolically, its intent is usually to mimic or represent some rendering of reality.[26] As has been widely criticized in film sound theory, sound too often serves to reify the image. It does this by copying and giving greater life to the image we see, rather than producing its own expression.

This representational index to *imagery* is not the same as a representation of *reality*. Aristotle also applied *mimesis* in a historical sense as "an imitation of human actions (*mimêsis praxeôs* [μίμησις πράξεως])."[27] (Cassin 2014). *Mimesis* initially expressed an inner reality (mime, dance, music) and not a reproduction of the external world. Only in the fifth century does it come to apply to the external world, which was Plato's concern. Sobchak (2012) contends that Aristotle's *mimesis* is not limited to "literal realism." Instead, ancient Greek stories imitate *other stories* and an echo of this can be found in cinema's current formal structures of genre. "In practical terms Greek writings are imitations of prior stories, redone, reshaped, given dramatic form or epic form as the case may be, but nevertheless imitations of fictions" (123). While Sobchak is applying *mimesis* to story imitation, one could also extract from this a way of conceiving *mimesis* in sonic terms. Plato's lunatic who screams animal sounds is as much a fiction as the classic film sound case of a punch to the face. Materially a cinematic punch has no semblance of fidelity to realism. A sound recordist may have struck a cow carcass with a baseball bat, or cracked celery stalks to imitate bones breaking.[28] These codes of sound are well known and in this sense film sounds imitate other film sounds in much the way that film stories and iconography imitate past films to uphold genre conventions. Insofar as film sound is *mimesis*, it represents (copies, mimics, imitates) *itself*. It is mimetic not as nature or reality, but *qua* cinema. Here we find Aristotle's lowest rung of *mimesis*—spectacle. Regarded in this manner of audience *expectation*—a prevailing attitude in film theory—sound design is neither diegetic nor its absence. It is *mimesis*. Here, film sound imitates at two levels: (1) it copies imagery in service to

---

[26] For more on the "real" versus the "rendered," see Chion (1994).
[27] Cassin, 2014. E-book chapter M, section "Mimesis."
[28] In film sound practice, this is called "sweetening"—a term that describes the combining of the natural sound recorded on set with additional sounds recorded later to give a heightened sense of emotional impact.

the image, (2) it copies prior film sound in service to genre. This is how standard film sound design functions in popular cinema. But if one instead conceives and practices film sound as "audible design," *mimesis* also fails. "Audible cinema" requires a concept that cannot be captured under any definition of *mimesis* or *diegesis*.

Logos: An Immanent Audibility

Ancient Greek, presentational and narrational concepts of cinema thus far described all conceive of storytelling and cinema in their delivery to the audience. Even sound gets wrapped up in the containers of presentation, text and spectatorship. This distance enables discursive analyses about a "work of art"—something seen and heard for the images and statements that can be read by some presumed audience. *Mimesis* and *Diegesis* function at the level of distance, which produces a privileged point of analysis to develop confused concepts of readings, representations and tellings. An audible approach removes these transcendent, distancing functions and instead opens to an immanent gathering. Acts of hearing and listening build and unfold the imagination as a gathering of time. It is an act within itself that is temporal, mnemonic, future-oriented, and generative. This opens to what makes cinema different—it unfolds *as itself*. It is immanent rather than transcendent. It has its own reality and a relationality within, one that exists entirely through its own flux of events as an expression of time. Taken as an expressive experience rather than a work of art, cinema represents neither a real nor a readable world. It is a *made* world. It has a *life* that is real, not to audience nor to camera but to the life that unfolds itself. This brings us to audible cinema as *logos*.

Logos is an extraordinarily complex term with a rich philosophical history. It is untranslatable to English, which is why it has often been appropriated to describe everything from discourse to the cosmos. Contemporary translations include "word," "statement," "ratio," "speech," and "reason." These terms are outcomes of their discursive function—and in some cases ontological ground—post-Aristotle. From Christian philosophy, *Logos* takes on a divine element as the wisdom and truth of God spoken through Jesus Christ. In today's philosophical discussions, it functions to describe a relationship in which an act of speaking comports to the preexisting truth of such an act. In such appropriations of *logos*, it is that which enables *its own* statement as an accordance with *one's own* sense of reason. This is evident in both Stoic and early Christian texts. It is also what contemporary structuralist and post-structuralist philosophy resists—that there is a prior statement waiting to be stated. These contemporary applications of the term are responses to Greek and, more specifically, Hellenistic thought. Through Plato's influence, truth lies in the forms as preexistent. In Aristotle lies an effort to categorize thinking toward the virtues of rhetoric.

Before all these appropriations, *logos* involved a relation—specifically, an audible relation. Through Heraclitus, *logos* describes the vital ethics of an *accounting* or *gathering* within the relational flux of self, nature and the cosmos. He is known for regarding the cosmos as fire, but this is meant to describe the change and flux of appearances.[29] *Logos appears* through the mechanisms of the everliving fire, but *logos* itself is neither appearance, language, substance or form. It is that which is given life in a relation of signs gathered through listening to what is unapparent.[30] *Logos* is the "expression" of fire as the stabilizing force in process (Kirk and Raven 1957, 200). There is no *logos* without the relation and its interpretation. Through fragments 1, 19, 50 and 108, interpretation comes not in seeing but in *listening*.[31] A true account comes not through listening to *someone*, but through listening to the *logos*. As Kirk & Raven point out, it is not *Heraclitus'* account that is important.[32] Rather, *logos* itself should be listened to—the cosmic order that hides from all appearances.

The *language* of Heraclitus is a reflection of his concepts of a natural account. Kahn illustrates how Heraclitus' *logos* is to be regarded both in

---

[29] Fire in Heraclitus is "the motive point of the cosmological process" that regulates all matter, while logos is "the measure and regulation of change," as described by Kirk and Raven (1957, 201). Brann describes Heraclitus' fire as "the quantifiability of all physical things, their mathematical second nature as well as their transformability, their capacity for elemental mutation. Fire enables the Logos to inform the cosmos with the most determinate relationality thinkable, that expressed in number-ratios" (Brann 2011, Part III, Section M).

[30] See Fragment 93 (*"The lord whose oracle is in Delphi neither speaks out nor conceals, but gives a sign."*) and Fragment 54 (*"An unapparent connexion is stronger than an apparent one."*) (quoting Kirk and Raven, 1957).

[31] The famous fragment 50 is usually translated as some variation of: *Listening not to me but to the* logos*, it is wise to acknowledge that all things are one*. Fragments 1 and 19 are about failures to listen, and fragment 108 is about hearing and understanding what is wise.

[32] See Fragment 50. Kirk & Raven write that what should be listened is not *his* account, "although the Logos was revealed in that account" (188). This is a confusing statement by the two revered scholars. What is "that" account they refer to? It is unclear in their analysis what "that" is if not "his."

its individual fragments and also as a whole (1979). Through Heraclitus' writings, *logos as word* is a puzzle, a game of language. Scholarly research on Heraclitus suggests that this interpretive element is his intent, rather than the popular post-Aristotelian denotation of "statement."[33] Indeed "statement" is a different word for Heraclitus—*diegesis*. In Heraclitus, *logos* is the relational element of any *diegesis*, marking a distinction between what is gathered and that which is described, instructed or explained from such a relation.

In his essay "Heraclitus on Logos: Language, Rationality and the Real," Enrique Hülsz (2013) mentions Heraclitus' use of the word διήγησις (*diegesis*) in his fragmented text *On Nature*. He writes that "after dealing with men's lack of understanding about a *logos* which is always the same (literally, 'always this') and by which all things happen, [Heraclitus] offers the earliest recorded description of what came to be called philosophy, when he goes on to characterize his own procedure as διήγησις [*diēgēsis*], a 'narrative explanation' dealing with 'words and deeds,' 'according to nature' (κατά φύσιν)" (283). In a footnote to the above reference, Hülsz expands on this *diegesis*: "The Greek noun διήγησις, meaning something like 'narrative exposition' and/ or 'explanation,' corresponds to the verb actually used, διηγούμαι[34] ('set out in detail,' 'describe'; LSJ s.v.)."[35] This is also evident in Aristotle's *Rhetoric* (2007), when he writes of *diegesis*—"narration of the facts"—as "judicial speech" (230). For Heraclitus, *diegesis* is the act of saying while *logos* is that to which and in which one has a relation. While *logos* may include what is sayable or said in one's taking account, it is not in itself the *saying*.[36] Explanation, *diegesis*, is not *logos* but *of logos*—a means of doing philosophy by narrating and explaining in the spoken word. To think in a Heraclitean conception, one's *relation* to the world is not *diegesis*. We are diegetic beings when we are

---

[33] See Kahn, C. H. (1979), McKirahan, R. D. (2010), Brann, E. (2011), Hülsz, E. (2013), Cassin, B. (2014).
[34] Roman-English phonetic: *diigoúmai*.
[35] LSJ: Liddell-Scott-Jones Greek-English Lexicon. Also, διηγούμαι, the "set out in detail" Hülsz refers to, comes from Fragment 1 (DK). Also translated as "set forth," in both cases meaning that which Heraclitus is explaining, describing, narrating, etc.
[36] I can find no literature to suggest that Heraclitus employed the word *lexis*, which Aristotle later used as the means, not the content, of speech, and which itself is divided into *diegesis* and *mimesis*.

in acts of *diegesis*. *Logos*, by contrast, is the immanent experiential relation—the gathering and the account.

Returning to Genette, his interest is not in narrating but in narrative.[37] *Narrative* is the text, statement or discourse. The term "narrative" lives in its relation to a story that is recounted, a discourse in its utterance. A Heraclitean *logos* has nothing to recount. Its account is immanent, only itself in its process of unfolding. *Logos* is an experiential accounting, one listened to and interpreted in the act of occurring. It is the unfolding of images, signs, sounds, imaginings and hearings brought about *through listening*. Such an act is a form of listening that is free of the *necessity* of sound. A cinematic *logos* is thereby a thought that unfolds, a relation of signs, born in the engagement of listening. The *logos relation* produces its account in its gathering. There is no statement, text, image or voice as necessary. A cinematic *logos* has no narrator, only the relation of those who live the film within and those who experience the film as this relation.

By conceiving cinema as *logos*, each film has its own logic, laws and relations. This returns to sensory relations as the core of engagement, specifically that imperative by Heraclitus to listen to what is underway. This listening is what *makes the account*. Cosmos, reason and the possibility of speaking are all wrapped up in the account, but *logos is* the relation. Plato had it backward: the "through" of *logos*, the *dia* of *logue*, is not speaking; it is listening. In this sense, dialogue takes on a new meaning. To engage in "dialogue" would thus be to stay silent and listen—to listen to what is in relation, the account that is underway in listening. Cinema becomes an audible act of listening through the film's own immanent unfolding. In such a conception, the art of cinema is a construction of such relations that manifest as imagery, as speaking, as reason, as logical. This reverses the standard analytical, textual distances of a reasoning consciousness that privileges a transcendent audience. An audible design, under the relational concept of *logos*, enables the thought of a cinema that lives itself.

Conclusion: A Cinematic *Logos*

The aim of a conception of "audible cinema" is to recognize that language—speech and reading—does not produce the images of cinema, as in

---

[37] See Genette (1980, 26-29) for more.

literature and Greek poetry. This has been a misstep in the history of film theory. Instead, audible cinema has its own expression that is immanent to a film's own reality. This is not to claim, therefore, that all cinema is *logos*, rather that *logos* provides *another cinematic expression*. Every film has its images and language; but it also has its own audible gathering and accounting of experience that lives alongside images and language. Further, it also has the capacity to create new imagery *from* listening. Altogether, this composes the "logic" of a film's own world, one which is not dependent on abstract truths or distanciations of observation, reading and analysis.[38] Such a *logos* is composed through this world's *own* laws of relationality—its own non-systemic structure—that constitutes its account. Such a concept requires two conceptual points of clarification:

1. *Logos* is listening to what is unapparent. It is an unseeing relation. Similarly, an audible cinema is an *unseeing* cinema. When one's audibility is decoupled from its visual and spatial verification, audibility takes on its own expression.
2. An audible cinema is thereby an *experiential* cinema. It expresses through hearings and listenenings within the film's own actuality. Such audibility forms a relation to audience that is affective, empathetic and immanent rather than received or read from a transcendent distance.

A cinematic *logos* is not given to a film audience, but unfolds as and within itself in its activity and through its relations. It is a concept of relations within the world the characters inhabit, and less about the external *fact* of a subject experiencing this world while sitting in the theater or in one's home. As *logos*, the distance is not so distant. The spirit of cinema is that its world reaches beyond itself to encompass that of the audience. Any individual who participates is the relation that ultimately "makes" the account that is already gathering within. We gather in time as we live the unfolding of the film's time. Living creatures that we are, we find our own empathetic attunement to this *logos as logos*. Such a cinema is neither mimetic nor diegetic to any other object, action, statement or genre, rather immanent and real *to its inhabitants*.

---

[38] We should keep in mind that in Bertolt Brecht's theater of alienation, the division of subconscious and conscious observation both remain at the level of the gaze (1964).

In my research, I can find only two writers who have considered a *logos* of cinema: Roger Munier and Jean Mitry. The latter quotes the former with the following: "'world, in its own terms and in the immanent expression of itself, puts itself at the service of a logos'" (Mitry 1997, 374). Mitry follows Munier's statement by stating that such a *logos* is discursive: "It is 'for-me' a means of existing in the world, of communicating to the world, of presenting to myself a discourse *about* the world: a discourse which appears as an expression *of* the world but one which has a duty to me to be what it is, into which I can completely project myself, the means to suggest the question and answer by creating the spectacle of my own illusions" (374-375). While effective in describing a created cinematic world into which one is projected and a *logos* organized of its relations, Mitry's adoption maintains discourse as the means of its expression. It confines *logos* to the denotation of *statement*. In its ancient connotation, *logos* is the *unseeing* relational potentiality—that which is made in such a relation, a listening relation *itself*. Early conceptions of *logos* connote an activity of *gathering*—not giving an account but *taking account*. It is not simply an act by an individual, rather that the *logos* is what comprises the activity, insofar as it is engaged.

Cinema as *logos* does not project sound through its speakers. It composes an immanent hearing and listening within itself as its own lived unfolding. Mitry is right that the creation of a cinematic *logos* is organizational rather than representational, composing its own "natural logic" that is other than the real world (375). But cinema as *logos* is best conceived in its *gathering* rather than its "communication," its *durations* of listening and hearing rather than its visible "facts." In its immanence, *logos* is the gathering and making of and from what is audible. Here, cinema produces its own affective relations and time-images from the audible engagement that *makes* such relations. This is not the voice making imagery, but a *poiesis* of its own making—the audibility that gathers and unfolds memory and imagination into new images, thoughts and feelings. The demands of the camera fade as audibility makes worlds. Such an expression composes something more ancient—a field of relations other than of the knowledge of discourse and things, which opens time to the possibilities of spirit and the unknown. This takes sound design far beyond any diegetic duality or mimetic reference, opening to unimagined possibilities.

Bibliography

Aristotle. *Poetics*. Translated by J. Sachs. Newburyport, MA: Focus Publishing, 2006.
Aristotle. *On Rhetoric: A Theory of Civic Discourse*. Translated by G. A. Kennedy. New York: Oxford, 2007.
Batcho, James. *Terrence Malick's Unseeing Cinema: Memory, Time and Audibility*. New York: Palgrave-Macmillan, 2018.
Bordwell, David and Kristin Thompson. "Fundamental Aesthetics of Sound in the Cinema." *Film Sound: Theory and Practice*, edited by Elisabeth Weis and John Belton, 181–199. New York: Columbia University Press. 1985.
Bordwell, David and Kristin Thompson. *Film Art: An Introduction*. (8th Ed.). New York: McGraw-Hill, 2008.
Brann, Eva. *The Logos of Heraclitus*. Philadelphia: Paul Dry Books, 2011. EPUB e-book.
Brecht, Bertolt. "Alienation Effects in Chinese Acting." *Brecht on Theater*, 91-99. New York: Hill and Wang, 1964.
Bresson, Robert. *Notes On Cinematography*. Translated by J. Griffin. New York: Urizen Books, 1977.
Cassin, Barbara, ed. *Dictionary of Untranslatables: A Philosophical Lexicon*. Princeton University, 2014. EPUB e-book.
Chion, Michel. *Audio-vision: Sound on Screen*. Translated by C. Gorbman. New York: Columbia University, 1994.
Chion, Michel. *Film: A Sound Art*. Translated by C. Gorbman. New York: Columbia University, 2009.
Doane, Mary Ann. "The Voice in the Cinema: The Articulation of Body and Space." *Film Sound: Theory and Practice*, edited by Elizabeth Weis & John Belton, 163-176. New York: Columbia University, 1985.
Elsaesser, Thomas and Malte Hagener. *Film Theory: An Introduction Through the Senses*. New York: Routledge, 2010.
Genette, Gerard. *Narrative Discourse: An Essay in Method*. Translated by J. E. Lewin. Ithica, NY: Cornell University, 1980.
Gorbman, Claudia. *Unheard Melodies: Narrative Film Music*. Bloomington, IN: Indiana University, 1987.
Halliwell, Stephen. "Diegesis - Mimesis." *The Living Handbook of Narratology*, edited by Peter Hühn, Jan Christoph Meister, John Pier and Wolf Schmid. Hamburg: Hamburg University Press, 2012. Accessed 30 November, 2014, http://wikis.sub.uni-hamburg.de/lhn/index.php/Diegesis_-_Mimesis.

Havelock, Eric A. *The Muse Learns to Write*. New Haven: Yale University Press, 1986.
Heidegger, Martin. *Being and Time*, translated by J. Stambaugh. Albany, NY: State University of New York, 2010.
Hülsz, Enrique. "Heraclitus on *Logos*: Language, Rationality and the Real." *Doctrine and Doxography: Studies on Heraclitus and Pythagoras*, edited by D. Sider and D. Obbink, 281-301. Berlin: De Gruyter, 2013.
Kahn, Charles H. *The Art and Thought of Heraclitus*. London: Cambridge, 1979.
Kirk, G. S. and J. E. Raven. *The Presocratic Philosophers*. London: Cambridge University, 1957.
McKirahan, Richard D. *Philosophy Before Socrates*. (2nd Ed.). Indianapolis, ID: Hackett Publishing, 2010.
Mendes, Sam, dir. *American Beauty*. United States: Jinks/Cohen Company, DreamWorks Pictures, 1999.
Metz, Christian. *Film Language*. New York: Oxford University, 1974.
Mitry, Jean. *The Aesthetics and Psychology of the Cinema*. Translated by C. King. Bloomington, IN: Indiana University, 1997.
Ong, Walter J. *Orality and Literacy*. New York: Routledge, 2002.
Plato. *Sophist*. Translated by E. Brann, P. Kalkavage and E. Salem. Newburyport, MA: Focus Philosophical Library, 1996.
Plato. *Republic*. Translated by C. D. C. Reeve. Indianapolis, IN: Hackett Publishing, 2004.
Shrivastava, Vinay. *Aesthetics of Cinema*. Dubuque, IA: Kendall Hunt, 1996.
Sinnerbrink, Robert. *New Philosophies of Film: Thinking Images*. New York: Continuum, 2011.
Sobchack, Thomas. "Genre Film: A Classical Experience." *Film Genre Reader IV*, edited by Barry Keith Grant, 121-132. Austin: University of Texas, 2012.
Stilwell, Robynn J. "The Fantastical Gap Between Diegetic and Non-diegetic." *Beyond the Soundtrack*, edited by In D. Goldmark, L. Kramer & R. Leppert, 184-202. Berkeley and Los Angeles, CA: University of California Press, 2007.
Taylor, Henry M. "The Success Story of a Misnomer." In *Offscreen 11*(8-9), 2007.
Wilder, Billy, dir. *Sunset Boulevard*. United States: Paramount Pictures, 1950.

Woodruff, Paul. "Aristotle on Mimesis." *Essays on Aristotle's Poetics*, edited by Amelie Rorty, 73-95. Princeton, NJ: Princeton University, 1992.

James Batcho, Ph.D.
Assistant Professor
International College
I-Shou University, Taiwan

Chapter Four

Augustine and Internet Addiction: Augustine on Desire and Will in the Age of Digitalisation

Andrew Tsz Wan Hung

This paper attempts to explore Augustine's ethics in light of internet addiction in the age of digitalization. According to cyber-psychologists, there are five subtypes of Internet addiction that are prevalent in modern society. They are cybersexual addiction, cyber-relationship addiction, net compulsions, information overload, and computer addiction; and among these the prevalence of cybersexual addiction is the most worrying. With such background, I then go on to explore Augustine's theory of will, desire, and concupiscence, and his debates with Julian, a supporter of Pelagius. Although many scholars, just like Julian, criticize Augustine's view of body and sexuality as too negative, in light of the prevalence of cybersexual addiction and other kinds of addiction, we can see Augustine's caution regarding concupiscence is a good reminder to us to be aware of the possible damage caused by an inordinate sexual desire. I then explore the psychological process of addiction and argue that it is consistent with Augustine's model of lust-habit-addictive necessity. I also defend Augustine's idea of concupiscence as desire against one's will and argue that it is also applicable to different kinds of internet addictions. For Augustine, human concupiscence comes from the Fall of the first parents which damaged our nature and free will and makes us remain in a state of weakness of will permanently so that we find it hard to resist the temptation of different enticing features of the internet and easily become internet addicted. However, our sin and weakness of will also remind us of our limitations and the need to seek the help of Divine grace.

1. Introduction

In the age of digitalization, information technology has invaded every aspect of our lives; it is changing our individual and social behaviour. In particular, use of the Internet has grown worldwide to 4.5 billion users, which is 58.8% of the world's population, and around 50.7% of internet users are in Asia.[1] Since Kimberly Young's work on Internet addiction, the issue of the Internet problem has attracted a great deal of attention.[2] Different statistics show that, generally, around 6 to 15% of internet users match the signs of internet addiction, and this goes up to 13 to 18% among college students, who seem to be the most at risk.[3] Chang-Kook Yang, in his studies, estimated that 10% of students met the criteria of addiction at the University of Taiwan.[4] In China, Lijuan Cui, Xin Zhao, Mingzheng Wu and Aihong Xu found that there are around 9.72% to 11.06% among young users who are serious addicts.[5] Once one is addicted to using the Internet, an individual has an escalating desire to use the Internet more and more; this means that the person becomes more tolerant to the excitement derived from use of the Internet. And when the Internet is taken away, it causes distress. These cravings are similar to alcohol and drug cravings which have great influence on individual well-being.[6]

The story of Augustine's inner struggle with sexual desire and celibacy is well-known. Many pastors and counsellors have also found that Augustine's story is helpful in counselling persons with sexual addiction. This also leads to many studies about his theology of will and sexual desire. However, research about Augustine's theology in light of the problems of Internet addiction is still rare. Fr. John Harvey's article is a rare one exploring Augustine's free will in responding to the problem of pornography

---

[1] "Internet World Stats 2019," *Internet World Stats*, accessed November 8, 2019. https://www.internetworldstats.com/stats.htm.
[2] Kimberly S. Young, "Internet Addiction: The Emergence of a New Clinical Disorder," *Cyberpsychology & Behavior* 1, no. 3 (1998): 237–244.
[3] Kimberly S. Young, Xiao Dong Yue and Li Ying, "Prevalence Estimates and Etiologic Models of Internet Addiction," in *Internet Addiction: A Handbook and Guide to Evaluation and Treatment*, ed. Young, K. S., & de Abreu, C. N. (Hoboken, NJ, US: John Wiley & Sons Inc., 2011), pp. 5-6.
[4] Chang-Kook Yang, "Sociopsychiatric Characteristics of Adolescents Who Use Computers to Excess," *Acta Psychiatrica Scandinavica*, 104, no.3 (2001): 217–222.
[5] Lijuan Cui, Xin Zhao, Mingzheng Wu and Aihong Xu, "A Research on the Effects of Internet Addiction on Adolescents' Social Development," *Psychological Science*, 1 (2006): 34–36.
[6] Mary Aiken, *The Cyber Effect* (Random House Publishing Group, 2016), p. 60.

today.[7] However, his article largely relies on *Confessions*. It does not cover Augustine's view of will and desires in his other writings. This paper thus attempts first to explore the nature of the cyber effect and then explore Augustine's ethics, in particular to conduct a substantial study on his theory of free will and desires in the age of digitalization. Hopefully, an understanding of the nature of the Internet and psychology of the use of the Internet and addiction thereto can shed light on our modern revision of Augustine's theology.

2. Cyber Effect and Internet Addiction

According to Young, there are five specific subtypes of Internet addiction: cybersexual addiction, cyber-relationship addiction, net compulsions (e.g. gambling or shopping on the internet), information overload (obsessed with staying up to date on the latest news or gossip), and computer addiction (excessive game-playing).[8] Among these different kinds of addictions, cybersexual addiction seems to be the most prevalent and the most serious problem among the youth. In Finland, while around 4.6 to 4.7% of the youth (12-18 yrs. old) match the signs of Internet addiction, the number of cases of cybersexual addiction is double this figure. An estimation based on survey data showed that 9% of users exhibit the signs of addiction related to sexually explicit material on the Internet.[9]

Why has the rise of the Internet led to such a disastrous problem of human addiction? According to Mary Aiken, a forensic cyber-psychologist, the Internet is not simply a neutral human tool. It has a special effect on us which is to magnify our capacity as well as our different kinds of desires. People who have been exposed to extreme content online will become easily addicted to social media, online gaming, cybersex and cyber-relationships. They easily feel freed up and emboldened online and may even indulge in certain risky behaviour. Such phenomenon of this emboldened behaviour online is explained in cyber-psychology as the

---

[7] Fr. John Harvey, "Saint Augustine, Freedom of Will, and Pornography," *The Linacre Quarterly*, 77, no. 1 (2010): 81-92.
[8] Kimberly S. Young, "Internet Addiction: Symptoms, Evaluation and Treatment," *Student British Medical Journal*, 7 (1999): 351–352. See also Mark Griffiths, "Gambling Addiction on the Internet," in *Internet Addiction: A Handbook and Guide to Evaluation and Treatment*, p. 100.
[9] Al Cooper, *Sex & the Internet: A Guidebook for Clinicians* (New York: Brunner-Routledge, 2002); Young, Yue & Ying, "Prevalence Estimates and Etiologic Models of Internet Addiction," p. 4.

"online disinhibition effect", which is facilitated by the environment of cyberspace, in which there is no authority, and everyone is anonymous and physically distanced. Furthermore, there is another cyber-psychological effect that is called "online escalation" which denotes that our problematic behaviour will become amplified online. Many of us have noticed this phenomenon in negative conversations with aggressive texts on online forums. What is worse is that online escalation can easily form a vicious cycle, that is, in order to feel better, the Internet user experiences a high from online activities, and that is followed by a guilty feeling, which further accelerates another cycle of impulsive online behaviour in order to feel high again. As Aiken states, "Whenever technology comes in contact with an underlying predisposition, or tendency for a certain behavior, it can result in behavioral amplification or escalation."[10] Thus, Aiken, states, the "Internet could be the most beguiling and enticing creation of humankind. Our evolutionary instincts, such as seeking, make it hard to resist." [11] And it is such cyber effect which causes the prevalence of Internet addiction. In the following, I will explore Augustine's ethics and his theory of will and desire.

3. Augustine's Eudaimonistic Ethics

Basically, the nature of Augustine's ethics is eudaimonistic virtue ethics which is similar to ancient eudaimonism.[12] For Augustine, human beings by nature desire good.[13] Ethics is an enquiry of the supreme good. And

---

[10] Aiken, *The Cyber Effect*, pp. 21-2, 65.
[11] Aiken, *The Cyber Effect*, p. 86.
[12] Bonnie Kent, "Augustine's Ethics," in *The Cambridge Companion to Augustine*, ed. Eleonore Stump and Norman Kretzmann (Cambridge University Press, 2001), p. 205.
[13] Augustine, *The City of God*, trans. Marcus Dods (New York: The Modern Library, 1952). Hereafter cited as *Civ. Dei* appeared parenthetically in the main text with an Arabic number indicating the book and the chapter. Augustine, *Confessions*, 2nd edition, trans. F. J. Sheed (Indianapolis: Hackett Publishing Company, 2006). Hereafter cited as *Conf.* appeared parenthetically in the main text with an Arabic number indicating the book and the chapter. Augustine, "The Happy Life," in *Augustine of Hippo: Selected Writings*, trans. and intro. Mary T. Clark (Paulist Press, 1984), pp. 167-93. Hereafter cited as *Beata vita* with an Arabic number indicating the book number. Augustine, *On the Trinity*, in *From Nicene and Post-Nicene Fathers, First Series, Vol. 3*, trans. Arthur West Haddan, ed. Philip Schaff (Buffalo, NY: Christian Literature Publishing Co., 1887). Revised and edited for New Advent by Kevin Knight,

happiness is the supreme good pursued by all human beings (*Beata vita* 10; *Civ. Dei* 10.1; *Conf.* 10.21; *Trin.*13.7.10).

However, unlike ancient eudaimonism, for Augustine, happiness can only be attained ultimately in the afterlife; and thus he criticizes the ancient philosophers for being arrogant in believing that people can attain happiness by philosophical endeavour in this life (*Civ. Dei* 19.4). Augustine argues that no one can reach happiness in the present life. However, those who accept the hope of the afterlife may be happy in the present life, not because of the present reality, but due to the future hope (*Civ. Dei* 19.20).

He criticizes the Epicureans for understanding happiness as freedom from all suffering and anxiety while denying immortality of the soul (*anima*) and searching for happiness in this life as inconvincible. People inevitably experience lots of suffering, anxieties and grieving in life. In order to set happiness as attainable in this life, they lower the goal of happiness so that it can be within one's own control. Such happiness brought about by the possession of goods will be lost when we die (*Trin.* 13.7.10).[14]

For Augustine, Stoicism is better than Epicureanism because Stoics consider happiness as derived from the virtue of mind rather than bodily pleasure. Augustine agrees that virtues help us live well, but are the means to happiness, not equivalent to happiness. Virtues by themselves are not the primary objects of nature; instead they are acquired through learning in order to fight against vice. For instance, the war between temperance and lust prevents our soul from assenting to wicked deeds (*Civ. Dei* 19.4). Virtues are the great goods, but only God is the absolute good who is the source of virtues and all good things (*Lib. arb.* 2.19.50). Furthermore, Augustine also criticizes Stoics' notion of virtue for being problematic. This is because, first of all, Stoics have neglected the influence of the body in the pursuit of happiness. Second, Augustine criticizes Stoics for being arrogant in overemphasizing the virtue of glory, while failing to see that virtue is also a gift from God rather than a human achievement.[15] For

---

http://www.newadvent.org/fathers/1301.htm. Hereafter cited as *Trin.* with an Arabic number indicating the book, the chapter and the section. Augustine, *On the Free Choice of the Will*, in *On the Free Choice of the Will, On Grace and Free Choice, and Other Writings*, trans. and ed. Peter King (New York: Cambridge University Press, 2010), pp. 3-126. Hereafter cited as *Lib. arb.* with an Arabic number indicating the book, the chapter and the section.
[14] Kent, "Augustine's Ethics", pp. 209-10.
[15] Kent, "Augustine's Ethics", p. 211.

Augustine, the definition of virtue is ordered love (*Civ. Dei* 15.22) which is oriented toward God, and in which charity is "the prime and necessary virtue, the loving union of God and his human creatures made possible by the divine gift of love from God who is love" (*Trin.* 15.18.32).[16]

According to Augustine, what one searches for should be something immutable; and the only supreme good that is able to fulfil our search for happiness is the immutable God (*Beata vita* 11; *Civ. Dei* 8.8; *Trin.*13.10). Thus, for Augustine, Platonism is a better pagan philosophy in teaching the idea of immortality of the soul; however, it is also wrong in believing that the human soul should seek happiness by being liberated from the body and emotions. Such devaluation of the body and emotions is inconsistent with the Christian doctrine of the incarnation and resurrection of the body (*Conf.* 7.9; *Civ. Dei* 14.9). However, Augustine ranks the significance of the soul higher than the body in his hierarchy of being because the body changes in time and place while the soul changes only in time (*Civ. Dei* 8.8, 14.23).[17] For Augustine, there is nothing closer to God than the rational soul (*animus*) or the mind because it is the image of God (*Civ. Dei* 11.26).

4. Augustine on Will and Desire

4.1. Augustine on Free will

According to Augustine, there are two kinds of human city. The city people live in according to the flesh is that of man, while the other city people live in according to the spirit is the city of God. Augustine clarifies that to live after the flesh not only includes those who pursue the pleasure of the flesh, but also those who reveal the vice of the soul. Thus, both Epicurean and Stoics are living after the flesh in Augustine's eyes (*Civ. Dei* 14.2). The central problem is not the nature of body itself. The devil has no body, but the devil's deeds are evil because they live according to themselves. What is crucial is the corruption of the body. It is the punishment of the original sin. And it is the sinful soul that causes the flesh to be corruptible (*Civ. Dei* 14.3). Human beings are sinful because they live according to themselves, which violates the original purpose of God's creation.

---

[16] George Lavere, "Virtue," in *Augustine through the Ages: An Encyclopedia*, ed. Allan D. Fitzgerald (Grand Rapids, Mich.: W.B. Eerdmans, 1999), p. 873.
[17] Roland Teske, "Soul," in *Augustine through the Ages: An Encyclopedia*, ed. Allan D. Fitzgerald (Grand Rapids, Mich.: W.B. Eerdmans, 1999), p. 808.

Although human beings have the will to seek happiness, not everyone can attain happiness. Augustine makes a distinction between the will to happiness and the will to uprightness (*Lib. arb.* 1.14-15). The will to happiness is inherited in human nature (*Conf.* 10.21.30; *Civ. Dei* 10.1). Although all people desire happiness, only good persons can attain true happiness by giving up their evil ways because of the will to uprightness. As Marianne Djuth states, "Evil persons lack the will of uprightness, obtaining a false happiness based on the temporal pleasure, and therefore they can never attain the true happiness based on the love of God."[18]

In *On the Free Choice of the Will* (*De libero arbitrio*; hereafter *On Free Will*), Augustine argues that free will is good because it is created by God. It is the condition of the possibility of moral goodness. However, it is just an intermediate good and it is possible to be misused and thus becomes a source of evil (*Lib. arb.* 2.18.47–2.19.53). Human beings, as rational creatures, possess knowledge of eternal laws, and have the freedom to "turn our love aside from temporal things and to turn it, purified, towards eternal things" (*Lib. arb* 1.5.32; trans. King 2010, 27). However, if human beings turn away from these eternal goods and love temporal mutable goods, we must take responsibility for our evil will because we are certain that we will (*Conf.* 7.3); and we commit sin and become slaves to lust voluntarily (*Lib. arb.* 2.19.53, 3.1.2). Thus, for Augustine, the central importance of attaining happiness is one's direction of one's will.

There have been numerous debates about whether Augustine's theory of will is libertarian or compatibilism. According to Jesse Couenhoven, in order to avoid attributing human sin to God, Augustine advocated a libertarian free will, or what Couenhoven calls "free-will theodicy", in his earlier writing such as *On Free Will*.[19] However, Augustine, in his later writings, such as *City of God* and *On Trinity,* rejected the idea of neutral will and the free-will defence; and endorsed compatibilism which asserts a consent theory of will that human beings were created to choose what delights them.

Indeed, many scholars agree that Augustine's view of free will and its relation to original sin and grace of God developed throughout his writings,

---

[18] Marianne Djuth, "Will (*voluntas*)," in *Augustine through the Ages: An Encyclopedia*, ed. Allan D. Fitzgerald (Grand Rapids, Mich.: W.B. Eerdmans, 1999), p. 881.

[19] Jesse Couenhoven, "Augustine's Rejection of the Free-Will Defence: An Overview of the Late Augustine's Theodicy," *Religious Studies*, 43, no. 3 (2007): 279-85.

in particular in his dialogue with Pelagians.[20] Augustine himself also admitted that he had further developed his view on the relationship between will and grace, and changed his view about the state of infants, and exposition of a passage in Roman. However, regarding his theory of free will in *On Free Will*, Augustine insisted that it was not wrong.[21] Basically, I would argue that we may find Augustine emphasizing different perspectives about free will in different works in response to different interlocutors and different questions. However, I cannot see that these views in different writings are mutually contradictory (except about the culpability of ignorance and weakness of will as I am going to discuss below); rather they can be complementary to each other. Thus, I will try my best to consider Augustine's different writings about free will as being compatible with each other, even though Augustine himself is not satisfied with his integrating of free will and faith as God's gift.[22]

4.2. Will, Desires and Emotions

According to Marianne Djuth, there are three definitions of will in Augustine's thought.[23]

(1) Sometimes, Augustine speaks of will as the power of free movement of the soul. In his debate with Manichean, Augustine defines will as "a movement of mind, no one compelling, either for not losing or for obtaining something"; and therefore, sin is the will to obtain what justice forbids and from which it is free to abstain.[24]

(2) Sometimes, Augustine speaks of will as consenting to certain desires. Indeed, regarding the relation between will and desire one should refer to his discussion about will and emotions.

---

[20] William Babcock, "Augustine on Sin and Moral Agency," *The Journal of Religious Ethics*, 16, no. 1 (1988): 34-41; Eleonore Stump, "Augustine on Free Will," in *The Cambridge Companion to Augustine*, ed. Eleonore Stump and Norman Kretzmann (Cambridge University Press, 2001), p. 130.
[21] Augustine, *Retractions (The Fathers of the Church: A New Translation, 60)*, trans. Sister Mary Inez Bogan (Washington, D.C.: The Catholic University of America Press, 1968), bk 1, ch. 9; Stump, "Augustine on Free Will," p. 130.
[22] Augustine, *On the Gift of Perseverance,* 8.18, in *On the Free Choice of the Will, On Grace and Free Choice, and Other Writings,* p. 230.
[23] Djuth, "Will (*voluntas*)," pp. 883-4,
[24] Augustine, *Of Two Souls,* in *From Nicene and Post-Nicene Fathers, First Series, Vol. 4,* trans. Albert H. Newman, ed. Philip Schaff (Buffalo, NY: Christian Literature Publishing Co., 1887). Revised and edited for New Advent by Kevin Knight, http://www.newadvent.org/fathers/1403.htm, ch. 10.14 – 11.14.

According to Augustine, our emotions and body are operated by will (*Civ. Dei* 14.24). The human soul involves four basic emotions: desire (*cupiditas*), joy (*laetitia*), fear (*metus*) and sorrow (*tristitia*)(*Civ. Dei* 14.3-6). Desire and joy are acts of will (*voluntas*) that are in agreement (*consensione*) with what we wish for. And fear and sorrow are acts of will that are in disagreement with the object we wish for. Emotions are indeed the expression of will. It is the outcome of the act of will when will is attracted or repelled to what we wish for or avoid. Desire is therefore the consent between what we seek and what we wish for. Therefore, for Augustine, desire is neutral and not necessarily bad. When our will is correctly directed, the desire is praiseworthy; and when it is wrongly directed, the desire is bad.

As Tornau states, Augustine moral psychology is indebted to the Stoic theory of assent. "As in Stoicism, the will to act is triggered by an impression generated by an external object (*visum*). To this the mind responds with an appetitive motion that urges us to pursue or to avoid the object (e.g., delight or fear). But only when we give our inner consent to this impulse or withhold it, does a will emerge that, circumstances permitting, results in a corresponding action."[25] According to Tornau, the appetitive motion is involuntary and a kind of impulse. Such impulse becomes temptation which is not personal sin, but due to original sin.[26] Will is thus the locus of our moral responsibility because our inner consent to certain action is within our power. If one wills to do something evil, one is guilty even though one fails to carry it out.

> (3) The most puzzling thing is that Augustine sometimes identifies will with love, and he also identifies love with desire. And love and desire drive us to pursue and embrace the object (*Trin.* 14.6.8-14.7.10).

In *On the Trinity* (*De Trinitate*) book 9, Augustine identifies will with love and desire of inquiry which move the learner to form a union with the object of their desire. In such pursuit of knowledge, it is will/love/desire that unites the knower with the target of knowledge (*Trin.* 9.12.18).[27]

---

[25] Christian Tornau, "Saint Augustine," in *The Stanford Encyclopedia of Philosophy* (2019, Winter Edition), ed. Edward N. Zalta, assessed on 2 July 2020, https://plato.stanford.edu/archives/win2019/entries/augustine/.
[26] Ibid.
[27] See also Djuth, "Will (*voluntas*)," pp. 883-4.

In *The City of God* (*De civitate Dei*), he distinguishes two kinds of love with reference to will's ends. He first examines the use of words in the Scripture and argues that there is no distinction between these different terms of love (*amor, dilectio,* and *caritas*) in John 21. What is important is the nature of the object it directs towards. As he states, "The right will is, therefore, well-directed love, and the wrong will is ill-directed love" (*Civ. Dei* 14.7). When someone aims at loving God and one's neighbour in accordance with divine commands, her/his will is directed to higher rather than lower goods. Such love is called "charity" (*caritas*), while the love of lower goods is a kind of carnally induced love of the temporal world which is called "concupiscence" (*concupiscentia*).[28]

In his *On Grace and Free Choice*, Augustine identifies *caritas* with liberty (*libertas*), that is, with the divinely bestowed ability (*posse*) to delight spontaneously in the goodness of God in the absence of the constraint of fear.[29] In *The Grace of Christ and Original Sin (De gratia Christi et de peccato originali)*,[30] Augustine argues that all human good deeds are rooted in love from God whether human beings realize it or not (*Grat. et pecc. or* 1.18.19-1.21.22; *Trin.* 12.10.15; 14.8.11). It is will (*voluntas*) or love that distinguishes human beings from animals.[31]

William Babcock is right in his analysis of Augustine's distinction between desire *(Cupiditas)* and charity *(Caritas)*. Desire *(cupiditas)* refers to the love of things that can be destroyed or vanished, while charity *(caritas)* refers to the love of the eternal—God, who alone cannot be lost. However, both are also kinds of love that are discriminated according to the object being loved. And the influence of two loves extends beyond their loved object to social order. While desire *(cupiditas)* will make persons stand against persons, charity *(caritas)* "in seeking and attaining

---

[28] Augustine, *On Christian Doctrine*, in *From Nicene and Post-Nicene Fathers, First Series, Vol. 2*, trans. James Shaw, ed. Philip Schaff (Buffalo, NY: Christian Literature Publishing Co., 1887). Revised and edited for New Advent by Kevin Knight. http://www.newadvent.org/fathers/12023.htm, bk, 3, ch. 10, sec. 16.

[29] Augustine, *On Grace and Free Choice*, 17.33-34 in *On the Free Choice of the Will, On Grace and Free Choice, and Other Writings*, pp. 168-171. Hereafter cited as *Grat. et lib. arb.* with an Arabic number indicating the chapter and the section.

[30] Augustine, *The Grace of Christ and Original Sin*, in *Answer to the Pelagians (Vol. I/23) The Works of Saint Augustine: A Translation for the 21st Century*, trans. Roland J. Teske, ed. John E. Rotelle (Hyde Park, N.Y.: New City Press, 1997), pp. 383-463. Hereafter cited as *Grat. et pecc. or.* with an Arabic number indicating the chapter and the section.

[31] Djuth, "Will (*voluntas*)," p. 884.

the eternal, also unites persons in the common bond of a love shared without threat or envy . . ."[32]

According to Carol Harrison, will and love are synonyms for Augustine. To will something is not simply about using our reason to choose, it is also to love and be moved by this love. Even if one plunders out of one's arrogance, or one uses their will inappropriately, one's action is still out of one's will and love; but such love is considered as concupiscence (*concupiscentia*).[33]

4.3. Two Levels of Will

Before we further discuss Augustine's idea of concupiscence, we have to deal with a puzzle that the third definition of will above seems to contradict with the first and second ones. On the one hand, Augustine sometimes identifies will with love and desire; on the other, Augustine defines will as free movement different from and undetermined by desires; and it can assent or reject the directions of desires. These two are incompatible. Indeed, Augustine stresses that our minds are more powerful than our desires, so it should dominate our desires and our desires should be ruled by the reason according to the eternal law (*Lib. arb.* 1.8.18, 1.10.20). So, are will and desire the same thing or different things?

I would argue that such puzzle brought about by the obscurity of the terms "will", "love" and "desire" can be explained in terms of two levels of will and desire. Inspired by Harry Frankfurt's distinction between "first-order volition" and "second-order volition", many scholars agree that Augustine's theory of will also involves two levels: first-order and second-order volitions.[34] While the first-order volitions are object-orientated and operate on all levels of soul, the second-order volitions are the ability to choose between conflicting first-order volitions. Eleonore Stump argues that Augustine is well aware of the case that will can command itself but such command is not always successful. This shows that "will can be divided against itself in various ways."[35] While one can have conflicts between

---

[32] William Babcock, "*Cupiditas and Caritas*: The Early Augustine on Love and Fulfillment". in *Augustine Today*, ed. Richard John Neuhaus (Grand Rapids: Eerdmans, 1993), p. 31.
[33] Carol Harrison, *Augustine: Christian Truth and Fractured Humanity* (New York: Oxford University Press, 2000), pp. 94-5.
[34] Tornau, "Saint Augustine"; Stump, "Augustine on Free Will," p.126.
[35] Stump, "Augustine on Free Will," p. 126.

first-order desires (eating chocolate or eating ice-cream) one can also be in conflict between first-order desires (eating chocolate) and second-order desires (not to eat chocolate for the sake of health). And this kind of conflict between will and desire is the result and punishment of sin (*Civ. Dei* 12.14). I think that such two levels of will can help us better understand the nature of three different definitions of will: while will as free movement and consent usually refers to the second-order volition, will as love and desire refers to the first-order volition. And when this first-order volition/desire turns away from God and towards what is temporal and mutable, it becomes concupiscence.

4.4. Lust and Concupiscence

Lust (*libido*) and concupiscence (*concupiscentia*) are the central theme of Augustine's doctrine of original sin.[36] Before Augustine, the term "concupiscence" (*concupiscentia*) had already been used by Tertullian to mean disordered desire.[37] In Augustine's earlier writing, concupiscence is not the main word used for this notion. For instance, in *Confessions*, he uses the words "lust" (*libido*) and "desire" (*cupiditas*) to express inordinate desire. Indeed, Augustine argues, the usage of two different words for desire (*cupiditas*) and concupiscence (*concupiscentia*), can be both used in a good sense or a bad sense. However, the default usage of desire and concupiscence is understood in a bad sense if the object is not defined (*Civ. Dei* 14.7). Thus, desire (*cupiditas*), concupiscence (*concupiscentia*) and lust (*libido*) are also used to refer to bad desire in Augustine's writings. In the anti-Pelagian works, "concupiscence" is persistently employed, and becomes a technical term for the disorder of the will inherited from Adam. In Augustine writings, the influences of concupiscence are mainly expressed in four ways: (1) a distaste for justice and a lustiness of iniquity, (2) divided will, (3) disordered human sexuality and (4) lust of the eyes.

---

[36] According to Richard Sorabji, the terms "*libido*" and "*concupiscentia carnis*" are interchanged in Augustine's writing, with *carnis* omitted when the context makes it redundant. Richard Sorabji, *Emotion and Peace of Mind: From Stoic Agitation to Christian Temptation* (New York: Oxford University Press, 2002), p. 404.

[37] Peter Burnell, "Concupiscence," in *Augustine through the Ages: An Encyclopedia*, ed. Allan D. Fitzgerald (Grand Rapids, Mich.: W.B. Eerdmans, 1999), p. 226.

(1) A Distaste for Justice and a Lustiness of Iniquity

In *Confessions* 8.5.10-12, Augustine attributes his own moral laziness, lack of moral freedom, compulsive desire to do wrong things and delay in conversions to human sins, including perversity of social environment, that is, the unfriendly friendliness of his companions (*Conf.* 2.9.17), the influence of individual bad habits, the innate core of moral distortion which is shown in infants' offensive spirit (*Conf.* 1.7.11). In particular, in the instance of robbery in the Pearl, Augustine confesses that he stole neither because of hunger, nor poverty. This was because he originally had enough of the thing he stole. Such evildoing was out of "contempt for it [justice] and an excess of iniquity" (*Conf.* 2.4.9).

(2) The Divided Will

Augustine then discusses his struggle between lust and the spirit. He states that his will was mastered and bound by the enemy. The perverted will caused lust, and he indulged in lust which became a habit. He rejects resisting this bad habit which became a kind of "addictive necessity".[38] On the other hand, he found that a new will developed in him, so that he can worship God freely. However, the new will is not yet strong enough to combat the old will; thus, his two wills contend with each other inside him and upset his soul. Unlike Manichean understanding of deliberation of two separated wills (one good and one evil), Augustine argues that the two wills are an expression of a single self, "it was I who willed to do it, I who was unwilling. It was I" (*Conf.* 8.10). His will is restored only when, at the end of *Confessions* 8, his will is healed by God's call which frees him immediately to choose an ascetic life.

Thus, in *On Man's Perfection in Righteousness*, in elaborating Paul's "doing the evil I do not want to do" (Rom. 7:16), Augustine states, "Now it is a good thing to avoid concupiscence, and this good the just man would, who lives by faith, and still he does what he hates, because he has concupiscence".[39]

---

[38] Tornau, "Saint Augustine"; see also *Conf.* 8.10-12.
[39] Augustine, *On Man's Perfection in Righteousness*, in *From Nicene and Post-Nicene Fathers, First Series, Vol. 5*, trans. Peter Holmes and Robert Ernest Wallis, and revised by Benjamin B. Warfield, ed. Philip Schaff (Buffalo, NY: Christian Literature Publishing Co., 1887). Revised and edited for New Advent by Kevin Knight, http://www.newadvent.org/fathers/1504.htm, ch. 11, sec. 28.

(3) Disordered Human Sexuality

Lust or inordinate sexual desire is the most obvious expression of concupiscence in Augustine's writings. As human beings sin through disobedience of God's commandment, God punished disobedience by using disobedience itself. The divine punishment makes the human body no longer obey the will which is shown in human desire, pain and death. Sexual desire or lust (*libido*) is especially uncontrolled by one's will. Sexual arousal can occur or stop without will's command. Even those who love this pleasure also cannot control their sexual desire as they wish (*Civ. Dei* 14.16). "Such lust does not merely invade the whole body and outward members; it takes such complete and passionate possession of the whole man, both physically and emotionally, that what results is the keenest of all pleasures on the level of sensation; and, at the crisis of excitement, it practically paralyzes all power of deliberate thought" (*Civ. Dei* 14.16). And thus, people feel shame in having sex in public, even legitimate sex between married couples (*Civ. Dei* 14.18, 14.23). As Gerard O'Daly (1999, 158) argues, lust is different from other emotions.[40] For instance, if anger leads to violence, such expression of emotions is assented by one's will. However, in the case of lust, the desire commands the bodily organ directly (*Civ. Dei* 14.19). Such lust becomes a problem for those who are committed to married life and the apostolic ideal. And in the book *On Marriage and Concupiscence*,[41] Augustine argues that concupiscence has even influenced the sexual intercourse of parents through which the original sin was transmitted to their children from generation to generation (*Nupt. et conc.* 1.24, 27).

According to Djuth, Augustine recognizes the presence of will in the soul's natural appetites or desires.[42] However, he disagrees that the natural appetites are evil in themselves. Instead he attributes their evil character to will's impotence in directing them to the proper goal. The most obvious example is that Augustine would consider the natural desire (*naturalis appetitus*) of the flesh for procreation as good, while he denounces the

---

[40] Gerard O'Daly, *Augustine's City of God: A Reader's Guide,* (New York: Oxford University Press, 1999), p. 158.

[41] Augustine, *On Marriage and Concupiscence,* in *From Nicene and Post-Nicene Fathers, First Series, Vol. 5*, trans. Peter Holmes and Robert Ernest Wallis, and revised by Benjamin B. Warfield, ed. Philip Schaff (Buffalo, NY: Christian Literature Publishing Co., 1887). Revised and edited for New Advent by Kevin Knight, http://www.newadvent.org/fathers/1507.htm. Hereafter cited as *Nupt. et conc.* with an Arabic number indicating the book and the chapter.

[42] Djuth, "Will (*voluntas*)," p. 882.

misdirected concupiscence in the flesh as rebellious to one's will which is the result of original sin (*Nupt. et conc.* 2.7, 17). In particular, the most conspicuous example for Augustine is the motion of the male sexual organ which disobeys the dictates of reason (*Nupt. et conc.* 2.31, 53).

In Augustine's newly discovered *Letter 6**, we can see Augustine further criticizes concupiscence for "disturbing us with such unruly and inordinate desires against our will even when there is no need... by insistent or even wicked desires, it seduces the hearts of even the faithful and the saints; it forces itself in by these turbulent movements even if we do not consent in the slightest."[43]

To be really free is to live according to one's wishes; and that is the precondition of human happiness. Augustine envisages that our prelapsarian sexual desire is obedient to our will and therefore there is no shame, guilt or obscenity (*Civ. Dei* 14.23). Augustine therefore argues that without the Fall, sexual desire would not have been the motor of our multiplication. He even states that those devoted persons would prefer to control their desire, to beget his children without suffering from this lust if they could (*Civ. Dei* 14.26).

(4) Lust of the Eyes

Apart from bodily desire which strives for sensual gratification, Augustine argues that lust of the eyes is another complicated form of temptation which is associated with an experience of temporal and corporal images. According to Augustine, the lust of the eyes originates from curiosity, which is an inordinate desire for knowledge derived from visual experience.[44] While it is in the name of learning knowledge, it actually strives for new experiences through the body. While the objects of pleasure are usually beautiful, harmonious, fragrant, savoury and soft, those for curiosity are not necessarily so, and can even be the opposite of these. In Augustine's words, the malady of curiosity causes people to see lacerated corpses, strange scenes shown in theatres, magical arts, seeing a dog chase a rabbit, and tempting God by asking for signs and wonders that are not for salvation. It is out of a desire to experiment and simply to test

---

[43] Augustine. *Letters, Volume 6 (1*–29*) (The Fathers of the Church, a New Translation, 81)*, trans. Robert B. Eno. (Washington, DC: Catholic University of America Press, 1989). *ep.* 6*.7–8. See also Richard Sorabji, *Emotion and Peace of Mind*, p. 405.

[44] Joseph N. Torchia, "Curiosity," in *Augustine through the Ages: An Encyclopedia*, ed. Allan D. Fitzgerald (Grand Rapids, Mich.: W.B. Eerdmans, 1999), p. 259.

God. All these trivial things just keep tempting his vain curiosity. These things distract him from serious thought. Augustine admits that if he was not awakened by showing his weakness by God and be elevated to the sight of God by deliberate act of thought, he would also become absorbed in such vain sights (*Conf.* 10.35). Indeed, today's people watching pornography is usually motivated both by the pursuit of inordinate sexual pleasure and curiosity. It is usually our sense of curiosity (lust of the eyes) which drives us to start assessing pornography which then leads to indulgence in sexual pleasure.

5. Augustine's Critics and Controversy with Julian

In his defences of marriage standing against the Manichaeans, Augustine argues that marriage is good because it leads to three goods: procreation, mutual fidelity and sacrament (*sacramentum*).[45] In *Retraction*, Augustine emphasizes that "Of this evil of passion conjugal chastity makes a good use for the procreation of children".[46] However, Augustine's understanding of concupiscence and sexuality was criticized by Julian, bishop of Eclanum and a supporter of Pelagius, as an opponent of marriage and was therefore Manichean. For Julian, concupiscence is just a natural desire created by God for the purpose of procreation. In consideration of Julian's criticism, Augustine further clarified his view of concupiscence by distinguishing the concupiscence of marriage (*concupiscentia nuptiarum*), which is the legitimate desire for offspring, from concupiscence of the flesh (*concupiscentia carnis*), "which we feel disturbing us with such unruly and inordinate desires against our will even when there is no need."[47] Augustine believes that there will be no concupiscence in paradise. However, for the sake of argument, he argues that even if concupiscence really exists in paradise, it would be a different type of concupiscence which is under the control of one's will in a way that will neither lead the

---

[45] Augustine, *Of the Good of Marriage,* in *From Nicene and Post-Nicene Fathers, First Series, Vol. 3*, trans. C.L. Cornish, ed. Philip Schaff (Buffalo, NY: Christian Literature Publishing Co., 1887). Revised and edited for New Advent by Kevin Knight, http://www.newadvent.org/fathers/1309.htm, sec. 32. See also David Hunter, "Marriage," in *Augustine through the Ages: An Encyclopedia*, ed. Allan D. Fitzgerald (Grand Rapids, Mich.: W.B. Eerdmans, 1999), p. 536; Sorabji, *Emotion and Peace of Mind*, p. 403.
[46] Augustine, *Retractions,* bk. 2, ch. 9.
[47] Augustine. *Letters, Volume 6 (1*–29*), ep.* 6*.7.

mind into sin nor into a struggle between lust and the spirit, but let it be upright and calm.[48]

Julian further criticizes Augustine's idea of concupiscence by comparing it with the feeling of hunger, thirst and digestion. According to Augustine's record in *Against Julian* 5. 5. 20, Julia makes a distinction between the command of one's will and the consent of one's will; and he refutes Augustine that although the male physical movements are not under the command of their will, they have the consent of their will, which is the similar to our feeling of hunger, thirst, and digestion. There is no point in regarding concupiscence as evil while accepting hunger, thirst and digestion as usual human desires. Augustine replies that although hunger, thirst and digestion, like concupiscence, also are not suffered by one's will, they are still different from concupiscence. This is because these are needs of the human body that we must sustain lest it be injured or killed. However, the body would not suffer injury if we don't give assent to concupiscence.[49] One more difference between concupiscence and hunger and thirst is the universal desire for the privacy of sex, as discussed before that people will generally feel shame if they have sex in public (*Civ. Dei* 14.18), which is not the case for eating or drinking. For Augustine, the feeling of shame concerning a lack of control of sex demonstrates that concupiscence is evil which starts only after the Fall of our first parents.

Richard Sorabji, after reviewing Augustine's debates with Julian, criticizes Augustine for grounding the evilness of lust on its disobedience to one's will as unsounded. In his words, "it must be wrong to take the fact of its being against the will as the reason for its badness. For it is against one's will only if one thinks it bad for *other* reasons."[50] Given Augustine's unique history, it is not surprising that Augustine considered concupiscence as wrong; however, it is not a sufficient reason to support the wrongfulness of concupiscence for everyone. It implies that Augustine's negative attitude towards sexuality fits only himself and is not applicable to general people. Sorabji's criticism has indeed raised two issues about Augustine's theory: negative view of sexuality and desire against one's will as bad.

---

[48] Augustine. *Letters, Volume 6 (1*–29*)*, ep. 6*.8; See also Sorabji, *Emotion and Peace of Mind*, p. 403; and Hunter, "Marriage," p. 537.
[49] Augustine, *Against Julian (Fathers of the Church Patristic Series)*, trans. Matthew A. Schuhmacher (The Catholic University of America Press, 2004), bk. 5, ch. 5, sec. 22. I have set aside Julia's criticism by comparison of sleep with concupiscence in *Against Julian* 5. 5. 21.
[50] Sorabji, *Emotion and Peace of Mind*, p. 414.

And in the following, first, I argue that instead of denying the value of sexuality, Augustine indeed affirms the function of procreation through sexuality, while being misgiving about the value of sexual pleasure. In light of the seriousness of internet addiction in the modern world, Augustine's caution regarding concupiscence and sexual pleasure is not altogether without reason and it is still relevant to modern society. Second, I cannot agree with Sorabji's criticism. I think that being against one's will is itself a sufficient reason to consider desire as bad.

5.1. Augustine's Rejection of Sexual Pleasure

Among atheists, agnostics and some Christians have always decried Augustine for his hatred of the body and sexuality because of the influence of Manichaean. However, they have neglected the fact that Augustine wrote at least six treatises against the Manichaeans.[51] Furthermore, Augustine's writing shows that he is positive towards marriage and sexuality for the purpose of procreation.

Indeed, in Augustine's earlier writings, his view on the body and sexuality seems to be negative and ambiguous. According to John Rist, in the *Confessions*, Augustine thought that human beings "are souls *fallen into* rather than with a body".[52] In *Of the Good of Marriage*, Augustine writes,

> whence could exist the progeny of the first men, whom God had blessed, saying, Increase, and be ye multiplied, and fill the earth; if they had not sinned, whereas their bodies by sinning deserved the condition of death, and there can be no sexual intercourse save of mortal bodies (*Of the Good of Marriage,* sec. 2).

Augustine then suggested that God probably would have enabled the first parents to produce children without sexual union, or the bodies of the first parents were originally mortal so that they could achieve sexual reproduction even if they had not sinned. At that time, Augustine seems to identify sexuality with a mortal body. However, in his later book *The Literal Meaning of Genesis*,[53] Augustine came to accept the originally

---

[51] Gabriel Hess, "Refuting the Claim that Augustine is Opposed to Corporeality," *Aporia* 23, no. 1 (2013): 30-1.
[52] John Rist, *Augustine: Ancient Thought Baptized* (Cambridge University Press, 1999), p. 112.
[53] Augustine, *The Literal Meaning of Genesis* in *On Genesis I/13 The Works of Saint Augustine: A Translation for the 21st Century,* trans. Edmund Hill, ed. John

created goodness of the human body and sexual reproduction (*Gen. litt.* 9.9.14–15). He concluded that the disembodied soul is incapable of enjoying God (*Gen. litt.* 12.35.68). However, for Augustine, after the Fall, sin has an immediate effect on the body, in particular on one's sexuality.[54] Before the Fall, human beings can command their body to reproduce "without any trouble or any sort of prurient itch for pleasure" (*Gen. litt.* 9.10.18).

Actually, Augustine's criticism of concupiscence seems to be based on his misgiving about sexual pleasure. As discussed above, Augustine makes a distinction between "concupiscence of marriage" and "concupiscence of the flesh". Indeed, I would rather call the former the "desire of offspring" while the later the "desire of sexual pleasure". It seems that for Augustine, sexual desires and activities are good only if they lead to procreation, and it is not good if it leads to sexual pleasure. From today's perspective, Augustine's uneasiness towards sexual pleasure may have neglected its positive function in constituting a conjugal relationship. However, it is exactly sexual pleasure which is so exciting that is appealing to and desired by everyone and leads to uncontrollable impulses and even sexual addiction, in particular in the age of digitalization.

On 30 November, 2011, *Newsweek Magazine* ran the article "The Sex Addiction Epidemic" which indicated that around 40 million people (about 13% of the US population) a day are logging into porn websites and around 9 million may qualify as sex addicts. Porn addictions have largely disturbed their work, and damaged their marriage and self-esteem.[55]

On 11 April, 2016, *Time Magazine* published the article "Porn and the threat to virility" which stated that around 40% of British youth (aged 14 – 17) regularly watch porn. And some youths have problems of porn-induced erectile dysfunction because of Internet indulgence which has changed how one's brain is wired. It means that the boys have a response

---

E. Rotelle (Hyde Park, NY: New City Press, 2002), pp. 155-506. Hereafter cited as *Gen. litt.* with an Arabic number indicating the book and the section.
[54] See also Hunter, "Marriage," pp. 356-8.
[55] Chris Lee, "The Sex Addiction Epidemic," *Newsweek Magazine*, December 2011, assessed on 11 November 2019, https://www.newsweek.com/sex-addiction-epidemic-66289.

toward woman, but their body is no longer cooperative. It responds only to the sight of pornography.[56]

Mary Eberstadt and Mary Anne Layden, in their book *The Social Costs of Pornography*, argue that the Internet has largely changed the ecology of pornography.[57] Online pornography is ubiquitous and easy to access, the images are ever-changing, and the hard core content is greatly increasing. More and more research and clinical experience have shown that online pornography is highly indulgent and affects normal sexual and marriage relationships. This is because exposure to pornography makes men rate their female partner as less attractive in comparison with porn actors, and to be less satisfied with sex with their female partner and have a greater desire for sex without emotional involvement. As philosopher Roger Scruton states, "Once they [men] have been led by their porn addiction to see sex in the instrumentalized way that pornography encourages, they begin to lose confidence in their ability to enjoy sex in any other way than through fantasy…And then the fear of desire arises, and from that fear the fear of love."[58] The prevalence of pornography also increases the risk of women being violated and trafficked. According to contemporary neuroscience, of all human activities, sexual activities will mostly increase our levels of dopamine, even though it still cannot compare with that generated by nicotine. Dopamine is a chemical in our brain. It produces feelings of pleasure and excitement; and it is the neurotransmitter in the brain's reward system. However, the reward system tells the brain that sexual activities feel high and that more of them are desired; which makes us vulnerable to addiction.[59] In light of today's problem of online sexual addiction, we can see that Augustine's cautious approach to concupiscence and indulgence of sexual pleasure is not unreasonable. Addiction is not concupiscence, but addiction is a probable outcome of concupiscence. Augustine's ethics has reminded us to be aware of the possible damage and temptation caused by inordinate sexual desire, as he himself experienced

---

[56] Belinda Luscombe, "Porn and the Threat to Virility," *Time Magazine*, April 2016, assessed on 31 October 2019, https://time.com/magazine/us/4277492/april-11th-2016-vol-187-no-13-u-s/.
[57] Mary Eberstadt and Mary Anne Layden, *The Social Costs of Pornography: A Statement of Findings and Recommendations* (The Witherspoon Institute, 2010).
[58] cited in Eberstadt & Layden, *The Social Costs of Pornography*, p. 38.
[59] Horvath, et al., "Sexual Addiction and Pornography Addiction". *Gulf Bend Center*, assessed on 12 November 2019, https://bit.ly/34R7SK4; David Fawcett, "Dopamine, Addiction, and Unnatural Rewards: Tips for Recovery," *Sex and Relationship Healing*, assessed on 29 October 2019, https://bit.ly/3ln9Bjk.

such emotional bondage due to sex, just like many addicts experience in today's world. And Augustine emphasized that it is only God's mercy and love that changed his life. God healed his lust for self-justification, forgave his remaining sins, redeemed his life from corruption and satisfied his desires with good things (*Conf.* 10.36).

5.2. Addiction as Against One's Will

Furthermore, the contemporary understanding of addiction also helps us to reflect on Augustine's view of "desire against one's will". According to Young, Yue & Ying, addictions are defined as "the habitual compulsion to engage in a certain activity or utilize a substance, notwithstanding the devastating consequences on the individual's physical, social, spiritual, mental, and financial well-being".[60]

Indeed, the scientific consensus today recognizes addiction as a chronic disease that changes both brain structure and function. In short, an addiction hijacks the brain and reduces one's self-control.[61] Basically, addiction involves three processes: learning process, tolerance and compulsion. As stated above, addictive behaviours (or substances) stimulate the reward circuit and then overload it. Repeated exposure to an addictive behaviour causes our brain to couple *liking* something with *wanting* it, in turn driving us to pursue the source of pleasure. This is the learning process. Over time, as brain receptors become overwhelmed by large amounts of dopamine, the brain will adapt by producing less dopamine or eliminating dopamine receptors. As a result, dopamine has less impact on the brain's reward system and addicts must indulge in the addictive behaviour more to obtain the same "high" as before -- an effect called "tolerance". And once tolerance occurs, compulsion will take over. While the pleasure associated with addictive behaviour decreases, the memory from the learning process and the desire to recreate such pleasure persists. These create an intense craving which contributes not only to addiction but to relapse even after sobriety. Indeed, the process of addiction discovered by today's scientific investigation is consistent with Augustine's model of habit in *Confessions* 8, in which the perverted will

---

[60] Young, Yue & Ying, "Prevalence Estimates and Etiologic Models of Internet Addiction," p. 6.
[61] Harvard Mental Health Letter 2011, "How Addiction Hijacks the Brain," *Harvard Mental Health Letter* (July 2011), assessed on 12 November 2019. https://bit.ly/34ERGP7.

leads to lust, and then lust to habit and habit to addictive necessity as discussed above.

The problem of addiction is that addicts do not really address life's obstacles, tackle daily stress, and/or confront past or present problems. They cannot but respond maladaptively by resorting to a pseudo coping mechanism at the expense of devastating results on the well-being of individuals and their families. In light of the problem of addiction, we can see how one's desire against one's will can damage our well-being; therefore, I defend Augustine in that it is a sufficient reason to arbitrate concupiscence as bad. Indeed, in light of the seriousness of internet addiction, apart from sexual indulgence, cyber-relationship, net gambling or shopping compulsions, information overload and excessive online game-playing can also be attributed to concupiscence, according to Augustine's definition. However, where does concupiscence, which makes us so addicted to different kinds of pleasure that are beyond the control of our will, come from?

6. Augustine on Original Sin and Divine Grace

6.1 Augustine on The Fall

According to Augustine, original human will by nature is good because all good things come from God. However, our first parents disobeyed God's commandant and ate the forbidden fruit. Augustine believes that evil will precede evil acts. It is just like an evil tree will bring forth evil fruit (*Civ. Dei* 14.12). And Augustine argues that such evil will, opposing its nature, indeed comes from its own nature, that is, because human beings were created out of nothing, "and thus (unlike God, who cannot sin) have the ontological possibility of falling away from the good."[62]

According to Augustine, the root of the Fall is pride (*Civ. Dei* 14.13). Pride makes human beings desire to elevate the self inordinately in which the soul cut itself off from the Sources, an immutable God, and makes the soul as the end to oneself. As Robert Markus argues, Augustine's understanding of pride shifted from his earlier understanding of turning away from higher to lower good that is a violation of divine order (*Conf.* 7.16.22) to perverted self-love deprived of a proper relationship with God,

---

[62] Couenhoven, "Augustine's Rejection of the Free-Will Defence," p. 287.

one's fellow and one's own self.[63] Actually, self-love or self-elevating by itself is not a problem. Self-love strives for true happiness by subordinating the self to God as part of the biblical commandments. However, excessive self-love which becomes a kind of pride and attempts to put the self in place of God is the root of sin (*Civ. Dei* 14.28).[64]

The fall of our first parents is so serious that it has damaged our nature. And the ignorance of the good and impotence in resisting concupiscence in human soul is the punishment of sin (*Lib. arb* 3.18.52). Our free will, ability to make free choices, is also damaged by original sin and therefore we are disturbed by our opposing passions. In his later debate with Pelagian, he further argues that original sin has so much damaged our will that it is impossible for us to overcome our sinful volitions; we thus permanently remain in the state of "*akrasia*", that is, weakness of will (*Civ. Dei* 19.4; *Nupt. et conc.* 1.35).[65] This makes it hard for us to resist the "beguiling and enticing" of the Internet that is so popular today, and easily fall into internet addiction.[66]

6.2 The Problem of Our Moral Responsibility Raised by the Doctrine of Original Sin

Actually, the idea of the original sin has raised another question about our moral responsibility. Are we, as the descendants of Adam and Eve, culpable for our wrongdoing if we sin without choice? Do we sin involuntarily? Babcock argues that Augustine's earlier view appeals to free will as essential to moral agency and argues that evils arise from the voluntary sin of the soul.[67] However, after his several conversations with Fortunatus, an elder of the Manichaeans, recorded in *A Debate with Fortunatus, a Manichean (Acta contra Fortunatum Manichaeum)*,[68]

---

[63] Robert A. Markus, *Conversion and Disenchantment in Augustine's Spiritual Career* (Villanova, PA: Villanova University Press, 1989), pp. 24-42.
[64] See also Tornau, "Saint Augustine."
[65] Augustine, *On Nature and Grace*, in *From Nicene and Post-Nicene Fathers, First Series, Vol. 5*, translated by Peter Holmes and Robert Ernest Wallis, and revised by Benjamin B. Warfield, ed. Philip Schaff (Buffalo, NY: Christian Literature Publishing Co., 1887). Revised and edited for New Advent by Kevin Knight, http://www.newadvent.org/fathers/1503.htm, Chapter 61-67.
[66] Aiken, *The Cyber Effect*, p. 86
[67] Babcock, "Augustine on Sin and Moral Agency," pp. 33-40.
[68] Augustine, *A Debate with Fortunatus, a Manichean,* in *The Manichean Debate (Vol. I/19) The Works of Saint Augustine: A Translation for the 21st Century,* trans.

Augustine no longer denied that sin is involuntary. Augustine changed his position to restrict the free exercise of will to only the first sin of the first parents. As Babcock says,

> And after the first sin, we sin involuntarily and are the moral agents of the evil that we do only in the sense that we are ourselves the authors of the condition in which we cannot help but sin.[69]

What concerns me here is Babcock saying that we sin "involuntarily". For Augustine, acting voluntarily is the main reason why Augustine attributes the responsibility of sin to human beings (*Lib. arb.* 3.1.2). Even in *A Debate with Fortunatus*, Augustine insists that we sin voluntarily; and "there is no sin if we do not sin by our own will" (*C. Fort.* 15, 17, 21). Although Augustine agrees that human beings are not able not to sin (*non posse non peccare*) after the Fall of the first parents (*C. Fort.* 22) and we are entangled in habit and addicted to not doing what we will, Augustine never gave up the idea of our responsibility for sinful acts and therefore our voluntariness in acting; in short, Augustine never says that we sin involuntarily; and this means that our evildoing is always within our power and therefore deserves punishment.

Augustine's idea of moral responsibility is made further obscure when he says, in *On Free Will*, Book 3, that neither ignorance nor weakness of will is culpable; rather what is culpable is that human beings reject to seek God who is willing to help us and to heal us (*Lib. arb.* 3.19.53). As he states,

> The soul is not held guilty because it is naturally ignorant and naturally incapable, but rather because it did not make an effort to know, and because it did not work enough to acquire the ability to act rightly (*Lib. arb.* 3.22.64).

Indeed, Augustine's view that ignorance and weakness of will are inculpable (*Lib. arb.* 3.19.53) has two problems. First, it seems to imply that if we have never heard of the Gospel and God's grace, we are blameless for our sin, which is certainly not what Augustine intended to argue. Second, it seems to be contradicting his earlier view that wrongdoing of the mind is blameworthy because it is voluntary (*Lib. arb.* 3.1.2). I would argue that his earlier view of responsibility based on voluntariness is more consistent with our religious experience. Even if when people fall into temptation,

---

Roland J. Teske, ed. Boniface Ramsey (N.Y.: New City Press, 2006), pp. 137-162. Hereafter cited as *C. Fort.* with an Arabic number indicating the section.
[69] Babcock, "Augustine on Sin and Moral Agency," p. 40.

and they do not receive immediate help from God after praying, people are still culpable for their own weakness and evildoing, and they cannot attribute the problem to God.

Fortunately, the Fall does not impugn God's work. God can make good use of evil. And the Fall allows God to exhibit his punishing power and his grace for those chosen people saved from the condemned masses (*civ. Dei* 14.26). While concupiscence leads us to betray God, it is also a means of grace which reminds us to search for God's help (*Lib. arb.* 3.22.65). Even reborn people may fail to obey commandments, "in order that, when we find ourselves lying in this diseased state, we might seek the medicine of Grace" (*Nupt. et conc.* 1.29.32). Thus, the prevalence of internet addiction caused by concupiscence and divine commandments should cause us to realize our limitations and our dependency on Divine grace.

6.3 Augustine on Divine Grace

For Augustine, the aspiration of the help of grace is the start of grace. Apart from grace as reminding, the most important function of grace is the empowerment of our first-order will. It is shown in his explanation of the difference between law and grace, in which Augustine emphasizes that grace produces sweetness rather than fear:

> If we are to call this grace "teaching"… with an ineffable sweetness in the depths and interior of the soul, not merely through those who externally plant and water, but also through himself who gives the increase secretly. In that way he not merely reveals the truth, but also imparts love… so that I am not forced to live under the law as a slave out of fear of punishment, but may find delight in the law with the love that makes me free (*Grat. et pecc. or.* 1.13.14).

Here the person uses his second-order volition to pray that God might strengthen his first-order will in goodness; and thus Augustine emphasizes that our will is helped by grace (*Grat. et pecc. or.* 14.15). Indeed, Augustine emphasizes that our turning towards God is determined by our free will with the assistance of God's gift (*Grat. et lib. arb.* 5.10, 17.33). Our will of faith is also out of God's grace; without the assistance of God's grace, we cannot turn to God.

For Augustine, we have shared our first parents' guilt and punishment. Human nature has been profoundly damaged by original sin; and thus we must continue to depend on God's grace profoundly.[70] As Augustine states,

> Therefore, the soul is ignorant of what it ought to do, precisely because it has not yet received it. but it will receive this, too, if it uses well what it has received: the power to search diligently and religiously, if it is willing. As for the fact that it cannot always accomplish what it recognizes it ought to do – well, the soul has also not yet received this…As a result, on account of that very trouble the soul is given a warning to call upon him Who helps in its perfection, the one Whom it perceives is the author of its inception (*Lib. arb.* 3.22.65).

As Stump states, "Here Augustine is apparently thinking of God as always willing to give grace to any person who wants God to give it to him."[71] It seems to assume that when the person is willing and prays to God, s/he will surely receive the power from God to be able to act rightly. However, how about the case when one has prayed to God to overcome certain weakness, but one is still trapped by the weakness of the will even after one's prayers? This is quite a common experience among believers; and we know that even if we pray, it does not mean that God will dramatically send us a dose of medicine which can immediately strengthen our will and overcome our weakness. Mostly, God's healing takes time. And throughout the process of recovery we may still be disturbed by our concupiscence and we may therefore commit sin which is blameworthy. However, God's hiddenness does not mean God's absence. In Catholic tradition, the experience of divine hiddenness, which is also called a "Dark Night of the Soul", is a spiritual transformative experience. It is a spiritual training process given by God. When it ends, one's life is transformed, and becomes more faithful and wondrous again.

7. Conclusion

This paper has explored Augustine's ethics in particular his theory of will, desire and concupiscence and its relevance to our life in the age of digitalization. In light of the prevalence of cybersexual addiction and other kinds of internet addiction, I argue that Augustine's cautions regarding concupiscence and indulgence of sexual desire, that are beyond the control of our will, should be highly evaluated and taken seriously. We are

---

[70] Kent, "Augustine's Ethics," p. 223.
[71] Stump, "Augustine on Free Will," p. 133.

vulnerable to internet addiction because human beings have suffered damage by the original sin and therefore inevitably remain in the state of weakness of will. However, our weakness in the face of the enticing features of the Internet just reminds us of our limitations and thus need to seek help from God's grace.

Bibliography

Reference of Augustine Theology

Augustine. *A Debate with Fortunatus, a Manichean.* In *The Manichean Debate (Vol. I/19) The Works of Saint Augustine: A Translation for the 21st Century*, translated and notes by Roland J. Teske, edited by Boniface Ramsey, 137-162. Brooklyn, N.Y.:New City Press, 2006.

Augustine. *Confessions*, 2nd Edition. Translated by F. J. Sheed, Indianapolis: Hackett Publishing Company, 2006.

Augustine. *Letters, Volume 6 (1*–29*) (The Fathers of the Church, A New Translation, 81).* Translated by Robert B. Eno, Washington, DC: Catholic University of America Press, 1989.

Augustine. *On Christian Doctrine.* In *From Nicene and Post-Nicene Fathers, First Series, Vol. 2*, translated by James Shaw, edited by Philip Schaff. Buffalo, NY: Christian Literature Publishing Co., 1887. Revised and edited for New Advent by Kevin Knight. Assessed on November 13, 2019. http://www.newadvent.org/fathers/12023.htm.

Augustine. *On Man's Perfection in Righteousness.* In *From Nicene and Post-Nicene Fathers, First Series, Vol. 5*, translated by Peter Holmes and Robert Ernest Wallis, and revised by Benjamin B. Warfield, edited by Philip Schaff. Buffalo, NY: Christian Literature Publishing Co., 1887. Revised and edited for New Advent by Kevin Knight. Assessed on November 13, 2019. http://www.newadvent.org/fathers/1504.htm.

Augustine. *On Marriage and Concupiscence.* In *From Nicene and Post-Nicene Fathers, First Series, Vol. 5*, translated by Peter Holmes and Robert Ernest Wallis, and revised by Benjamin B. Warfield, edited by Philip Schaff. Buffalo, NY: Christian Literature Publishing Co., 1887. Revised and edited for New Advent by Kevin Knight. Assessed on November 13, 2019. http://www.newadvent.org/fathers/1507.htm.

Augustine. *On Nature and Grace.* In *From Nicene and Post-Nicene Fathers, First Series, Vol. 5*, translated by Peter Holmes and Robert Ernest Wallis, and revised by Benjamin B. Warfield, edited by Philip Schaff. Buffalo, NY: Christian Literature Publishing Co., 1887. Revised and edited for New Advent by Kevin Knight. Assessed on November 13, 2019. http://www.newadvent.org/fathers/1503.htm.

Augustine. *On the Free Choice of the Will, On Grace and Free Choice, and Other Writings.* Edited and translated by Peter King. New York: Cambridge University Press, 2010.

Augustine. *Of Two Souls.* In *From Nicene and Post-Nicene Fathers, First Series, Vol. 4*, translated by Albert H. Newman, edited by Philip Schaff. Buffalo, NY: Christian Literature Publishing Co., 1887). Revised and edited for New Advent by Kevin Knight. Assessed on November 13, 2019. http://www.newadvent.org/fathers/1403.htm.

Augustine. *Retractions (The Fathers of the Church: A New Translation, 60).* Translated by Sister Mary Inez Bogan, Washington, D.C.: The Catholic University of America Press, 1968.

Augustine. *The City of God.* Translated by Marcus Dods (New York: The Modern Library, 1952

Augustine. *The Grace of Christ and Original Sin.* In *Answer to the Pelagians (Vol. I/23) The Works of Saint Augustine: A Translation for the 21st Century*, translated and notes Roland J. Teske, edited by John E. Rotelle, OSA, 383-463. Hyde Park, N.Y.:New City Press, 1997.

Augustine. "The Happy Life." In *Augustine of Hippo: Selected Writings*, translated and introduced by Mary T. Clark, 167-93. Paulist Press, 1984.

Augustine. *The Literal Meaning of Genesis.* In *On Genesis I/13 The works of Saint Augustine: a Translation for the 21st Century*, translated by Edmund Hill, edited by John E. Rotelle, 155-506. Hyde Park, NY: New City Press, 2002.

Babcock, William S. "Augustine on Sin and Moral Agency." *The Journal of Religious Ethics* 16, no. 1 (1988): 28-55.

Babcock, William S. "*Cupiditas and Caritas*: The Early Augustine on Love and Fulfillment." In *Augustine Today*, edited by Richard John Neuhaus, 1-34. Grand Rapids: Eerdmans, 1993.

Burnell, Peter. "Concupiscence." In *Augustine through the Ages: An Encyclopedia*, edited by Allan D. Fitzgerald. 223-7. Grand Rapids, Mich.: W.B. Eerdmans, 1999.

Couenhoven, Jesse. "Augustine's Rejection of the Free-Will Defence: An Overview of the Late Augustine's Theodicy." *Religious Studies* 43, no. 3 (2007): 279-298.

Djuth, Marianne. "Will (*voluntas*)." In *Augustine through the Ages: An Encyclopedia*, edited by Allan D. Fitzgerald, 881-5. Grand Rapids, Mich.: W.B. Eerdmans, 1999.

Fr. Harvey, John, "Saint Augustine, Freedom of Will, and Pornography." *The Linacre Quarterly* 77, no. 1 (2010): 81-92.

Harrison, Carol. *Augustine: Christian Truth and Fractured Humanity*. New York: Oxford University Press, 2000.

Hess, Gabriel. "Refuting the Claim that Augustine is Opposed to Corporeality." *Aporia* 23, no. 1 (2013): 27-36.

Hunter, David G. "Augustine on the Body." In *A Companion to Augustine*, edited by Mark Vessey, 353–64. Malden: Blackwell Publishing Limited, 2012.

Hunter, David G. "Marriage." In *Augustine through the Ages: An Encyclopedia*, Allan D. Fitzgerald ed., 535-7. Grand Rapids, Mich.: W.B. Eerdmans, 1999.
Kent, Bonnie. "Augustine's Ethics." In *The Cambridge Companion to Augustine*, edited by Eleonore Stump and Norman Kretzmann, 205-33. Cambridge University Press, 2001.
Lavere, George J. "Virtue." In *Augustine through the Ages: An Encyclopedia*, edited by Allan D. Fitzgerald ed., 871-4. Grand Rapids, Mich.: W.B. Eerdmans, 1999.
Markus, Robert A. *Conversion and Disenchantment in Augustine's Spiritual Career.* Villanova, PA: Villanova University Press, 1989.
O'Daly, Gerard. *Augustine's City of God: A Reader's Guide.* New York: Oxford University Press, 1999.
Rist, John, *Augustine: Ancient Thought Baptized.* Cambridge University Press, 1999.
Sorabji, Richard. *Emotion and Peace of Mind: From Stoic Agitation to Christian Temptation*, New York: Oxford University Press, 2002.
Stump, Eleonore. "Augustine on Free Will." In *The Cambridge Companion to Augustine*, edited by Eleonore Stump and Norman Kretzmann, 124-47. Cambridge University Press, 2001.
Teske, Roland J. "Soul." In *Augustine through the Ages: An Encyclopedia*, edited by Allan D. Fitzgerald, 807-12. Grand Rapids, Mich.: W.B. Eerdmans, 1999.
Torchia, N. Joseph. "Curiosity." In *Augustine through the Ages: An Encyclopedia*, edited by Allan D. Fitzgerald, 259-61. Grand Rapids, Mich.: W.B. Eerdmans, 1999.
Tornau, Christian. "Saint Augustine." In *The Stanford Encyclopedia of Philosophy* (Winter Edition), edited by Edward N. Zalta. Assessed November 19, 2019.
https://plato.stanford.edu/archives/win2019/entries/augustine/.

Reference of Internet and Addiction

Aiken, Mary. *The Cyber Effect*. Random House Publishing Group, 2016.
Cooper, Al. *Sex & the Internet: A Guidebook for Clinicians*. New York: Brunner-Routledge, 2002.
Cui, Lijuan, Xin Zhao, Mingzheng Wu and Aihong Xu. "A Research on the Effects of Internet Addiction on Adolescents' Social Development." (Chinese Article) *Psychological Science*, 1 (2006): 34–36.

Eberstadt, Mary and Mary A. Layden. *The Social Costs of Pornography: A Statement of Findings and Recommendations*. The Witherspoon Institute, 2010.

Fawcett, David. "Dopamine, Addiction, and Unnatural Rewards: Tips for Recovery." *Sex and Relationship Healing*. Assessed October 29, 2019. https://bit.ly/3ln9Bjk.

Griffiths, Mark. "Gambling Addiction on the Internet." In *Internet Addiction: A Handbook and Guide to Evaluation and Treatment*, edited by Young, Kimberly S. and Cristiano Nabuco de Abreu, 91-112. Hoboken, NJ, US: John Wiley & Sons Inc., 2011.

Harvard Mental Health Letter. "How Addiction Hijacks the Brain", *Harvard Mental Health Letter*, (2011). Assessed November 12, 2019. https://bit.ly/34NOb5G.

Horvath, et al. "Sexual Addiction and Pornography Addiction." *Gulf Bend Center*. Assessed November 12, 2019. https://bit.ly/34R7SK4,.

"Internet World Stats 2019." *Internet World Stats*. Assessed November 20, 2019. https://www.internetworldstats.com/stats.htm.

Lee, Chris. "The Sex Addiction Epidemic." *Newsweek Magazine*, (December 2011). Assessed November 11, 2019. https://www.newsweek.com/sex-addiction-epidemic-66289.

Luscombe, Belinda. "Porn and the Threat to Virility." *Time Magazine*, (April 2016). Assessed October 31, 2019. https://time.com/magazine/us/4277492/april-11th-2016-vol-187-no-13-u-s/.

Yang, Chang-Kook. "Sociopsychiatric Characteristics of Adolescents Who Use Computers to Excess." *Acta Psychiatrica Scandinavica* 104, no. 3 (2001): 217–222.

Young, Kimberly S. "Internet Addiction: The Emergence of a New Clinical Disorder." *Cyberpsychology & Behavior* 1, no. 3 (1998): 237–244.

Young, Kimberly S. "Internet Addiction: Symptoms, Evaluation and Treatment." *Student British Medical Journal* 7 (1999): 351–352.

Young, Kimberly S., Xiao Dong Yue and Li Ying. "Prevalence Estimates and Etiologic Models of Internet Addiction." In *Internet Addiction: A Handbook and Guide to Evaluation and Treatment*, edited by Young, Kimberly S. and Cristiano Nabuco de Abreu, 3-18. Hoboken, NJ, US: John Wiley & Sons Inc., 2011.

Andrew Tsz Wan HUNG
Division of Social Sciences, Humanities and Design
College of Professional and Continuing Education, The Hong Kong Polytechnic University.

CHAPTER FIVE

JUSTIFICATION BY FAITH AND ARISTOTLE'S CONCEPTS OF *DUNAMIS* AND *ENERGEIA*

LE CHIH HSIEH

"*Paul is perfectly aware of the typical Greek opposition*—which pertains both to categories of language and thought—between potentiality (*dunamis*) and act (*energeia*)."[1] In this paper, I will explore how the concepts of *dunamis* and *energeia* might help us understand Paul's claim in Gal 2:16: "no one is justified by the works of the law but by the faith of Jesus Christ." Although the words *dunamis* and *energeia* do not appear in this particular sentence, what Paul expresses through these words is fundamentally connected to *dunamis* and *energeia*: work (*ergon*) is intrinsically related to *energeia* as the law is related to the works of sin (Rom 7:5, 8, 13, 17, 20), while faith is at work in those who are in Christ, and Christ is placed in conjunction to *dunamis* in the phrase "*dunamis* of Christ" (2 Cor 12:9).[2] Thus, it would be fruitful to explore how these two concepts—*dunamis* and *energeia*—might help us better understand Paul's statements concerning "works of the law" and "faith of Jesus Christ."

Aristotle is the one responsible for the widespread presence of these two concepts in Greek philosophy.[3] Therefore, I will focus in this paper on Aristotle's use of these concepts and explore how these concepts might help us better understand Paul's theology of justification.

---

[1] Giorgio Agamben, *The Time That Remains: A Commentary on the Letter to the Romans* (Stanford, Calif.: Stanford University Press, 2005), 90, see also 96.
[2] We shall have more to say about these connections in the latter part of the paper.
[3] Anna Marmodoro and Irini-Fotini Viltanioti, *Divine Powers in Late Antiquity* (Oxford: Oxford University Press, 2017).

1. Aristotle's concepts of *dunamis* and *energeia*

The concepts of *dunamis* and *energeia* are crucial to Aristotle's philosophy. He employs this pair of concepts in almost every facet of his work.[4] These concepts are not only found ubiquitous in Aristotle's writings, but also foundational to his philosophical thinking. His studies on substance and being center around these two concepts.[5] He uses them to make the crucial distinction between motion (*kinesis*) and activity (*energeia*).[6] This distinction is important because Aristotle understands being in terms of matter and form, and form is none other than the activity (*energeia*) of the matter (which he interprets as *dunamis*). I will argue in the latter part of this paper that the phrase "works of the law" is used as a reference to a series of actions that are best characterized as motion; whereas "faith of Jesus Christ" refers to actions that are best characterized as activity. To begin, I will first explore how *dunamis* and *energeia* help differentiate motion and activity.

In Book 9 of the *Metaphysics*, Aristotle makes the distinction between motion (*kinesis*) and activity (*energeia*):

> We should call one group motions, and the other activities. Every motion is incomplete (ἀτελής): slimming, learning, walking, building; these are motions and are indeed incomplete. For one cannot at the same time be walking and have walked, or be building and have built, nor be coming to be and have come to be, nor be being moved and have been moved; the two things are different (ἕτερον), as in general are moving and having moved. But at the same time one has seen and sees; these are the same thing, as are thinking and having thought. So the latter of these I call an activity, and the former a motion. (*Metaphysics* 9.6, 1048b18-34; trans. Kosman)

The difference between motion and activity is that motion is incomplete (*a-telos*). By incomplete Aristotle does not mean that motions have no *telos*, but that motions have no *telos in and of themselves*. The *telos* of a motion is always something other than itself. The *telos* of walking is to

---

[4] This pair of concepts appears in Aristotle's discussions on metaphysics, physics, biology, and ethics.
[5] Louis Aryeh Kosman, *The Activity of Being: An Essay on Aristotle's Ontology* (Cambridge, Mass.: Harvard University Press, 2013).
[6] *Energeia* is used in two different senses. First, it is placed in contrast to *dunamis*; second, it is placed in contrast to motion. We might call the first sense the general sense of *energeia*; the second, the proper sense. In Aristotle's understanding, motion involves both *dunamis* and *energeia* (general sense of energeia).

arrive at a certain destination; the *telos* of building is to build a certain structure. To have arrived at a certain destination requires a previous process of walking during which its perfection has yet to take place. When perfection takes place and the *telos* is achieved, the motion ceases. The motion and the *telos* are not the same.[7]

Activities are different. The *telos* of the activity is intrinsic to the activity itself. To have seen is at the same time to see. The *telos* of seeing a certain thing does not require a previous process during which the *telos* is taking place but has not yet taken place. The *telos* of the activity is in the very moment of its being enacted. Also, unlike motion, the *telos* of the activity does not cancel out the activity itself, for the *telos* of the activity is found in the activity itself.

Aristotle defines motion as "the realization of what is able to be [something] as such" (ἡ τοῦ δυνάμει ὄντος ἐντελέχεια ᾗ τοιοῦτον; *Physics* 3.1, 201a11). The meaning of the phrase "as such" is a much debated issue in modern scholarship. Kosman argues that "as such" refers to "the ability to be something."[8] The wood lying on the floor has the ability (*dunamis*) to be built into a fence, or to be built into a door, or to be built into a window. None of these abilities are realized when the wood is lying on the floor. The instant when the ability (*dunamis*) to be built into the door is realized (becomes an actuality [*energeia*]) is when the wood is in the motion of being built into the door. When the door is completed the wood's ability to be built into the door is exhausted and disappears, replaced by the wooden door. When the door is completed, the wood as buildable into a door no longer exists, it is fully realized.

Here we have two different levels of realization (*energeia*). The first level of realization takes place when motion begins. As motion begins, the wood lying on the floor realizes its ability to be built into a door. The second level of realization takes place when motion ceases. As motion ceases, the wood, formerly buildable, is now built into a door. The first level of realization is constitutive, whereas the second level of realization is privative. The wood's ability to be built into the door is realized (the first level of realization) when motion takes place; the wood's ability to be

---

[7] Kosman, *The Activity of Being*, 45-53.
[8] Louis Aryeh Kosman, "Aristotle's Definition of Motion," *Phronesis* 14 (1969): 40-62. See also Coope, Ursula. "Change and Its Relation to Actuality and Potentiality". In *A Companion to Aristotle*, ed. G. Anagnostopoulos (Oxford: Wiley-Blackwell, 2009), 277-291.

Justification by Faith and Aristotle's Concepts of *Dunamis* and *Energeia* 119

built into the door is exhausted (the second level of realization) when the motion ceases. The *ability* [of the wood] *to be built into the door* is realized and exhausted as motion begins and as motion ends. Thus, motion is defined by Aristotle as the realization of *an ability to be something*, as such.

We must remember that the wood lying on the floor, however, does have the ability to be built into the door. That ability is, however, latent in the wood. It is latent together with different kinds of abilities, the ability to be built into a fence, the ability to be built into a house, and so on. When motion begins, that ability to be built into the door is realized and will be exhausted when the motion ceases. From the perspective of the completed wooden door, the wood lying on the ground is potentially potentially a wooden door, while the same wood in the process of being built into a door is actually potentially a door.

                          (first level of realization)   (second level of realization)
wood on the floor → **wood being built into a house** → **wooden house**
Has double potentiality
to be a wooden house
                The actuality (*energeia*) of the double potential
                Has the potentiality [or ability] (*dunamis*) to be a wooden house
                                        The fully realized actuality
                                        of the potential to be a wooden house

Activities have a similar structure. Take language speaking as an example. A baby human being, unlike other animals, has the ability to speak Chinese. However, people who have learned to speak Chinese also have the ability to speak Chinese. These two abilities are different. The baby's ability is the ability to have the ability to speak Chinese. The baby is only potentially potentially a Chinese speaker. The one who has learned to speak Chinese fully is the one who has realized the baby's ability to learn Chinese. The one who has learned to speak Chinese, unlike the baby who does not have the ability to communicate in Chinese, can communicate to others by actually speaking Chinese.

                          (first level of realization)   (second level of realization)
baby able to learn C. → **adult who has learned C.** → **adult who is speaking C.**
Potentially potentially a Chinese speaker
                The actuality (*energeia*) of the double potential
                Has the potential (*dunamis*) to be an active Chinese speaker
                                          The actuality of the potential
                                          to be an active Chinese speaker

Thus, both motion and activity have a similar three tier structure: double potentiality, actuality (of the double potentiality) as potentiality, and actuality. There are however important differences between the two. In motion, when a potentiality (*dunamis*) is fully realized, the potentiality is used up, consumed, and destroyed; whereas in activity, when a potentiality (*dunamis*) turns into actuality (*energeia*), the potentiality is not destroyed, but preserved, strengthened, and perfected.

Human beings exist as a kind of activity (*energeia* proper). The body is a potentiality; whereas the soul is the first level of actuality. The soul could be further actualized by putting the *ergon* of the soul to work (*energeia*). For the soul to be actively-at-work is the actuality of the soul. The end (*telos*) of the soul is the work of the soul. The soul is fully actualized when the *ergon* of the soul functions in excellence, that is, when the soul attains virtue.

I will argue in the following that the phrase "works of the law" marks a series of actions that are best characterized as motion; whereas "faith of Jesus Christ" marks a series of actions that are best characterized as activity.

2. Motion and works of the law

Paul states in Galatians that "we know that no one is justified by the works of the law but by the faith of Jesus Christ" (οὐ δικαιοῦται ἄνθρωπος ἐξ ἔργων νόμου ἐὰν μὴ διὰ πίστεως Ἰησοῦ Χριστοῦ; Gal. 2:16). By "works of the law" Paul is referring to the characteristic functions of the law.[9] In the Greco-Roman philosophical tradition, every substance has an *ergon* (ἔργον) (Plato, *Resp.* 352d-354a; Aristotle, *Eth. nic.* 1.7.14-15; Epictetus, *Ench.* 1; *Diatr.* 2.5.4; 4.1.71-75). The *ergon* is the form of the substance that determines the essence of a substance. For example, a horse is a horse because it performs the *ergon* of the horse, that is, it does what horses characteristically do. For this reason, the *ergon* of a horse is closely related to the being of the horse. The two cannot be separated. The *ergon* of the

---

[9] Le Chih (Luke) Hsieh, "Works of the Law as Functions of the Law," *Sino-Christian Studies* 25 (2018): 7-40. How one is supposed to interpret the phrase "works of the law" is a much debated issue in NT studies. For a survey of the different interpretations see: Thomas R. Schreiner, "'Works of the Law' in Paul," *Novum Testamentum* 33 (1991): 225-38. Ronald Y. K. Fung, A *Commentary on the Epistle to the Galatians* [Chinese] (Taiwan: Campus Evangelical Fellowship Press, 2008), 526-45.

horse is what makes the horse the horse, just as the *ergon* of the eye is to see and to see is what makes the eye the eye. To see is what the eye characteristically does and does best.

In Paul's understanding, the works of the law have to do with distinguishing good and evil, rewarding those who do good and punishing those who do evil.[10] The law, having such a function, is considered in its nature to be good and just (Rom 7:12).[11] The law and its function is to maintain justice and make justice possible. However, in Romans 7, in discussing the relationship between sin and the law, Paul points out that the law not only fails to bring about good but instead activates sin and participates in the works of sin in producing death.

Sin was said to be "dead" (νεκρά 7:8) before the coming of the law. Not that it did not exist, but that it existed only potentially: "for before the law was given, sin was in the world, but there is no accounting (οὐκ ἐλλογεῖται) for sin when there is no law" (Rom. 5:13). The sin exists but is not put into words (*en-logos*). It is not in language nor in thought. The coming of the law does not create sin, but revives (ἀναζάω) sin. The law activates sin from its potentiality.[12]

Sin through the law comes to language and to thought. Sin becomes an activity at work in producing death. Before the coming of the law, sin lies dormant in the world. Sin is at this stage only potentially potentially death. The law in reviving sin brought sin to its first level of realization. After having achieved the first level of realization, sin then had the *dunamis* (potentiality) that could be realized and produce death. Paul could, therefore, say that "the *dunamis* of sin is the law" (1 Cor. 15:56), in the sense that the law produces the *dunamis* of sin. The *dunamis* of sin is both at the same time the *realization* of a double potential and the *potential* that if realized produces death.

---

[10] Hsieh, "Works of the Law as Functions of the Law," 40.
[11] According to Fitzmyer, the law as intended for life. Fitzmyer, J. A., (2008). *Romans: A New Translation with Introduction and Commentary* (New Haven: Yale University Press), 469.
[12] The use of the verb ἀναζάω is significant for it places the law in parallel to Christ. The law like Christ brings life to the death. Human beings were dead in sin, but by participating in Christ's death and resurrection they experience the newness of the life.

	(first level realization)	(second level realization)
Sin "dead" →	**Sin "revived"** →	**Sin fully realized**
potentially potentially death	potentially death	death

Paul more than once speaks of sin at work in producing evil and death:

> For while we were in the flesh, the sinful passions....were at work (ἐνηργεῖτο) in the members of our body to bear fruit for death. (Rom. 7:5)

> Sin, taking opportunity through the commandment, produced (κατειργάσατο) in me coveting of every kind. (Rom. 7:8)

> It was sin, so that sin might be shown to be sin, through what is good working death (κατεργαζομένη) in me. (Rom. 7:13)

> No longer am I the one doing it (κατεργάζομαι), but sin which dwells in me. (Rom. 7:17)

> If I am doing the very thing I do not want, I am no longer the one doing it (κατεργάζομαι), but sin which dwells in me. (Rom. 7:20)

The word that Paul uses most often for the work of sin is κατεργάζομαι. The verb is different from ἐνεργέω in that it emphasizes the result and the end product of the work.[13] Sin produces evil deeds and ultimately death. Moreover, Paul emphasizes that the law is involved in the κατεργάζομαι of sin. Like a house builder who not only brings the brick to its first level of realization (activating the *dunamis* that was dormant), but also continuously moves the bricks so that the bricks' *dunamis* might be fully realized and become a house, so too, the law not only brings sin to its first level of realization, but also continuously moves sin, and as a result the *dunamis* of the sin is fully realized and produces death.

The involvement of the law in the workings of sin is expressed by Paul through the use of prepositional phrases:

> The sinful passions, **by the law** (διὰ τοῦ νόμου), were at work in our members our body to bear fruit for death. (Rom 7:5)

> Sin, taking opportunity **by the commandment** (διὰ τῆς ἐντολῆς), produced in me coveting of every kind (Rom. 7:8)

---

[13] BDAG: "to cause a state or condition, bring about, produce, create." Arndt, W., Danker, F. W., and Bauer, W. *A Greek-English Lexicon of the New Testament and Other Early Christian Literature* (Chicago: University of Chicago Press, 2000), 531.

> Sin, taking an opportunity **by the commandment** (διὰ τῆς ἐντολῆς), deceived me and through it killed me. (Rom. 7:11)

> It was sin, so that sin might be shown to be sin, **by what is good** (διὰ τοῦ ἀγαθοῦ) working death in me. (Rom. 7:13)

The prepositions express not only means but also agency.[14] The law is not only the initiator that revives sin, but also the agent that sustains sin and puts sin in motion. Both the law and sin are at work in producing death.[15] It is for this reason, Paul can speak of salvation in terms of the de-activation (καταργέω) of both law and sin.[16]

> But now we have been de-activated (κατηργήθημεν) from the Law, having died to that by which we were bound, so that we serve in newness of the Spirit and not in the oldness of the letter. (Rom. 7:6; see also 7:2)

In other words, salvation delivers human beings from the law. As a result, sin is no longer at work in producing death. The motion is said to be de-activated, that is, it is no longer at work. Apart from the law, sin is reduced back into its potentiality. However, Paul not only speaks of the de-activation of sin apart from the law, but also he speaks of the de-activation of the law itself.

> For if what is made inactive (καταργούμενον) was with glory, much more that which remains is in glory. Therefore having such a hope, we use great boldness in our speech, and are not like Moses, who used to put a veil over his face so that the sons of Israel would not look intently at the end of what was made inactive (καταργουμένου). But their minds were hardened; for until this very day at the reading of the old covenant the same veil remains unlifted, because it is made inactive (καταργεῖται) in Christ. (2 Cor. 3:11-14)

The law is made inactive by Christ, for Christ has accomplished what the law could not do, that is, "to condemn sin in the flesh so that the just

---

[14] Dunn notes: "διὰ τοῦ νόμου as elsewhere in Romans denotes the divinely intended function of the law, the agency of the law in accordance with God's will." James D. G. Dunn, *Romans* (Word Biblical Commentary; Nashville, Tenn.: Thomas Nelson, 1988), 364.

[15] The law in activating sin and producing death is therefore called by Paul "the law of sin and death" (Rom 8:2).

[16] Agamben notes: "Katargeō is a compound of argeō, which in turn derives from the adjective argos, meaning 'inoperative, not-at-work (a-ergos), inactive.'" (*The Time that Remains*, 95)

requirements of the law might be fulfilled in us" (Rom 8:3-4). The law is holy, and the commandment is holy and just and good (Rom 7:12), but neither the law nor the commandment brings justice to human beings. Instead, Christ is the one who brings justice and sanctification and redemption to those who believe (1 Cor 1:30).[17]

It is important to note that when Paul speaks of the law and sin at work in producing death, he is not speaking in abstract terms, but of the real-life experiences that he himself has experienced at first hand. Whenever the law appears in the ecclesia of Christ, the law triggers the sinful desires among its members; as a result, the ecclesia is divided into factions contending with one another. This internal dissension is precisely what Paul has in view when he speaks of members at war with one another in Romans 7. It is this internal *stasis* that brings death to the community. The body spoken of in Romans 7 is the body of the ecclesia.[18] The "I" in Romans 7 is the ecclesia "writ small." Unlike the Greco-Roman political theorist who argues that the law is necessary for the salvation, safety, justice, and peace of the *polis* (Solon, "Eunomia" (Poem 4); Plato, *Rep.*; Aristotle, *Eth. nic.* 10.9.8; Epicurus, *Principle Doctrines* 38), Paul instead argues that the law brings sin, *stasis*, and ultimately death.

Stasis is precisely what happened in the ecclesia in Galatia.[19] Jewish preachers came preaching the law, claiming that in order to become true heirs of Abraham those who believe in Christ must be circumcised, and only by circumcision could they inherit the blessings of Abraham.[20] These

---

[17] Ben Witherington III. *Conflict and Community in Corinth: A Socio-Rhetorical Commentary on 1 and 2 Corinthians* (Grand Rapids, Mich.: Eerdmans, 1995), 117.

[18] Romans 7 should be read along with Romans chapters 12-15. Those whom Paul calls "weak" (Rom 14:1-2; 15:1) are those who follow the law in observing the day (Rom 14:5), the dietary laws (Rom 14:14) and circumcision (Rom 15:8). The law has come and caused internal division among the weak and the strong in the ecclesia of Rome.

[19] Galatians as discourse on concord, see Smit, Joop. "The Letter of Paul to the Galatians: A Deliberative Speech". In *The Galatians Debate*, ed. Mark D. Nanos (Peabody, Mass.: Hendrickson, 2002), 58; Ben Witherington III. *Grace in Galatia: A Commentary on St. Paul's Letter to the Galatians* (Edinburgh: T&T Clark, 1998), 27, 36.

[20] Richard N. Longenecker notes that: "Paul's opponents were Jewish Christians—or, more accurately, Christian Jews—who came from the Jerusalem church to Paul's churches in Galatia with a message stressing the need for Gentiles to be circumcised and to keep the rudiments of the cultic calendar, both for full acceptance by God and as a proper Christian lifestyle. Undoubtedly they presented their message as being theologically based and claimed to be only interested in

teachings and promises ignited desires (Gal 5:16, 24), vainglory (Gal 5:26), and envy (Gal 5:26) among the members of the ecclesia. Those who adhere to the law thought of themselves as being the true heirs of Abraham having the privilege to inherit the blessings of Abraham. This kind of thinking provoked tension and conflict within the community.

Paul says that the ecclesia was being "stirred up" (ταράσσω) by the preachers (Gal 1:7; 5:10, 12). Ταράσσω is a technical term that is often used to describe political *stasis*.[21] As a result, community members acted like beasts devouring one another causing death (Gal 5:15). "Devouring one another" is an image that is often used by political theorists to describe the downfall of the *polis*, as the *polis* loses civilization and is reduced to its original state (Dio Chrysostom, *Nicom.* 17; Plutarch, *Adv. Col.* 30).[22]

3. Activity and faith of Jesus Christ

Events caused by the works of the law are characterized as *motion*. On the contrary, Paul often correlates Christ with the concept of *morphe*, a concept that Aristotle relates not to motion but to *activity*. *Morphe*, we recall, is the first realization of matter. The relationship between *morphe* and matter, in the case of the human being, is the relationship between the

---

Gentiles being fully integrated into the chosen people of Israel, and so full recipients of the blessings of the Abrahamic covenant." However, Longenecker is wrong in saying that the message of the opponents were aimed at the libertinism within the Gentile-based church. Galatians chapter 5-6 is not a message for the cure of the libertinism within the church but a cure for the *stasis* caused by the opponents. Richard N. Longenecker, *Galatians* (Word Biblical Commentary; Dallas: Word Books, 2002), xcv. See also J. D. G. Dunn, *The Epistle to the Galatians* (Peabody, MA: Hendrickson, 1993), 9-11.

[21] Ταράσσω is a political term originating from the age-old political metaphor of the state being like a ship sailing on the sea. Political turmoil (ταράσσω) is like the wind and the waves that break the ship and cause it to sink. Cf. Solon, *Frg.* 12; Isocrates, *Callim.* 44; Dionysius of Halicarnassus, *Ant. rom.* 32.4; Philo, *Abr.* 1.27.

[22] Stasis as "devouring one another" is most vividly depicted by Josephus in his account of the stasis that caused the fall of Jerusalem (Josephus, *J.W.* 375-6). At the pinnacle of the Jerusalem stasis Josephus pictures the horrifying scene of certain Jerusalemite named Mary devouring her own children (Josephus, *J.W.* 5.1-4). See Honora Howell Chapman, "Josephus and the Cannibalism of Mary (BJ 6.199-219)," in *Companion to Greek and Roman Historiography* (ed. John Marincola; Malden, Mass.: Blackwell, 2007), 419-26.

soul and the body. The body is the organ that carries out the functions of life, whereas the soul is the set of functions that resides in the body. [23]

Both Jews and Gentiles, before they are called to Christ, have their bodies serve as instruments for sin. Paul calls this body "the body of sin" (Rom 6:6), or the body that is "enslaved to sin" (Rom 6:7). The body, as a result, can only function in a sinful manner. After being called to Christ, human beings experience a transfer of lordship: no longer are they under the dominion of sin but are now free to serve God (Rom 6:10-14). Their bodies are no longer instruments for sin but are capable of doing good and acting justly (Rom 6:16). Their bodies are like being created anew, acquiring a new set of functions. This new life is made possible by participating in Christ's death and resurrection. Christ is in them (Gal 4:19; Rom 8:10; 2 Cor 13:5; cf. Col 1:27; Eph 3:17) and they are in Christ (*passim*). The body takes up a new form, a new way of life, displaying a new set of functions. Paul describes this experience of renewal as taking up *the form of Christ*.

Paul says in Rom 8:29: "For those whom he foreknew he also predestined to be conformed to the image of his Son (συμμόρφους τῆς εἰκόνος τοῦ υἱοῦ αὐτοῦ), that his Son would be the firstborn among many brothers and sisters" (Rom. 8:29). The use of the word icon recalls Gen 1:26-27, where Adam is created as the image of God. [24] Adam represents the old humanity; whereas Christ represents the new humanity. Those who conform to the image of Christ are members of the family of Christ. The familial language is significant, for the family is a type of friendship (Aristotle, *Eth. nic.* 8.7.1; 8.10.4-6; Dio Chrysostom, *Conc. Apam.* 41; Plutarch, *Frat. amor.* 479c-d) where all things are shared in common, not only material goods, but also the mind and the spirit. To share a form is to share a way of living.

Paul also speaks of the *morphe* of Christ in Gal 4:19. Salvation, according to Paul, comes through the transfer of lordship (Gal 1:4; 5:1; 6:14). Paul uses various metaphors to describe the radical transformation brought about by the salvation of Christ. The image that appears most frequently is the transfer from slavery to freedom (Gal 5:1; 4:21-31; 2:4).[25] Also, there

---

[23] Kosman, *The Activity of Being*, 104-111.
[24] Dunn, *Romans*, 483.
[25] Sam Tsang, *From Slaves to Sons: A New Rhetoric Analysis on Paul's Slave Metaphors in His Letter to the Galatians* (Studies in Biblical Literature; New York: Peter Lang, 2005), 63-80.

is the image of putting on new clothes (Gal 3:27). But the most powerful image used to describe the process of transformation is the image of the new creation (Gal 6:15) and the image of new birth (Gal 4:19, 29). Like the new-born, those who are saved are given a new life. And to have a new life is to have a new soul (*morphe*), as Paul would say in Gal 4:19: "My children–I am again undergoing birth pains until Christ is formed in you (μορφωθῇ Χριστὸς ἐν ὑμῖν)."

Paul worries that the Galatians who are willing to be circumcised are cutting themselves off from Christ and are falling away from grace (Gal 5:4). Law and Christ are not compatible. To be under the law is to lose the new life in Christ. And to lose the new life is to lose the *morphe* that constitutes the new life.

The *morphe* of Christ marks the beginning of the life of the Christian. Christians obtain the *morphe* of Christ when they are saved by Christ. However, the *morphe*, like the sin revived by the law, is both a potentiality (*dunamis*) and an actuality (*energeia*). The *morphe* is the realization of the matter. However, the *morphe* is also a *dunamis* that can be perfected by practice.

For this reason, Paul not only speaks of obtaining the *morphe* of Christ at the moment of salvation, but also the perfecting of the *morphe* of Christ as a process at work throughout the life of the Christian.[26] The *morphe* of Christ is often mentioned in relation to Paul's ethical teachings. Paul repeatedly exhorts Christians *to be conformed to Christ by practicing acts that are exemplified by Christ.*

2 Corinthians 3 demonstrates the close relationship between *morphe* and ethics. Chapter 3 is part of Paul's *apologia* for his frank speech toward the Corinthian community.[27] The *apologia* begins in 2 Cor 2:14 and ends in 7:4. Repeatedly in this section, Paul speaks of his frankness toward the Corinthians (2 Cor 2:17; 3:12; 4:1, 13, 16; 5:6, 8, 20). The whole section ends with the climax that he has his "mouth wide open" (2 Cor 6:11) toward the Corinthians, wishing that they would accept his words with a wide-opened heart (2 Cor 6:13; 7:2). Paul speaks in frankness for he wants the Corinthians to *live a holy life*: "let us cleanse ourselves from every

---

[26] J. D. G. Dunn notes that for Paul "Conformity to Christ is a lifelong process" (*The Theology of Paul's Letter to the Galatians* [Cambridge: Cambridge University Press, 1993], 120).
[27] David E. Garland, *2 Corinthians* (The New American Commentary; Nashville, Tenn.: Broadman & Holman, 1999), 135ff.

defilement of body and of spirit, making holiness perfect in the fear of God" (2 Cor 7:1).

In the Greco-Roman world, friends have the duty to speak frankness so as to build virtue in one another.[28] Paul gives moral exhortation to the Corinthians not only because he as a friend has the duty to do so, but also because he is confident that the Spirit through which he speaks gives life (2 Cor 3:3, 6; 4:12; 5:14-15). Speaking through the spirit that gives life, Paul is confident that his *moral exhortations* (spoken of through frank speech) will help *transform* (μεταμορφούμεθα the Corinthians to the icon of the Lord (2 Cor 3:18). The verb μεταμορφούμεθα is set in the present tense reminding his readers that the transformation is an ongoing and continuous process.[29]

In Romans 12:1-2, Paul begins his moral exhortations with a thematic statement:

> I exhort you (Παρακαλῶ)...to present your bodies as a living sacrifice, holy and acceptable to God, which is your spiritual worship. Do not be conformed to this world but be transformed (μεταμορφοῦσθε) by the renewal of your mind that you may prove what is the will of God, what is good and acceptable and perfect" (Rom. 12:1-2).

Paul often begins his moral exhortations with the word παρακαλῶ (1 Cor 1:10; 4:16; Phil 4:2; 1 Thess 4:1; 5:14; 2 Thess 3:12; Philem 1:9) as Greco-Roman moralists often do (Aristides, *De pace* 23). His exhortation is that Christians should not be conformed to the world but be transformed *to Christ*. Though Christ is not explicitly mentioned in the text, this can be inferred through context with confidence. Repeatedly in his exhortations, Paul asks the Roman Christians to act in accordance with Christ (Rom 13:14; 14:5-9; 15:1-3, 5).

---

[28] David E. Fredrickson, "Parrhsia in the Pauline Epistles," in *Friendship, Flattery, and Frankness of Speech: Studies on Friendship in the New Testament World* (ed. John T. Fitzgerald; Leiden: E. J. Brill, 1996); J. Paul Sampley, "Paul's Frank Speech with the Galatians and the Corinthians," in *Philodemus and the New Testament World* (ed. John T. Fitzgerald, Dirk Obbink, and Glenn Stanfield Holland; Leiden: E. J. Brill, 2004); Le Chih (Luke) Hsieh, "*Paul as a* Parrhesiastes," in *Sino-Christian Studies* 18 (2014): 7-31.

[29] William B. Barcley comes to a similar conclusion: "Paul depicts the transformation into the image of Christ as progressive. This is indicated by the present tense verb, μεταμορφούμεθα, as well as by the phrase ἀπὸ δόξης εἰς δόξαν" (*Christ in You: A Study in Paul's Theology and Ethics* [New York: University Press of America, 1999], 86).

The transformation is possible by means of renewal of the mind (Rom 12:2b). The mind is one of the faculties of moral reasoning. With a renewed mind comes moral discernment capable of knowing what is good and pleasing and perfect.[30] The implication is that by moral discernment and moral practice, Christians will be transformed into the image of Christ. In other words, the form of the Christians will be perfected (becoming like Christ) by putting into practice actions in accordance with Christ.

Paul also speaks of conformity to Christ in Philippians 3:10. Here, he speaks specifically of "conformity to his death" (συμμορφιζόμενος τῷ θανάτῳ αὐτοῦ). He does so because the moral exhortations in this letter are closely tied to the death of Jesus Christ. Paul's exhortation in this letter is: "Do nothing from selfish ambition or conceit, but in humility regard others as better than yourselves" (Phil 2:3). The humility that Paul speaks of is exemplified by Christ who "humbled himself and became obedient to the point of death, even death on a cross" (Phil 2:8).

In sum, conformity to Christ is closely linked to Paul's moral exhortations. Christians obtain the form of Christ when they are saved, but they are also told to perfect the form of Christ throughout their lives. The *morphe* is the *ergon* of the human being. The *ergon* of the human being achieves perfection through actively exercising the *ergon*. Another way of saying this is to say that virtue is achieved by doing virtuous acts (Aristotle, *Eth. nic.* 2.1.5, 2.1.7). Similarly, the *morphe* of Christ is perfected by actively practicing activities that are in accordance with Christ.

              (first level of realization)   (second level of realization)
body → *morphe* of Christ → active exercise of the *morphe* of Christ

We note that for Aristotle *morphe* is a *dunamis*.[31] Paul, for this reason, speaks not only of the *morphe* of Christ, but also of the *dunamis* of Christ:

> He said to me, "My grace is sufficient for you, for the *dunamis* is perfected in weakness;" most gladly, therefore, I will boast in my weaknesses, that the *dunamis of the Christ* may dwell on me. (2 Cor 12:9)

---

[30] I take the infinitive phrase εἰς τὸ δοκιμάζειν as modifying ἀνακαινώσει.
[31] Klaus Corcilius, "Faculties in Ancient Philosophy," in *The Faculties: A History* (ed. Dominik Perler, Oxford Philosophical Concepts; Oxford: Oxford University Press, 2015), 32-38.

Paul speaks of perfecting the *dunamis* of Christ through weakness.[32] By weakness, he is referring to the weakness of the gospel message (1 Cor 1:18-2:15). In other words, the *dunamis* of Christ is perfected by practicing acts in accordance to the gospel of Christ. Or, we might say that the *ergon* (*dunamis*) of Christ is perfected by practicing the *ergon* of Christ (the characteristic work of Christ). Paul shows that the *telos* of the *dunamis* lies within itself. The realization of the *dunamis* is not something other than itself, but in its performance, just as the *telos* of being is not something other than itself, but in its well-being.

Paul exhorts Christians to be conformed to Christ. Conformity to Christ is achieved by performing acts in accordance with Christ. Paul uses the word *pistis* to describe the act of aligning oneself to Christ. Faith is directed toward Christ, not as a given entity, nor as an object of thought, but as Lord of all.[33] Faith as faith toward Christ as lord means that faith is obedience (Rom 1:5; 16:26). Faith is obedience to Christ living lives that are worthy of Christ (Phil 1:27). Faith is at work through love (πίστις δι' ἀγάπης ἐνεργουμένη; Gal. 5:6) fulfilling the law of Christ (or the law that is Christ) (Gal 6:2). In other words, faith is the *energeia* of the *dunamis* of Christ. Thus, we find Paul repeatedly associates faith with *energeia* (Gal 3:4; 5:6; Col 1:29).[34]

In sum, by faith of Jesus Christ, Paul is referring to the faith that is energizing the *dunamis* of Christ perfecting the *dunamis* as the *dunamis* is put to work. Paul is depicting an activity (*energeia*) that finds its *telos* in the active working of the *dunamis* itself.

Conclusion

Paul says in Gal 2:16: "no one is justified by the works of the law but by the faith of Jesus Christ." This statement is true for Paul, for he has observed that whenever the *ergon* of the law is at work it not only fails to produce justice but instead activates sin and further energizes sin in working out death. On the contrary, whenever faith is at work there are acts in

---

[32] Richard Kearney, "Paul's Notion of *Dunamis*: Between the Possible and the Impossible," in *St. Paul among the Philosophers* (ed. John D. Caputo and Linda Alcoff, Indiana Series in the Philosophy of Religion; Bloomington, Ind.: Indiana University Press, 2009), 150-154.
[33] Matthew W. Bates, *Salvation by Allegiance Alone: Rethinking Faith, Works, and the Gospel of Jesus the King* (Grand Rapids, Mich.: Baker Academic, 2017).
[34] Agamben, *The Time that Remains*, 90.

accordance with Christ perfecting the form of Christ that one has when being saved. The *ergon* of the law characterizes motion that leads to death. Faith of Jesus Christ characterizes activity that finds its *telos* in active being.

In describing these two different dynamics, Paul in his letters employs a set of concepts that is widely used by Greco-Roman philosophers: *ergon, energeia, dunamis, morphe, telos, katargeō*. A good understanding of how these concepts relate to one another helps us better understand Paul's theology. Like Aristotle, Paul values activity over motion. However, unlike Aristotle, Paul values not the law but the form of the one who has died on the cross: a thought that would never have crossed Aristotle's mind.

Bibliography

Arndt, W., Danker, F. W., & Bauer, W. 2000. *A Greek-English Lexicon of the New Testament and Other Early Christian Literature* (Chicago: University of Chicago Press).

Agamben, Giorgio. 2005. *The Time That Remains: A Commentary on the Letter to the Romans.* Stanford, Calif.: Stanford University Press.

Barcley, William B. 1999. *"Christ in You": A Study in Paul's Theology and Ethics.* Lanham, MD: University Press of America.

Bates, Matthew W. 2017. *Salvation by Allegiance Alone: Rethinking Faith, Works, and the Gospel of Jesus the King.* Grand Rapids, Mich.: Baker Academic.

Coope, Ursula. "Change and Its Relation to Actuality and Potentiality." In *A Companion to Aristotle*, edited by G. Anagnostopoulos, 277-291. (Oxford: Wiley-Blackwell, 2009).

Corcilius, Klaus. "Faculties in Ancient Philosophy." In *The Faculties: A History*, edited by Dominik Perler, 9-58. (Oxford Philosophical Concepts. Oxford: Oxford University Press, 2015).

Dunn, James D. G. 1998. *Romans.* Word Biblical Commentary. Nashville, Tenn.: Thomas Nelson, 1988.

—. 1993. *The Epistle to the Galatians.* Peabody, MA: Hendrickson.

—. 1993. *The Theology of Paul's Letter to the Galatians.* Cambridge: Cambridge University Press.

Fredrickson, David E. "Parrhsia in the Pauline Epistles." In *Friendship, Flattery, and Frankness of Speech: Studies on Friendship in the New Testament World*, edited by John T. Fitzgerald, 163-83. (Leiden: E. J. Brill, 1996).

Fung, Ronald Y. K. 2008. *A Commentary on the Epistle to the Galatians* [Chinese] (Taiwan: Campus Evangelical Fellowship Press, 2008).

Garland, David E. 1999. *2 Corinthians*. The New American Commentary 29. Nashville, Tenn.: Broadman & Holman.
Chapman, Honora Howell. "Josephus and the Cannibalism of Mary (BJ 6.199-219)." In *Companion to Greek and Roman Historiography*, edited by John Marincola, 419-426. (Malden, Mass.: Blackwell, 2007).
Hsieh, Le Chih (Luke). "Works of the Law as Functions of the Law." *Sino-Christian Studies* 25 (2018): 7-40.
—. "Paul as a *Parrhesiastes.*" *Sino-Christian Studies* 18 (2014): 7-31.
Kearney, Richard. "Paul's Notion of *Dunamis*: Between the Possible and the Impossible." In *St. Paul among the Philosophers*, edited by John D. Caputo and Linda Alcoff, 142-159. (Indiana Series in the Philosophy of Religion; Bloomington, Ind.: Indiana University Press, 2009).
Kosman, L. A. "Aristotle's Definition of Motion." *Phronesis* 14 (1969):40-62.
—. 2013. *The Activity of Being: An Essay on Aristotle's Ontology.* Cambridge, Mass.: Harvard University Press.
Longenecker, R. N. 2002.*Galatians*. Word Biblical Commentary. Dallas: Word Books.
Marmodoro, Anna, and Irini-Fotini Viltanioti. 2017. *Divine Powers in Late Antiquity.* Oxford: Oxford University Press.
Sampley, J. Paul. "Paul's Frank Speech with the Galatians and the Corinthians." In *Philodemus and the New Testament World*, edited by John T. Fitzgerald, Dirk Obbink and Glenn Stanfield Holland, 295-321. (Leiden: E. J. Brill, 2004).
Schreiner, Thomas R. "'Works of the Law' in Paul." *Novum Testamentum* 33 (1991): 225-38.
Smit, Joop. "The Letter of Paul to the Galatians: A Deliberative Speech". In *The Galatians Debate*, edited by Mark D. Nanos, 39-59. (Peabody, Mass.: Hendrickson, 2002).
Tsang, Sam. 2005. *From Slaves to Sons: A New Rhetoric Analysis on Paul's Slave Metaphors in His Letter to the Galatians.* Studies in Biblical Literature 81. New York: Peter Lang.
Witherington III, Ben. 1995. *Conflict and Community in Corinth: A Socio-Rhetorical Commentary on 1 and 2 Corinthians.* Grand Rapids, Mich.: Eerdmans.
—. 1998. *Grace in Galatia: A Commentary on St. Paul's Letter to the Galatians*. Edinburgh: T&T Clark.

Le Chih Hsieh
China Evangelical Seminary, Taiwan

Chapter Six

Ancient Philosophers in the Age of Digitalisation

Yip Mei Loh and Bernard Li

The concept of digitalisation and its relationship to ancient Greek philosophy and Christianity is, at first sight, an unlikely one, perhaps because we set so much store on the results and benefits of digitalisation that we forget its origins. Thus this article will set out to examine the relationship between these three major fields: finding the source of the digital concept in the Bible, the birth of modern science and technology and the work of the ancient Greek philosophers.

The four sections of this article will trace the development of human intelligence from these three subjects, presenting insights in such a way as to guide the reader more easily to understanding. The meaning of the very term 'digit' is examined, from its appearance as Michelangelo's 'Finger of God' to its modern manifestation as the driver of all modern technological function.

1.

Most people whose lives are guided by digital devices everywhere may find it hard to imagine that the field of digitalisation is inseparable from that of the philosophy of ancient Greece, which is the cradle of human speculative thought, and which nourishes the formation of early Christian theology. The former is concerned with technology, which is our means to facilitate, while the latter is from the domain of humanity, that is the practice of life; and between them they should stimulate enquiry into the reasons for this apparent relationship.

Why are they so intertwined? First, an examination of the term 'technology', which is comprised of the Greek terms '*technē*' and '*logos*', reveals their interconnection, and we can discover that technology is essentially derived from humanity, that is, the liberal arts. Martin Heidegger holds that the term '*technē*' belongs to the human activity of '*poiēsis*' which means an engagement in creation or invention.[1] In other words, the term '*technē*' refers to conceptual universal rule, which is revealed by experiential and experimental observation of nature, and which is inherent in things themselves, so it is unchangeable and common to all who use it. Hence Heidegger defines it as 'a mode of revealing'[2] to arrive at the sphere of *alētheia* (truth)[3], which Plato read as mathematical proportion in the *Republic* 486d, in such a way that a mathematical proposition that is examined by the first principle is called a '*theorema*',[4] whose law and truth are unalterably present and common to all who behold it.[5] To that extent the concept of '*technē*' cannot be independent of that of *theōria*, which itself derives from two sources: '*théa*' and '*theos*'.[6]

One of them originally means 'beholding' or 'contemplating', and which could be composed of two Greek terms '*théa*' (sight) and '*horaō*' (to behold)[7], whose Aorist is '*eidon*' (Form), and whose aorist infinite is '*idein*', on the strength of which Plato's concept of either '*to eidos*' or of '*he idea*' means 'beholding'. Walter Mesch defines it as 'perception of a vision' (das Wahrnehmen einer Schau (*thea*))[8]. In Plato's *Cratylus* 389a-b, Socrates holds that all kinds of the weaver's shuttles must contain the form of shuttles, so that when the carpenter makes one, he is beholding its Form

---

[1] Martin Heidegger. *The Question Concerning Technology and Other Essays*, (The US: Garland Publishing, Inc., 1977), p. 13.
[2] Ibid.
[3] Ibid., p. 12.
[4] Dorothy Emmet. 'Theoria and The Way of Life' in *The Journal of Theological Studies*, p. 38, April 1966, New Series, Vol. 17, No. 1, pp.38-52.
[5] Augustine. *De Libero Arbitrio*, II, 29, p. 171, Zweisprachige Ausgabe, eingeleitet, übersetzt und herausgegeben von Johannes Brachtendorf, (Paderborn/Germany: Ferdinand Schöningh, 2006).
[6] Walter Mesch. 'theôrein/theôria' in *Wörterbuch der antiken Philosophie*, Herausgegeben von Christoph und Christof Rapp, (München/Germany: C.H. Beck oHG, 2002), S. 436.
[7] Christoph Riedweg. *Pythagoras*, translated from German by Steven Rendall, (Ithaca and London: Cornell University Press, 2005), p.96. Cf. Dorothy Emmet, 'Theoria and The Way of Life' in *The Journal of Theological Studies*, p. 38, April 1966, New Series, Vol. 17, No. 1, pp.38-52. Cf. D. N. Rodowick. 'Theoria as Practical Philosophy' in the *Elegy for Theory*, pp.7-8, particularly footnote 7, published by Harvard University Press, pp7-12.
[8] Walter Mesch (2002). 'theôrein/theôria', S. 436.

to make it, thereby his *technē* is the exhibition of Form, which inhabits his work. And in the *Gorgias* 503d-e Socrates says that all craftsmen direct their work not at random but with the function (*ergon*) of their *technē* in mind so that what each produces will have a certain form, 'each *technē* has exactly a function (*ergon*), and a function is handled by exactly a *technē*'[9] based upon its *theōria*. For example, the medical *technē* studies the nature of health; and the doctor is obliged to follow its universal rules to give accounts of health and to look after his patients according to it. So 'every *technē* deals with the whole of the function, not just partial aspects'[10]. In brief, every *technē* is founded upon its universal rule, that is, *theōria*, which it reveals, and from which it is distinguished, since it is also included with repeated practice through learning. So *technē*, the exercising (*poiēsis*) of professional ability, involves experience to reveal truth or Forms; and things that are in the phenomenal world participate in the world of Forms.

In his *Republic* 507b and 508b-509a Plato claims that Forms, which are the offspring of the Good that the Good produced in proportion to itself, and which are 'goodlike'(*agathoeidēs*), can be known by the mind (*noeisthai*), not seen (*horasthai*), so the forms of geometry and the *technē* of artificial things in the phenomenal world that is understood with the help of sense-perception are the exhibition of Forms.[11] Likewise, Augustine thinks that *theōria* can be in the mind (*nous*) alone, and *technē* joins imitation with reason in soul.[12] In 511c Plato further holds that reality and the mind are contemplated (*theōroumenon*) by the science of dialectical discussion in thought (*dianoia*) without using senses. Clearly, Plato's concept of '*theōria*' (contemplating sight) here is to emphasize participating in the sight of the intelligible part, not on the unity with the Good (*to agathos*).

The other source of the term '*theōria*' might be found in the two Greek terms '*theos*' (God) and '*horaō*', contrary to those scholars who link

---

[9] Nussbaum. 'Technē-Analogie' in *Platon Handbuch – Leben-Werk-Wirkung*, Christoph Horn, Jörn Müller, Joachim Söder (Hg.), 2. Auflage, (Stuttgart/Deutschland: J.B. Metzler, Springer-Verlag GmbH, 2017), S. 344.
[10] Ibid.
[11] Plato. *Republic*, BK VI, 511a, edited and translated by Chris Emlyn-Jones and William Preddy (London/England: Harvard University Press, 2013), pp.100-101.
[12] Saint Augustine. 'On Music' in *The Father of the Church*, Vol 4, ch.4, 5-8, (The US/Washington, D.C.: The Catholic University of America Press, 1947), pp.176-182.

theōria with theatre, where official visitors (*theoroi*) attended festivals and consulted oracles;[13] for example, Walter Mesch understands it as 'the awareness of a god (das Gewahren eines Gottes(*theos*)) that occurs when ambassadors attend religious festivals but only watch'.[14] However, Rodolphe Gasché boldly offers an interpretation whereby although theory and theatre derive from the same root, they might not have any intrinsic relation,[15] since a philosopher such as Socrates possesses a pedagogical aim to search for and reveal truth, so *theōria* can derive from *theos* because its main concern is to associate with the divine.[16] For example, in the *Theaetetus*150c-d, Plato depicts Socrates as a divine teacher who is compelled by god to act as a divine midwife (*maieuesthai me ho theos anagkazei*), that is, Socrates emulates god in inspiring his followers with love of knowledge itself to behold the divine wisdom; and in 155d he further describes the philosopher as a god Thaumas, who initiates the pursuit of wisdom. In the *Apology* 31c-d Socrates says that there is a divine or a *daimon* who has been coming to him since he was a child, so that his divine sign (*to daimonion sêmeion*)[17] is the practical life of *theōria* wherein he contemplates the vision of his divine. And he devotes his whole life to communicate with, or to unify with, his divine, and sacrifices himself for persistent inquiry into truth.

In the *Republic* 519c-d Plato claims that for a lover of wisdom, the most important thing is 'to see the Good' (*ideĩn te to agathon*) that Forms originate. And in 492a and 526e respectively Plato emphasizes that the nature of the philosopher's soul is by every means to strive for seeing (*ideĩn*) the most blessed part or the highest virtue, i.e. the Good. Furthermore, Plotinus defines '*theōria*' as 'contemplating the nature of the Good (*tên tou agathou physin*)'[18], which is the principle of all living beings.[19] Mark Edwards seems to concur with Plotinus in putting it that the concept of '*theōria*' is 'the vision of the Good[20]', which is the

---

[13] Cf. Christoph Riedweg (2005). *Pythagoras*, p. 97.
[14] Walter Mesch. 'theôrein/theôria', S. 436.
[15] Rodolphe Gasché. *The Honor of Thinking – Critique, Theory, Philosophy*, (Stanford/California: Stanford University Press, 2007), p. 190.
[16] Ibid., p. 200.
[17] Plato. *Republic*, BK VI, 496c, pp.48-49; cf. *Euthyphro*, 3b, pp.8-9; *Apology* 31c-32a, pp.112-115 and *Symposium*, 173d-e, pp.84-85.
[18] Plotinus. *Ennead* VI, 7, 15, 14, translated by A.H. Armstrong, (Cambridge/England: Harvard University Press, 1988), p.134.
[19] Ibid., VI, 7, 14, 15-20, pp.134-137 and Ibid., VI, 7, 16, 23-32, pp.138-141.
[20] Mark Julian Edwards. *Origen against Plato* (USA: Ashgate Publishing Company,

perfection of an inquiry for Socrates.[21] He seems to hold that Plato's *theōria* is purely emphasis on the contemplation of the Good, a view I would like to explore and explain further. Firstly, it might be that Prof. Edwards refrains to mention that for Plato's Socrates, being divine-like, the goal of the true philosopher is to unite with the Good to possess a perfect life (*kalos agathos*), the *theōria* of the philosopher's soul, since Socrates's life is dedicated to the fulfilment of the divine's commands, in both his instruction and action. Furthermore, he might not discuss the claim of Augustine's wisdom, which says that only when man is able to contemplate the highest Good is he able to possess that truth.[22] Accordingly, Plato might be the first philosopher to endow a new connotation of *theōria* from participation in Forms to ascend towards union with the Good or god. This in turn had its influence on Plotinus.

Likewise, In Matthew 5:8 Jesus says 'Blessed are the pure in heart, for they will see God (*ton theon opsontai*)'. So in the role of being the apostles of Jesus, they imitate Him in dedicating themselves towards a life of *theōria*, that is *visio Dei* (the vision of God) for union with the Father. Whether or not the Christian Apostles, like the author of Matthew, acquire it from Platonic philosophy, is not the point of this paper. However, in Christian faith the early theologians, particularly Origen, wear the mantle of Greek philosophy not only to absorb the Greek *paideia* but also to make use of its rich conceptual vocabulary and its literary means of interpreting their biblical concept of oneness of the divine principle.[23] Hence Mark Edwards believes that for Origen *theōria* is not only in his *visio Dei*, but also in his union with Him, which is the *visio* of his duty within his exegesis,[24] thereby he devotes his life to his faith to imitate Christ in being a martyr. Jaeger says that Origen is a late heir to the Greek scientific spirit, his philosophical theology being immersed in Plato's spirit, and that he dedicates his life to *theōria*.[25] From this point of view, Origen's

---

2002), p. 137. Cf. 馬克愛德華斯。《歐利根駁斥柏拉圖》，羅月美譯，(台北：五南出版社，2020 年 5 月)，231 頁。

[21] Ibid.

[22] Augustine. *De Libero Arbitrio*, II, 26; II, 28; II, 29, Zweisprachige Ausgabe, eingeleitet, übersetzt und herausgegeben von Johannes Brachtendorf, (Paderborn/Germany: Ferdinand Schöningh, 2006), p. 164, p. 169, p. 171.

[23] Werner Jaeger. Early Christianity and Greek Paideia, (London/England: The Belknap Press of Harvard University Press, 1961), pp.29-33.

[24] Mark Julian Edwards. *Origen against Plato*, p. 137. Cf. 馬克愛德華斯，《歐利根駁斥柏拉圖》，羅月美譯，231 頁。

[25] Werner Jaeger. Early Christianity and Greek Paideia, p. 58.

understanding of *theōria* does not exceed Plato's understanding.

Meanwhile the term 'logos' means 'principle', 'ratio' or 'reasoned discourse'. It follows that the term 'technology' means the principle (*archē*) or the ratio of *technē*. If we follow the universal rules which are inherent in things themselves, and which are indestructible, then things can be invented. The Gospel of John says that 'in the beginning was the Word (*Logos*), the Word is with God, and the Word is God'. The principle of the cosmos is God, who made all things, so He is the principle of the creation. In other words, God at the beginning endows us with His principles, to understand Him, and to utilise them in the invention of our own material products. So the technology used by human beings is along the principles of the universal rules that are changeless truth, and its purpose is to achieve its functions in performance of its end. Thus, our innovation (*poiēsis*) is simply to copy His principles to create our needs for the purpose of understanding God. Using these technological means, what kinds of function would God want us to exhibit Him with? Ecclesiastes 7: 26 gives us the answer, which says 'I turned my mind to understand, to know and to search out wisdom and <u>number</u>' (*Lustrávi univérsa ánimo meo, ut scirem et considerárem, et quaérerem sapiéntiam et <u>ratiónem</u>*), to such an extent that Augustine believes that the inseparability and immutability of wisdom and number are also shown in the Bible, in that they are one and same thing because of their participation in the unchangeable truth.[26]

Secondly, if we explore the term 'digitalisation', we wonder how we can invent these omnifunctional marvels of technology that can fit in the palm of our hand, such as the Apple watch or the smartphone. Now the first thing that I would like to do is to breakdown the term 'digitalisation'. This can be derived from both the adjective 'digital' and the noun 'digit', and 'digit' comes from the Latin '*digitus*', which means 'finger', and which also stands for the Arabic numbers zero and one in binary code.[27] Alan Turing was the first to use binary code to compute data on to tape. The

---

[26] Augustine. *De Libero Arbitrio*, II, 31-32, pp. 174-177. Cf. Christoph Horn. 'Augustins Philosophie der Zahlen', S. 389-415, in *the Revue des Études Augustiniennes* 40 (1994), S. 397.

[27] Cf. Yip Mei Loh. 'The Allegory of Pistis and Eikasia in Plato's Divided Line and Social Media Bespoke Groups as Virtual "Ekklesia" in Taiwan', in Цифровизация общества и будущее христианства: Материалы V Международной научной конференции 24.01.2019 / Отв. ред. И. П. Рязанцев, ред.-сост. Р. М. Плюснин. – М.: Изд-во (ПСТГУ, 2019), p. 40. ISBN 978-5-7429-1251-4.

term 'digital' can be referred to the way a computer works, which processes data with binary numbers - zeros and ones. In summary, the concept of digitalisation implies that an instrument that is manipulated by binary digits with fingers to calculate a function, can be called an 'artificial mind' or 'human-like brain', and is a form of intelligence, which is invented to resemble the human mind. Furthermore, in the Bible 'the finger of God' is '*digitus Dei*' in Latin and '*daktulos theou*' in Greek. In Luke 11:20 Jesus says '*Porro, si in dígito Dei eício daemónia, profécto pervénit in vos regnum Dei*'(*ei dè én daktulôi theou [egô] ekballô ta daimónia, ara ephthasen eph' hymas he basileía tou theou*)[28]. And in Exodus 8:19, '*Et dixérunt maléfici ad Pharaónem: Dígitus Dei set hic*'.[29] The finger of God is to cast out evil and to endow man with a purified life.

With this background we are reminded of Michelangelo's painting, *The Creation of Adam*, which depicts God giving life to Adam through His finger. So when God uses his finger to give us life, and we use our finger to give function or life to artificial intelligence, technology is shown to be derived from human innovation; it should conform with human nature to assist us in the pursuit of beauty, goodness, truth and love, and not to abuse it. If we employ Plato's *Timaeus* 22a-c, wherein the old Egyptian priest chided Solon and his fellow Greeks for being children in their souls, then we can analogise the antiquity and sagacity of Egypt with the philosophy of early Christianity, while the youthful, bright but shallow knowledge of the Greeks is our modern phenomenon of digitalisation. The priest warns Solon about old forgotten disasters; but the modern entity that is technology, as well as bringing huge benefits, also bears risks of existential moment. Threats abound to the well-being of vast swathes of humanity, from lonely individuals to entire nations; and emanate from one nation to another or even one nation's government to its own people.

2.

Plato's *Republic* 530d holds that the Pythagoreans discovered astronomy and harmony, which by allegorical interpretation can be grasped through the eyes and ears, and are brothers in science.[30] According to Diogenes

---

[28] St. Jerome translated. Secundum Lucam 11:20, in the Bibliaa Sacra, Vulgatae Editionis, (Edizioni San Paolo s.r.l., 2003, Seconda edizione 2012), p. 1061.
[29] Ibid., p. 74.
[30] Plato. *Republic*, 530d, Bk VII, edited and translated by Chris Emlyn-Jones and William Preddy (London/England: Harvard University Press, 2013), pp.164-165. Cf. Anthony Kenny. *Ancient Philosophy – A New History of Western Philosophy*,

Laertius, Thales was the first to study astronomy and the first to predict the eclipse of the sun and to fix the solstices.[31] Furthermore, he also was the first to discover the seasons of the years and to divide it into 365 days.[32] In the *Timaeus* 37d Plato, the 'Pythagorean', claims that god makes time an eternal image of eternity in unity moving according to number, and at the same time brings order to the cosmos. Obviously, for Plato the cosmos comes into being with time[33], which is eternal. In the *Timaeus* 32b-c he says that the Demiurge creates the body of the cosmos with four particular elements – fire, water, earth and air – a symphony of proportion. So number is an essential constituent of the thesis that the cosmos is a world-order, which is beautiful and good, consonant with Augustine's assertion that 'beauty pleases us because of number'[34]. According to Aristotle's *Metaphysics* 986a, the Pythagoreans hold that all bodily things are composed of numbers, which are the principles (*archai*) of all existing things. The movement of the cosmos is rooted in numbers, giving our understanding of time, and exists in a state of *Harmonia* (fitting together); thus its movement is a harmonious symphony based on arithmetical ratio.[35] Albeit the ancient philosophers asserted that numbers are the substantive constituents of the book of the cosmos, it took Galileo (1564-1642) and his successors to prove their assertion true.[36] Relative to the ancient philosophers, modern science is a child.

The term 'mind' in Plato speaks of '*nous*', which is the resemblance of man to his maker. In the *Timaeus* 29e-30b Plato holds that god is good. He is free of jealousy and wants everything to become as much like himself as possible. He put intellect or mind (*nous*), which is made in the likeness of

---

(the US: Oxford University Press, 2004), Vol. 1, p. 9.

[31] Diogenes Laertius. *Lives of Eminent Philosophers*, edited with an introduction by Tiziano Dorandi, Liber I, 23:20-22, (the UK: Cambridge University Press, First published 2013), p.80.

[32] Ibid., Liber 1, 27: 56-59, p.82.

[33] St. Epiphanius. *Panarion*, translated by Frank Williams, (Leiden/The Netherlands: Koninklijke Brill, 2009), Bk.1, p.24.

[34] Christoph Horn. *Augustinus*, (München/Germany: Verlag C.H. Beck oHG, 2012), 2 Auflage, S.55.

[35] Plato. *Republic* VII, 531b-c (London/England: Harvard University Press, first published 2013), pp. 166-167. Cf. Christoph Riedweg. *Pythagoras- his Life, Teaching, and Influence*, translated by Steven Rendall in collaboration with Christoph and Andreas Schatzmann (Ithaca and London: Cornell University Press, 2002), p. 80.

[36] Anthony Kenny. *Ancient Philosophy – A New History of Western Philosophy*, Vol. 1, p. 9.

god, into the soul (*psychê*), and the soul in the body (*sôma*). Thus for Plato it follows that man possesses mind, soul and body. In other words, the body has both soul and mind.[37] Origen, in his *Against Celsus*, holds that the God of the cosmos is mind, or superior to mind and being – simple, invisible and incorporeal. He cannot be comprehended by any save the one who has come to be in the image of that mind.[38] That is, God can be understood by Christ, who is God's mind, since the similar can be known by the similar; as Plato says in the *Republic* 507b, the Forms can be perceived by the mind only. Indeed, Origen proclaims that the faculty of sense perception is inferior to that of the mind; where sight is connected with colour, shape and size, and hearing with the voice and sound; whereas the mind itself is the intellectual image (*intellectualis imago*) of God, and enables us to understand the divine nature to some degree.[39] Furthermore, he claims that God is mind, which 'needs intellectual magnitude, because it grows in an intellectual and not in a physical sense'[40], the capacity of the human mind can be cultivated by means of hard mental exercise, so that man's intelligence is not dependent on his physical age, but on the extent of the depth of his learning.[41]

3.

Now man creates an artificial intelligence, which resembles his mind, with binary numbers. It follows that the principle of the artificial mind is binary numbers. And if the artificial mind is created by man according to binary numbers, and resembles the human mind, is our mind made of numbers as well?

---

[37] Cf. Yip-Mei Loh. '*The Sōma and The Psychē In The Gospel Of Matthew and In Plato's Timaeus*' in the *People: International Journal of Social Science* 2 (1): 557-590 (2016), pp.585-586; and Yip-Mei Loh. 'The Allegory of Pistis and Eikasia in Plato's Divided Line and Social Media Bespoke Groups as Virtual "Ekklesia" in Taiwan', p. 40.

[38] Origen. *Contra Celsum*, VII: 38, translated by Henry Chadwick. (The UK: Cambridge University Press, first published 1953), p.425. Cf. Mark Julian Edwards. *Origen against Plato*, p.57.

[39] Origen. *On First Principles*, edited and translated by John Behr, 1.1.7 (The UK: Oxford University Press, First edition published in 2018), pp.36-37.

[40] Origen. *On First Principles*, translated into English, together with an Introduction and Notes by G. W. Butterworth, 1.6 (The US: Harper & Row, Publishers, 1966, Reprinted, 1973), p. 11.

[41] Ibid.

In Plato's *Sophist* 238a, the Eleatic Stranger assumes that 'all number (*arithmon*) is among the things which are'[42], through which Plato seemingly holds that number is intermediary between the phenomenal world and Forms, and that we can understand the world of Forms with the help of number.[43] In his *Timaeus* 29a he holds that mind (*nous*) is the image of the eternal model, which the Demiurge is looking at when he is moulding *nous*, and, as in 41d-e, Plato tells us that the Demiurge makes our souls with the same ingredients as he made the soul of the cosmos (save their purity is not as rich); and their number is equal to the stars, so that each person is unique. Then the Demiurge sows each human soul into the instrument of time, thereby our souls are composed of numbers (*arithmoi*). After that he puts nous (mind) into our souls.[44] So our mind dwells in our souls, and is not our souls, but our souls possess it. In other words, our souls are the sanctuary of the mind. In *Ennead* VI Plotinus goes so far as to say that the soul as a substance (*ousia*) is a number.[45] And Augustine considers that our soul is made by God, and is like God because he makes it immortal in his own likeness; while the artificial mind lives within its body - but for only as long as the 'device' exists.[46] Once the device is damaged or corrupted in some way the data within - the mind - is lost. Thus any artificial intelligence we create, any artificial mind, can only benefit from an artificial immortality; that is, this digital immortality is subject to the durability of the physical environment wherein it resides.

Hence there are two kinds of knowledge in the intelligent world, one is the knowledge of soul, which is called mathematics, that can be comprehended by soul; the other the knowledge of mind - the knowledge of Forms - which can be intellectually and speculatively intuited by pure mind alone, by means of dialectics. Our mind is the image of the eternity that is *monas*. It follows that there are two Platonic notions of time, one is eternity (*Aiôn*), or the eternal present, which can be contemplated by our mind alone; the other is the image of eternity or everlasting likeness (*eikôn*), which is not

---

[42] Plato. *Sophist* 280a, with an English Translation by Harold North Fowler, (Cambridge/England: Harvard University Press,1921), pp. 342-343.
[43] Cf. Svetla Slaveva-Griffin. *Plotinus on Number* (New York/the US: Oxford University Press, 2009), p. 59.
[44] Plato. *Timaeus* 30b, also see footnote 37.
[45] Plotinus. *Ennead* VI, 6, 16, 45, translated by A.H. Armstrong, (Cambridge/England: Harvard University Press, 1988), pp.64-65.
[46] Saint Augustine. 'The Magnitude of the Soul' in *The Father of the Church*, Vol 4, ch.2 (The US/Washington, D.C.: The Catholic University of America Press, 1947), pp.61-62.

only moving according to number, but also has a beginning, past, present and future, and which is counted and computed by our intellectual soul in the passage of time. Hence the Demiurge, who produces an imitation by keeping to the proportions of the length, breadth, and depth of his model, possesses the *technê* of likeness-making, not of appearance-making, whose purpose is to appear like the true thing without proportions, like a painter.[47]

In the *Republic* 525a-e Plato holds that all calculation and arithmetic are to do with numbers, which lead our souls toward truth. It is not only guardians who should study mathematics for the purpose of war, but the philosopher has also to be conversant with it, because it can help him to turn the soul away from transience to truth and substance (*aletheia kai ousia*). For Plato, the study of calculation is preparation for philosopher-kings, enabling them to contemplate truth and substance without the disturbance of sense-perception. Also it enables *technē* because of its determinacy, as demonstrated in the tracking of Covid-19 patients. For example German Chancellor Angela Merkel, presented her government's strategy on 1st May 2020, to forecast likely numbers of infected patients to manage the extent of the national health threat. She said that 'if we have 40,000 people infected in total and 1,500 new infections every day, then it's possible for our 400 public health offices to trace that. That was the goal all along. Where were we successful? We were successful when a Chinese woman infected 16 other people at Webasto (the company), there we could trace every single case.'[48] Therefore, when facing a crisis, the employment of reason, or numeric calculation, lends the possibility of solving the crisis, because numbers can help us to predict the possible future and adopt preventative measures in a timely manner. To a certain extent, Plotinus correctly interprets man as living a rational life (*zôn logikên ho anthrôpos*)[49], that is, a life of computation. Augustine endorses Evodius in saying that *ratio* (meaning computation, or calculation) enables our reason and intellect to grasp working with numbers, albeit more easily for some than for others; and that for those who understand it, it is absolute. Even if

---

[47] Plato. *Sophist* 235d-236c, pp.332-335.
[48] Accessed 12th August 2020:
https://www.facebook.com/deutschewellenews/videos/707885133281457/UzpfST EwMDAwNzkxOTA0OTg1NDoyNjAwNzU2NDkwMTk4Mjk0/?fref=search&__tn__=%2Cd%2CP-R&eid=ARBynvu8we7Fr4D7FDef53lTXBCbHp97300Etg8dy LnflfMbgzqD3dQn-R8FoQwsii93GzFnkmPXg2Uy.
[49] Plotinus. *Ennead* VI, 7, 4, 34, translated by A.H. Armstrong, (Cambridge/England: Harvard University Press, 1988), pp.100-101.

we make a mistake, it remains true and complete. On the contrary, the less we know of it, the greater the mistakes we make.[50]

Plato thinks that number, as something which can be conceived mentally, can lead a philosopher to a state of moderation (*sôphrosune*), and that a true philosopher is the one whose soul can ascend to the world of Forms, to behold the truth. He holds that only the pure mind alone can grasp the true goal of the intelligible world, which is from the journey of calculation to that of dialectic; that is, from the journey of reason to that of the mind itself. To uplift the best part of the soul toward the contemplation of the best in things that are in the real world,[51] is what Aristotle echoes, and urges us to pursue the life of contemplation inasmuch as the mind is our real self.[52]

In the Bible number is allegorized by the finger of God. Psalm 8:4-9 implies that the cosmos is made by the fingers of God, which give life to all His creations. Isaiah 64:8 says that we are the work of God's hand (*manus*). The sun, the moon, and the stars all follow their own orbits and keep a certain distance without derailment in that the order of the universe is moved according to number. And scientists delve the mysteries of the universe by dint of their comprehension of number. Without numbers nothing is possible. Numbers are the essence of all rational creation. As Plotinus would have it, the soul can apprehend the melody in the intelligible world in that man can understand the forming principle (*logos*) in imitation, to create our civilization;[53] man is imitating God's creation with number in the course of his own innovation. In brief, the civilization of digitalisation is the exhibition of God's power. Psalm 8: 4 says,

> *Quóniam vidébo caelos tuos, ópera <u>digitórum</u> tuórum, lunam et stellas quae tu fundásti.* (For I will behold thy heavens, the works of thy fingers: the moon and the stars which thou hast founded.)

---

[50] St. Augustine. *De libero arbitrio*, Bk. II, VIII, 20, Band 9, zweisprachige Ausgabe, eingeleitet, übersetzt und herausgegeben von Johannes Brachtendort, (München/Deutschland: Ferdinand Schöningh, 2006), S. 156-157,.
[51] Plato. *Republic* 532b-c, pp. 170-171.
[52] Aristotle. *Die Nikomachische Ethik*, 1178a, Grechisch-deutsch, Übersetzt von Olof-Gigon, neu herausgegeben von Rainer Nickel (Artemis & Winkler, 2001), S.445. Cf. Mark Julian Edwards (2002). *Origen Against Plato*, p. 95.
[53] Plotinus. *Ennead* VI, 7, 6, 12, pp.102-103.

To this extent, numbers are the instrument with which God creates the world and by means of which He keeps in perfect order; numbers in this sense stand for God, understood as the Holy Spirit, according to Christoph Horn.[54]

4.

Although Diogenes Laertius has Pythagoras being the first person to call himself a *philosophos*,[55] which is composed of '*philo*' and '*sophos*' - meaning 'friend of wisdom' or 'loving wisdom'-, it is still arguable whether he is the inventor of the Greek term '*philosophia*' due to insufficient evidence.

However, the term occurs in Plato's dialogues relatively often. He interprets '*philosophia*' as 'striving for wisdom' in his *Symposium*, and in *Phaedrus* 278d he refers to the philosopher as a lover of wisdom, who engages in the activity of *vita contemplative*, that is a life of union with the Good or god. And his path is to inquire into the truth of God's creation and to seek the first principles because of '*to thaumazein*' (wonder), which is the beginning of love for wisdom.[56] Aristotle says that it is wonder which causes men to philosophize, and to concern themselves with the movement of the universe.[57]

In the Bible God is Wisdom itself. All creations are manifestations of His Wisdom. In 1 Corinthians 1:24 Paul proclaims Christ as the wisdom of God (*theou sophia*) and the power of God (*theou dunamis*). Origen in his *First Principles* not only says that Christ by nature is the same as Wisdom, but also re-asserts Paul's claim.[58] He further likens wisdom as an

---

[54] Christoph Horn. *Augustinus* (München/Germany: Verlag C.H.Beck oHG, 2010), S.68. Cf. 克里斯多夫‧霍恩著。《奧古斯丁—哲學思想導論》，羅月美譯，(台北：五南出版社，2021 年 03 月)，80 頁。
[55] Diogenes Laertius. *Lives of Eminent Philosophers*, Liber I, 1:12 (the UK: Cambridge University Press, first published 2013), p.73.
[56] Plato. *Theaetetus* 155d with an English translation by Harold North Fowler, (London/England: Harvard University Press, first published 1921), pp.54-55.
[57] Aristotle. *Metaphysics*, BK I, 982b12-14, BK I-IX, with an English translation by Hugh Tredennick, (London/England: Harvard University Press, first published 1933), p.12.
[58] Origen. *On First Principles*, Ch. II.1, being Koetschau's Text of the *De Principiis* translated onto English, together with an introduction and notes by G. W. Butterworth. Introduction to the Torchbook edition by Henri De Lubac, (the US: Harper & Row, Publishers, 1973), p. 15.

interpreter of the mind's secrets.[59] In the *Philebus*, Plato depicts the true mind as divine and king of heaven and earth;[60] and that the task of the philosopher is to interpret the divine's wisdom with words, by means of which he possesses the 'love (*agape*) of knowledge[61]'. Origen also understands Wisdom as the Word (*logos*) of God.[62] John, in 1:1, says that 'in the beginning was the Word and the Word was with God. And the Word was God'. God, Jesus and Wisdom are the same. They are inseparable and tripartite so that all science is the exhibition of God's wisdom, and all innovation is in the interpreting of His word. As it says in Ecclesiastes 1:9,

> What has been will be again, what has been done will be done again; there is nothing new under the sun.

Everything is foreknown by God, like the functions of computer programs, which have been pre-set, and are foreseen by us. Man imitates God's wisdom to invent artificial intelligence. Hence, we have to humble ourselves to know God's magnificent creation by means of state-of-the-art digitalisation.

It is inevitable that advanced digitalisation will, where employed properly, provide excellent tools to inhibit the spread of rampant infectious diseases like the current COVID 19 pandemic. For example, during the early incubation period of this disease, the Taiwanese authorities were able to call upon big health insurance databases, phone apps and other technologies to rigorously record and contact-trace international arrivals at the country's ports and airports, including many from the stricken cruise ship, *Diamond Princess*.[63] These measures, along with active quarantining, enabled the country to record among the lowest infection

---

[59] Ibid., p. 16.
[60] Plato. *Philebus* 22c, 28c (London/England:Harvard University Press, first published 1925), pp.238-239, pp. 260-261.
[61] Ibid., 63e, pp. 382-383.
[62] Origen. *On First Principles*, Ch. II.1 (1973), p. 16.
[63] Chi-Mai Chen, MD, MSc; Hong-Wei Jyan, MSc; Shih-Chieh Chien, PhD; Hsiao-Hsuan Jen, PhD; Chen-Yang Hsu, PhD, MD; Po-Chang Lee, MD, MSc; Chun-Fu Lee, MSc; Yi-Ting Yang, MSN; Meng-Yu Chen, MD, MSc; Li-Sheng Chen, PhD; Hsiu-Hsi Chen, PhD; Chang-Chuan Chan, ScD. 'Containing COVID-19 Among 627,386 Persons in Contact With the Diamond Princess Cruise Ship Passengers Who Disembarked in Taiwan: Big Data Analytics', originally published in *the Journal of Medical Internet Research* (http://www.jmir.org), 05.05.2020.

and death rates in the world. However, the fact that other countries performed rather more poorly – particularly in the West – may be found in the obstructions caused by data protection laws. The will, and indeed, the mechanism to suspend these laws is much less developed in the West, thereby the infection runs amok while policy makers agonise over the necessary subversion of their data protection legislation. Such conundrums were faced and dealt with a decade and a half earlier in Taiwan, when the Infectious Disease Control Act was mandated in 2007.[64] This allows the government to waive the provisions of data control for the purposes of containing the spread of a major infection, and demonstrates the importance of collaboration between people and government in the face of catastrophe. According to the Taiwanese digital minister, Audrey Tang, the Taiwan government, in embracing digitalisation since 1998, has had the aim that democracy should be an everyday process, as a prerequisite for digital services. In other words, everyone's business with everybody's help, so when the Taiwanese people fought the pandemic, they did so without the need for lockdown. They fought the information damage with this, and there were no takedowns. All these are centered around the idea of the social sector, the citizen-oriented groups that open the door and invite everyone in the public to contribute to the design process, and therefore, instead of working for the government, they work with the government, and instead of the government working for the people, the government needs to work with the people, and even after the people.[65]

Nevertheless, through digitalisation the tools exist for us to do wonderful things, or terrible. The choice, as ever, is up to us. As Origen says we are the author of evil. God is good and just for both the good and the wicked, who are of one nature, but the consequences of these two people are different by their own free choice of the will (*autexousion*).[66] Likewise, in *De libero arbitrio* Augustine holds that God is not responsible for the wrongness that has been done by our bad will. We should condemn those who misuse the free choice of the will (*libero voluntatis arbitrio*) for evil. God endows us with free choice of the will, because He wants us not only to live justly, but to be served with just punishment and reward.[67]

---

[64] Ibid.
[65] https://www.youtube.com/watch?v=LWtzU3sPPC4, (Accessed 26th November 2020).
[66] Origen. *On First Principles*, Vol. II, 3.1.9-10. Edited and Translated by John Behr. (Oxford/United Kingdom: Oxford University Press, 2017), pp. 309-315.
[67] St. Augustine. *De libero arbitrio*, Bk. I, XI, 21-23, S. 104-107, Bk. II, XVIII,

Conclusion

Wisdom is God's effluence, digitalisation is man's innovation, a product of the effluence of wisdom. It follows that we must make the best use of technology to glorify God's wisdom. We know that Thales, Pythagoras and Plato went to Egypt, then a centre of civilization, to absorb advanced knowledge for the establishment of their doctrines. And the philosophy of early Christianity founded in Egypt, obliges us to bear it in mind when developing the Christian faith in our age of digitalisation, particularly as Egypt was also the place where Moses led the Jews from enslavement to freedom. Its lesson teaches us that 'the free cheese is often in the mousetrap'. This is from an early time in human history which shows that there is a price for the pursuit of freedom.

Today when we use advanced digital equipment, we must not forget its close relationship with humanistic thought, and its rich and nourishing composition, so that we are enabled not only to improve the quality of human life, to enhance and secure the right of freedom of speech without censorship, but also to maintain peace in the world, if we use it justly.

Bibliography

Aristotle. *Die Nikomachische Ethik*, 1178a, S. 445, Grechisch-deutsch, Übersetzt von Olof-Gigon, neu herausgegeben von Rainer Nickel, Düsseldorf/Zürich: Artemis & Winkler Verlag, 2001.

—. *Metaphysics*, with an English translation by Hugh Tredennick. London/England: Harvard University Press, first published 1933.

Chi-Mai Chen, MD, MSc; Hong-Wei Jyan, MSc; Shih-Chieh Chien, PhD; Hsiao-Hsuan Jen, PhD;
  Chen-Yang Hsu, PhD, MD; Po-Chang Lee, MD, MSc;Chun-Fu Lee, MSc; Yi-Ting Yang, MSN; Meng-Yu Chen, MD, MSc; Li-Sheng Chen, PhD; Hsiu-Hsi Chen, PhD; Chang-Chuan Chan, ScD.
  'Containing COVID-19 Among 627,386 Persons in Contact With the Diamond Princess Cruise Ship Passengers Who Disembarked in Taiwan: Big Data Analytics', originally published in *the Journal of Medical Internet Research* (http://www.jmir.org), 05.05.2020.

Edwards, Julian Mark. *Origen against Plato*. England: Ashgate Publishing Limited, 2002.

一.《歐利根駁斥柏拉圖》，羅月美譯，台北：五南出版社，2020年05月。

Emmet, Dorothy. 'Theoria and The Way of Life' in *The Journal of Theological Studies*, April 1966, New Series, Vol. 17, No. 1, pp.38-52.

Heidegger, Martin. *The Question Concerning Technology and Other Essays*. The US: Garland Publishing, Inc, 1977.

Horn, Christoph. *Augustinus*. München/Germany: Verlag C.H.Beck oHG, 2010.

一.《奧古斯丁—哲學思想導論》，羅月美譯，台北：五南出版社，2021年03月。

—. 'Augustins Philosophie der Zahlen' in *the Revue des Études Augustiniennes* 40 (1994), S. 389-415.

Horn, Christoph, und Christof Rapp. *Wörterbuch der antiken Philosophie*. München/Germany: Verlag C.H.Beck oHG, 2002.

Kenny, Anthony. *Ancient Philosophy – A New History of Western Philosophy*, Vol. 1., the US: Oxford University Press, 2004.

Laertius, Diogenes. *Lives of Eminent Philosophers*, edited with introduction by Tiziano Dorandi. the UK: Cambridge University Press, first published 2013.

Loh, Yip-Mei. '*The Sōma and The Psychē In The Gospel Of Matthew and In Plato's Timaeus*', in the *People: International Journal of Social Science* 2 (1): 557-590 (2016).

—. 'The Allegory of Pistis and Eikasia in Plato's Divided Line and Social

Media Bespoke Groups as Virtual "Ekklesia" in Taiwan', in the Цифровизация общества и будущее христианства: Материалы V Международной научной конференции 24.01.2019 / Отв. ред. И. П. Рязанцев, ред.-сост. Р. М. Плюснин. – М.: Изд-во ПСТГУ, 2019. ISBN 978-5-7429-1251-4.

Nussbaum. 'Technē-Analogie' in *Platon Handbuch – Leben-Werk-Wirkung*, Christoph Horn, Jörn Müller, Joachim Söder (Hg.), 2. Auflage, Stuttgart/Deutschland: J.B. Metzler, Springer-Verlag GmbH, 2017.

Origen. *Contra Celsum*, translated by Henry Chadwick, the UK: Cambridge University Press, first published 1953.

—. *On First Principles*, edited and translated by John Behr, the UK: Oxford University Press, first edition published in 2017.

Origen. *On First Principles*, being Koetschau's Text of the *De Principiis* translated onto English, together with an introduction and notes by G. W. Butterworth. Introduction to the Torchbook edition by Henri De Lubac. the US: Harper & Row, Publishers, 1973.

Plato. *Euthyphro*, *Apology*, with an English translation by Harold North Fowler. Introduction by W. R. M. Lamb, London/England: Harvard University Press, first published 1914.

—. *Republic*, edited and translated by Chris Emlyn-Jones and William Preddy, London/England: Harvard University Press, 2013.

—. *Philebus*, with an English translation by Harold N. Fowler, London/England: Harvard University Press, first published 1925.

—. *Timaeus*, with an English Translation by R. G. Bury, London/England: Harvard University Press, first published 1929.

—. *Sophist*, with an English translation by Harold North Fowler, London/England: Harvard University Press, first published 1921.

—. *Symposium*, with an English translation by W. R. M. Lamb, London/England: Harvard University Press, first published 1925.

—. *Theaetetus*, with an English translation by Harold North Fowler, London/England: Harvard University Press, first published 1921.

Plotinus. *Ennead* VI. 6-9, translated by A.H. Armstrong, Cambridge/England: Harvard University Press, 1988.

Riedweg, Christoph. *Pythagoras- his Life, Teaching, and Influence*, translated by Steven Rendall in collaboration with Christoph Riedweg and Andreas Schatzmann, Ithaca and London: Cornell University Press, 2002.

Rodowick, D. N. 'Theoria as Practical Philosophy' in the *Elegy for Theory*, published by Harvard University Press, pp7-12.

Saint Augustine. 'On Music' in *The Father of the Church*, Vol 4, The

US/Washington, D.C.: The Catholic University of America Press, 1947.

—. 'The Magnitude of the Soul' in *The Father of the Church*, Vol 4, the US/Washington, D.C.: The Catholic University of America Press, 1947.

—. *De libero arbitrio*, Band 9, zweisprachige Ausgabe, eingeleitet, übersetzt und herausgegeben von Johannes Brachtendort, (München/Deutschland: Ferdinand Schöningh).

Slaveva-Griffin, Svetla. *Plotinus on Number*, New York/the US: Oxford University Press, 2009.

St. Epiphanius. *Panarion*, translated by Frank Williams, Leiden/The Netherland: Koninklijke Brill, 2009.

St. Jerome translated (Seconda edizione 2012). Secundum Lucam, in the Bibliaa Sacra, Vulgatae Editionis, Edizioni San Paolo s.r.l., 2003. Link cited: https://www.facebook.com/deutschewellenews/videos/707885133281457/UzpfSTEwMDAwNzkxOTA0OTg1NDoyNjAwNzU2NDkwMTk9Mjk0/?fref=search&__tn__=%2Cd%2CP-R&eid=ARBynvu8we7Fr4D7FDef53lTXBCbHp97300Etg8dyLnflfMbgzqD3dQn-R8FoQwsii93GzFnkmPXg2Uy, (Accessed 12th August 2020).

Audrey Tang interview: https://www.youtube.com/watch?v=LWtzU3sPPC4, (Accessed 26th November 2020).

Yip Mei Loh
Full time Assistant Professor
Graduate School of Religion
Chung Yuan Christian University, Taiwan
Part time Assistant Professor
Fu Jen Catholic University, Taiwan

Bernard Li
Chair Professor
Department of Philosophy
Fu Jen Catholic University, Taiwan

CHAPTER SEVEN

NOTES ON TWENTIETH-CENTURY TRANSLATION OF GREEK AND LATIN PHILOSOPHY

MARK EDWARDS

In the twentieth century, reading of Greek and Latin in the original has almost been confined to professional classicists and their pupils.[1] The frequency with which an author has been translated for the common reader is a measure of his standing in the popular or the academic canon. So far as it is possible to distinguish them, the latter is represented by the university imprints and the Loeb Library, the former by such ventures as Everyman's Library, the World's Classics and Penguin Classics. If the idiom of a translation is a fair diagnostic of its intended readership, it could once have been said that Loeb conceded most and Penguin least to the general reader. The later twentieth century, however, has seen a great expansion of university education in western societies, a corollary of which is that any text in common demand will also be felt to need an academic edition. Free translations are of no use to students, and when it is assumed that the majority of those reading any text will be preparing for an examination of some kind, copious annotation becomes a necessary instrument of pedagogy. This trend conspires with another – the demand for published "research" as a condition of tenure for many academics – to ensure that footnotes will grow on increasing in detail and volume, and that translations will become ever more pedantic. As postgraduate students come to form a large minority or even a majority, of academic readers, translations of this kind will serve as instruments for a preliminary reconnaissance of literature in a field which is being proposed for doctoral

---

[1] I am grateful for the advice of Professor Christopher Pelling and Lawrence Venuti.

study; if acquisition of the original language is deemed unnecessary, they may act as permanent substitutes for the original text.

My aim in the present paper is not to denounce these tendencies but to draw attention to some of their consequences for the study of Greek and Latin philosophy up to the renaissance. I shall comment particularly on the part that the mere existence of translations can play in the widening of knowledge, and at the same time on the injury or enhancement to an established reputation that can arise from the absence or availability of new academic versions. I shall make some comparisons between notable translations of the same author that have been produced at different times or for different audiences. Since the original research for this paper was undertaken more than a decade ago, I have made only passing reference to translations published in the twentieth century: to attempt a more adequate survey would have doubled the length of the paper without revealing any new tendencies or any falling off in those to which I have drawn attention. If my remarks were valid at the end of the twentieth century, I doubt that they have lost anything in cogency or substance as we approach the next quarter of the twenty-first.

The toils of Platonism

Plato, if not the greatest of philosophers, is the great artist among philosophers, and to reproduce his peculiar combination of felicities in English would require powers that are not commonly united in a committee. Consequently no one hand is likely to supplant the complete translation of his works by Benjamin Jowett, Master of Balliol College and Regius Professor of Greek at Oxford in the later nineteenth century.[2] Except for its mistakes, this is as faithful as the prevailing canons of elegance permitted, though, in his character as an Anglican clergyman, Jowett is unable to give a candid account of passages which celebrate homosexual love, and tends to use "God" as a proper name where other translators might seek a different rendering of *theos*. Translations of individual texts have multiplied since Jowett's day, and the appearance of one in a series of classics generally foreshadows an attempt upon the whole corpus. Both the genuine and the contested dialogues have been assiduously translated for the Loeb Library, each translator aiming to reproduce, according to his own principles, what his author said in Greek.

---

[2] Benjamin Jowett, *The Complete Dialogues of Plato* (Oxford: Oxford University Press 1871), often reprinted.

Prefaces and footnotes offered further assistance to readers, but even the Greekless reader of Paul Shorey's copious notes to the *Republic* (1930), strewn as they are with brusque assurances that "the translation is correct", will be able to see how many questions are foreclosed by the decisions of the scholar.[3]

The barriers to appreciation of Plato lie not only in the language but in his jokes, his harsh transitions and the argumentative quibbling of his interlocutors. These, if they cannot be disguised, can at least be palliated by a commentary, and the digressions become less arduous if the itinerary is laid out stage by stage. F.M. Cornford's versions of the *Theaetetus, Sophist, Timaeus* and *Parmenides* are divided into segments with interlocking summaries and italicised synopses.[4] Accusing Shorey of having devised an English that was intelligible only to those who could read the Greek original, Cornford eased the prose of its complexities and the text of its digressions. His method is pursued, without abridgement but also without the same richness of annotation, in Skemp's *Statesman* (1952) and Hackforth's *Phaedrus* (1952).[5] These are not books designed for the common reader, whose trepidation is apt to be increased by measures designed to curtail the labours of the student. Penguin is the first publisher to have commissioned a representative translation of Plato's works for a public wholly unacquainted both with Greek and with the world in which it was spoken. The enterprise has given rise to a noun, 'Penguinification', first employed by Trevor Saunders in an article which served as a manifesto for his translation of the *Laws*.[6]

Saunders notes that the reading of a difficult and unpopular text can be leavened by synopses of the content. At the same time, since the purpose of a translation is to draw the reader into the author's world, he does not favour a style that hides the idiosyncrasies of the Greek. Where Plato is grand, the translator should aim at dignity; where he is idiomatic, it is permissible to convey the change of register with an English colloquialism.

---

[3] Paul Shorey (*Plato: Republic*, 2 vols. (Cambridge, Mass.: Harvard University Press, Loeb Classical Library 1930).
[4] Francis M. Cornford, *Plato's Theory of Knowledge*. (London: Routledge and Kegan Paul 1935); *Plato's Cosmology*. (London: Routledge and Kegan Paul 1937); *Plato and Parmenides*. (London: Routledge and Kegan Paul 1939).
[5] J.B. Skemp, *Plato: Statesman*. (London: Routledge and Kegan Paul 1952); P.M. Hackforth, *Plato: Phaedrus*. (Cambridge: Cambridge University Press1952)
[6] Trevor Saunders, "The Penguinification of Plato", *Greece and Rome* 22 (1975), 19-28; Trevor Saunders, *Plato: The Laws* (Harmondsworth: Penguin Classics, 1970).

Consistency in the rendering of the same terms is desirable, but ought not to be pursued where it obscures the true meaning of the text. These precepts were tacitly acknowledged by most translators of Plato in the Penguin series, but are particularly fruitful when applied to a work that sits, like the *Laws*, on the margins of the canon. It follows, as a corollary to this last remark, that the boundaries of the canon may be ossified by the history of translation. Thus the *First Alcibiades*, which appears among the *spuria* in standard editions of Plato, escapes translation (except in Jowett[7]) because it is deemed to be inauthentic, with the consequence that the presumption against its authenticity has become intractable.

Faces of Aristotle

Translations from Aristotle have not so much confirmed as circumscribed the canon of his writings. The Loeb Library and Oxford University Press have both employed a battery of scholars to put the whole corpus into English; in series designed to serve the common reader, on the other hand, it is generally assumed that only the *Politics*, the *Poetics* and the *Nicomachean Ethics* will be of interest, though the World's Classics has added the *Physics*,[8] Everyman the *Metaphysics*,[9] Penguin the *Art of Rhetoric* and *On the Soul*.[10] Headings, synopses and the relegation of digressive matter to footnotes are among the measures adopted in such works to make Aristotle speak as though he were our contemporary. Lesser but seminal writings are translated in a much less popular idiom for Oxford's Clarendon Aristotle Series, in which the object is to translate with extreme fidelity, making no choice between interpretations of a disputed passage. The bald prose that results is bewigged in notes, more formidable than the asperities of the text itself to a reader who approaches it with only a general interest in philosophy. The series does not yet offer a full translation of the *Politics* or *Nicomachean Ethics*, nor has any been produced elsewhere with a similar apparatus of scholarship. To the reader

---

[7] Benjamin Jowett, *The Dialogues of Plato*, vol. 2 (Oxford: Oxford University Press 1892), 458ff. See further A. M. Archie, "The Philosophical and Political Anatomy of Plato's *Alcibiades Major*", *History of Political Thought* 32 (2011), 234-252.
[8] Robin Waterfield, *Aristotle: The Physics* (Oxford: Oxford University Press, World's Classics 1996).
[9] The books are rearranged by John Warrington, *Aristotle's Metaphysics* (London: Dent 1956) for the thousandth volume in the Everyman library.
[10] Hugh Lawson Tancred, *Aristotle: The Art of Rhetoric* (Harmondsworth: Penguin Classics 1992); *Aristotle: On the Soul* (Harmondsworth: Penguin Classics 2004).

who approaches him through an English filter, therefore, there are two Aristotles - neither of whom is the Aristotle of 'common readers' in the ancient world, who knew him chiefly through his more perishable, 'exoteric' works.

Classicists are apt to complain that little has survived of the Greek philosophers, yet half of what remains is not only unread but unknown by title to the majority of scholars. One of the great accomplishments of philology at the end of the nineteenth century was the editing of the Aristotelian commentators under the auspices of the Prussian Academy in Berlin. The series, running to 15.000 pages, was for a long time little more than a mausoleum for the remains of Alexander of Aphrodisias, Ammonius, Philoponus, Simplicius and a handful of less prolific commentators. During the 1980's Richard Sorabji, then Professor of Philosophy at King's College London, secured "generous and imaginative" funding from a coalition of British, Italian and American patrons which has enabled him to commission and supervise, book by book, the translation of this corpus into English. Of his collaborators few are novices, and many are academics of high distinction. Each has been expected to translate the Greek as closely as English idiom would permit, and to render every salient term with a single term, or batch of terms, that could be matched against the original in a glossary appended to the volume. Uniformity of nomenclature is not required, but is encouraged by the practice of submitting each translation in draft to a body of experts, most of whom are at work on other volumes. Each of the volumes, published by Duckworth, is heavily annotated, and concludes with a bibliography, an index of citations, a subject index and an index of the chief Greek terms according to the pagination of the Berlin edition, which is printed in the margins of the translation. The best fruits of the enterprise have been plucked for Sorabji's anthology in three volumes, *The Philosophy of the Commentators*,[11] a book rather more ambitious than its title, as its purpose is to facilitate comparison between exegetic and speculative treatments of the same topics in the writings of Aristotle. To this end, it juxtaposes gatherings from his own series with materials from Plotinus and his successors, newly translated and in some instances translated for the first time.

---

[11] Richard Sorabji, ed., *The Philosophy of the Commentators 200-600 A.D.* Vol 1: *Psychology (with Ethics and Religion)*. Vol 2: *Physics*. Vol 3: *Logic and Metaphysics*. (London: Duckworth 2004).

Greek Antipodes

The intended beneficiary of Sorabji's project and the Clarendon series is the university student, not the elusive common reader. As I observed in my preface, however, even the reader of a Penguin Classic is now assumed to require a battery of notes and a translation that could function as a crib. Earlier contributions to the series have been overhauled, augmented or superseded; authors such as Lucian and Plutarch, who have mastered the thoughts of other men but declined to play master to any school, have no place on the syllabus and therefore cannot hope to be honoured in their entirety with a fresh translation.[12] On the other hand, as no curriculum in the study of ancient thought can neglect its origins, an audience can now be found for an inexpensive version of the fragmentary and inelegant remains of the Presocratics. Jonathan Barnes's commentary in the Penguin Classic is meagre, his translations unavoidably tendentious and his choice of authors governed by conventions that he has no opportunity to examine.[13] For the maturing scholar there are volumes dedicated to single authors, in which every phrase of the English text is set beside the Greek and vindicated by an ample commentary. The sophists of the fifth century, however, are most conveniently studied in the anthology compiled for Penguin Classics by John Dillon and Tania Gergel in 2003.[14]

Tradition seems to have hallowed an anomaly in the case of Marcus Aurelius, whose *Meditations* (properly, admonitions *To Himself*) are almost studiously devoid of originality. It was in Matthew Arnold's notice of a new rendering by the schoolmaster George Long that he acquired his modern character as a shepherd for homeless Christians.[15] Long's version has been reprinted many times, although its style may seem more likely to numb the ears than to touch the conscience of today's reader: "When thou art offended at any man's fault, forthwith turn to thyself and reflect in what like manner thou dost err thyself." For all Matthew Arnold's strictures

---

[12] Thus Lucian is represented only by Paul, Turner, *Lucian: Satirical Sketches* (Penguin: Harmondsworth 1961) and Plutarch by a mere five of his *Moralia* in Rex Warner, *Plutarch: Moral Essays* (Harmondsworth: Penguin 1971).
[13] Jonathan Barnes, *Early Greek Philosophy* (Harmondsworth: Penguin Classics 1987).
[14] John Dillon and Tania Gergel, *The Greek Sophists* (Harmondsworth: Penguin Classics 2003).
[15] Matthew Arnold, "Marcus Aurelius", in *Essays in Criticism* (London: Dent), 207-230, first published in 1862. He is commenting on George Long, *The Meditations of Marcus Aurelius Antoninus* (Chicago: Chicago University Press 1990), also first published in 1862.

on the pedantry of Long, this rendering gallops by comparison with that of the Loeb translator, C.R. Haines: "Doth another's iniquity shock thee? Turn incontinently to thyself and bethink thee what analogous wrongdoing there is of thine".[16] The clergyman Maxwell Staniforth conveys the point without forced tropes or gratuitous archaism for Penguin Classics: "When another's fault offends you, turn to yourself and consider what similar shortcomings there may be in you".[17] Martin Hammond's new translation for Penguin is even closer to the original in sense and force: "When you are offended at the wrong done by another, move on at once to consider what similar wrongs you are committing" (2006: 101).[18] Perhaps few common readers will be so common as to prefer the effort of G.R. Hays for Phoenix Books: "When faced with people's bad behaviour, turn around and ask when you have acted like that".[19] Yet even this may not be an incongruous guise for the one philosopher of the ancient world who can still be read with the innocence of a disciple.

Latin: Prose or Verse?

A translation of a Latin philosophical text must be artful, or it had best not be undertaken. Everyman chose the latter course with Seneca, and he is poorly represented in paperback series. His letters to Lucilius appeared in Penguin as *Letters from a Stoic* (Robin Campbell, 1969), a change of title that deflects interest from the teaching to the man. Cicero's *De Officiis* (once commonly known in English as Tully's *Offices*) have also been translated under new titles both as political classics and as masterpieces of literature.[20] The *De Natura Deorum* (*On the Nature of the Gods*) is also frequently translated; on the other hand, one must go to the indefatigable Loeb Library for unabridged translations of the *De Finibus* (another work whose title defies an English gloss), of his two treatises in defence of scepticism (called in Latin the *Academica*), and of his dialogue with his

---

[16] C.R Haines, *Marcus Aurelius: Meditations* (Cambridge, Mass.: Harvard University Press, Loeb Classical Library 1916), 281-283.
[17] Maxwell Staniforth, *Marcus Aurelius: Meditations* (Harmondsworth: Penguin Classics, 1964), 132.
[18] Martin Hammond, *Marcus Aurelius: Meditations*, with introduction by Diskin Clay (Harmondsworth: Penguin Classics 2006), 101.
[19] Gregory Hays, *Marcus Aurelius: Meditations*. (London: Phoenix Books 2004), 165.
[20] Miriam Griffin, *Cicero: On Duties* (Cambridge: Cambridge University Press Texts in the History of Political Thought 1991); Peter Walsh, *Cicero: On Obligations*. (Oxford: Oxford University Press, World's Classics 2001).

brother *On Divination*.[21] The consequence of this neglect, however, has been to diminish his reputation as a thinker, and to foster the illusion that he was more a Stoic than a Sceptic, more handy with scissors and paste than with the instruments of critical analysis, and never profound except when quoting Greek.

The poem by Lucretius *On the Nature of Things* possesses a double interest, as an indisputable masterpiece of verse and as the one compendious system of Epicurean thought that remains to us from antiquity. While prose is the favoured vehicle of translators, it might be urged that metre permits a closer approximation to the quaint beauties which are forced upon Lucretius by the rigidity of the hexameter. In fact, verse neither bestows nor impairs the ability to distinguish the ornamental from the essential which is the test of a good translation. Lucretius' term for atoms, *corpora prima*, may have been chosen under metrical duress, but is rendered equally well by W.H.D. Rouse for Loeb as "first bodies", and by William Ellery Leonard in blank verse as "primal bodies".[22] Latham's "primary particles" and Ferguson-Smith's "ultimate particles"[23] may be felt impose too mature a vocabulary on a poet whose very words are the *corpora prima* of philosophy in his own tongue.

Most blank verse translations have, like Leonard's, been as blank as prose in diction and metronomic in their scansion. Anthony Esolin, by contrast, undertakes the task as the knowing pupil of an age in which blank verse can be written only in boxing-gloves.[24] He can make Agamemnon "shove his fleet off on a *bon voyage*" (1995: 28) without any warrant in the sense or spirit of the original Latin, while argumentative passages are sometimes introduced with a jaunty colloquialism – "it's simple too to figure out how lightning" (1995: 40) - reminding us of the techniques by which some

---

[21] Harris Rackham, *Cicero: On Ends* (Cambridge, Mass: Harvard University Press 1914); W. A. Falconer, *Cicero: On Old Age, On Friendship, On Divination* (Cambridge, Mass.: Harvard University Press 1923); Harris Rackham, *Cicero: On the Nature of the Gods, Academics* (Cambridge, Mass.: Harvard University Press 1933).

[22] W.H.D. Rouse, *Lucretius*, revised by Martin Ferguson-Smith (Cambridge, Mass.: Harvard University Press, Loeb Classical Library 1975), 7; William Ellery Leonard, *Lucretius: On the Nature of Things*. (New York: Dutton 1916), 4.

[23] R.E. Latham, *Lucretius: On the Nature of the Universe,* revised by J. Godwin. (Harmondsworth: Penguin Classics 1951), 28; Martin Ferguson-Smith, *Lucretius: On the Nature of Things*. (Indianapolis: Hackett 1969), 4.

[24] Anthony Esolin, *Lucretius: On the Nature of Things* (Baltimore: Johns Hopkins Press 1995).

scientists have cajoled the public ear in recent years. Lucretius, however is not colloquial, any more than he is mischievous or ironic: he writes in verse because Latin affords no models of expository prose. The English tongue, on the other hand has forked since the days when the same words could express the thoughts of a Milton and of a Newton (Latham, 1951: 16). Blank verse can become a vehicle for argument by becoming as blank as prose and aping the homogeneous diction of twentieth-century philosophy; but that is not the way of the professional poet, who teases his reader by abrupt transitions, startling shifts of accent and a trick of putting much of his thought in suggestion rather than statement.

One prose text whose aureate style is sometimes thought to demand a verse translation is the tale of Cupid and Psyche, which was embedded by Apuleius in his novel, the *Golden Ass* or *Metamorphoses*, and is felt by every reader to be an allegory, though no-one is yet agreed to have found the key. Robert Bridges' version in rhyme royal – miraculously literal, for all that it is divided into twelve books, each containing as many stanzas as there are days in the corresponding month – has been forgotten, though hardly superseded.[25] Another verse translation (1912) is from the pen of a clergyman, George Ratcliffe Woodward, who falls somewhere between John Gower and William Morris as he gallops in rhymed octosyllabic couplets through nine cantos, each named after one of the Muses, like the nine books of Herodotus.[26] Such ventures, however whimsical they may seem, give a truer notion of the blending of philosophy with the mysteries in this tale than the esurient translation of Robert Graves for Penguin Classics, which is the version most in use.[27]

There is no doubt that Boethius was a poet, or that his *Consolation of Philosophy*, done into English by King Alfred and Geoffrey Chaucer, is still a desideratum in any library of world literature. It is also a prime example of the Menippean style, in which prose alternates with an exceptional variety of metres. Chaucer used prose throughout, and the translator of the Penguin Classic blithely embraced this precedent[28]. The Loeb Boethius – now revised, and still the one bilingual edition

---

[25] Robert Bridges, *Eros and Psyche* (London: Bell).
[26] Geo. Ratcliffe Woodward, *Cupid and Psyche, from the Latin of Apuleius.* (London: Herbert and Daniel 1912).
[27] Robert Graves, (1950), *Apuleius: The Golden Ass* (Harmondsworth: Penguin Classics).
[28] V.E. Watts, *Boethius, The Consolation of Philosophy.* (Harmondsworth: Penguin Classics 1969)

purchasable by the general reader – matches the poetry line for line, with no pretence of metrical regularity (Tester, 1973).[29] More recently, the appearance of a fine academic monograph on the poetry of Boethius[30] (O'Daly, 1991) has emboldened two translators to render these passages in lines whose stresses match the long quantities in the Latin original.[31] The result, even when then stresses are marked with accents on the page, is an acoustic labyrinth, in which some ears will find less melody than in Chaucer's liquid prose.[32]

Plotinus[33]

The rediscovery of the Neoplatonists has at once enriched the literary culture of the British Isles and shaped a new course in academic studies. Plotinus of Alexandria (204/5-270) is now universally recognized as the father of Neoplatonism, and hence the most seminal thinker in the Greek tradition after Plato and Aristotle. Nevertheless, the first complete translation of his *Enneads* into English did not appear until 1930.[34] The author, Stephen MacKenna, was an Irish man of letters and a friend of the poet Yeats. Studies of the latter have portrayed him as a sceptical disciple of Plotinus, though he might be described with more truth as an admiring adversary. Before Yeats had MacKenna's book before him, the Alexandrian was but one in a group of magi whom he knew through the work of Thomas Taylor, polymath, mystic and voluble freethinker of the early nineteenth century.[35] MacKenna's new translation of the *Enneads* ensured that, while the works of Plotinus' students fell out of print and out

---

[29] J. K.Tester, *Boethius*: *De Consolatione Philosophiae*, with the *Tractates*, translated by various hands (Cambridge, Mass.: Harvard University Press, Loeb Library 1973).
[30] Gerard O'Daly, *The Poetry of Boethius*. (London: Duckworth 1991).
[31] Peter Walsh, *Boethius, The Consolation of Philosophy*. (Oxford: OUP, World's Classics 2000); S. Renihan, *Boethius: On the Consolation of Philosophy* (Indianapolis: Hackett 2001).
[32] See R. Morris, *Chaucer's Translation of Boethius'* De Consolatione Philosophiae (Oxford: Oxford University Press 1868).
[33] Since this was first written, a new translation of the whole of Plotinus into English has appeared, and it is characteristic of the modern age that it is the work of several hands: see Gerson (2018) in Plotinus bibliography.
[34] Stephen Mackenna, *Plotinus: The Six Enneads* (Chicago: University of Chccago Press 1990), initially published in stages from 1917 to 1930, then revised by B.S. Page (London: Faber, 1956).
[35] Thomas Taylor, *Select Works of Plotinus*, ed. G.R.S. Mead (London: Bohn 1929). First published 1817.

of histories of philosophy, those of the master himself would at last become current in a form accessible to the general reader.

The triumph of this version over Taylor's cannot be ascribed to its greater elegance, lucidity or fidelity to the original: Taylor's Saxon and monosyllabic "flight of the alone to the alone" (1929: 322) is a perfect equivalent for the Greek in the peroration to the last *Ennead*, which loses half its sense and all its melody in MacKenna's Latinate substitute, "the passing of the solitary to the solitary" (1990: 678). Again, in the opening sentence of the same treatise, it is Taylor who preserves the demotic vigour of his text – "all beings are beings through the one" (1929: 299) – whereas MacKenna slips once more into Latin: "it is by virtue of unity that all beings are beings" (1990: 671). Add to this his occasional choice of hinged abstractions – "intellectual-principle" for *nous* where most are content with "mind" or "intellect", and "reason-principle" for the more difficult *logos* – and it appears that he is aiming less at euphony than at a marriage of the exotic with the austere, more characteristic of translation from Chinese or Indian sources.[36] The new translation for Loeb by Hilary Armstrong – the soul of Plotinian scholarship in English for half a century – returns to the conventional equivalents for *nous* and *logos*, and is generally as simple as Taylor but more periodic: his version of the last *Ennead* begins, "It is by the One that all beings are beings"[37] Yet he purposely eschews the most famous phrase in Taylor's version, on the plea that it has nurtured a false conception of Plotinus as a mystic. Instead he translates the last words of the *Enneads* as "escape in solitude to the solitary", which is smoother than MacKenna's attempt but further from the Greek.

Other Neoplatonists

The only work by Porphyry to have been translated three times since the turn of the twentieth century is the *Isagoge* or introduction to logic. Like P.V. Spade's translation of 1994, that of E.W. Warren is designed for the student of mediaeval logic, who, unlike the student of classical thought,

---

[36] On the other hand, his rendering of *to hen* as "unity" rather than "the One" forestalls the common error of treating the One as a thing with which the soul may aspire to union.
[37] A.H. Armstrong, *Plotinus, Enneads*, 7 vols. (Cambridge, Mass.: Harvard University Press, Loeb Classical Library 1966-1984), 344-345.

has never been expected to know much Greek.[38] A new translation for Classicists by Jonathan Barnes is prefaced by a note that observance of English idiom and fidelity to the Greek are "mutual enemies," and in his own practice the Greek has rather the better of the English. "It being necessary, Chrysaorius, even for a schooling in Aristotle's predications, to know what is a genus and what a difference …"[39] (2003: 3) is a proem that seems designed to send the reader to his commentary. Warren's version – 'To understand Aristotle's categories, Chrysaorius, one must know the nature of genus, difference etc.' (1975: 27) – is intended for those who wish to read this work, as Augustine read it, without a master (*Confessions* 4.16.28).

Proclus has continued to be regarded, by the English-speaking classicist, as a study for bibliophiles, or for theologians. The reader who lacks both Greek and French must return to Thomas Taylor if he wishes to consult Proclus' majestic commentaries on the *Timaeus* and the *Republic*. His first translator in the twentieth century was E.R. Dodds, an Irish scholar who held the Regius chair of Greek at Oxford, and turned to the Neoplatonists, like his countrymen Yeats and MacKenna, in the hope of something better than religion. The stringent rationalism of Plotinus was in his view the only creed of late antiquity that had not been overthrown by modern science; if took up Proclus, it was because he offered more scope to an editor, and he revealed his own bias by choosing the most schematic, and hence the least characteristic of Proclus' works, the *Elements of Theology*. The beginning, as in all projects of this kind, is a manifesto and an augury. The rubric to the first proposition runs into English literally as "Every manifold partakes in some way of the one". The typically agglutinative sentence that follows opens conversationally, "For if it did not partake in any way". adopts a more academic register, "Every manifold in some way participates unity", then makes a sentence by itself of the following clause, "For suppose a manifold in no way participating unity".[40] The transitive use of the verb 'participate' looks back to Milton and Hooker; the clinical phrasing and atomic syntax, on the other hand, are dictated by the conventions of analytical philosophy. Thus we lose the conversational

---

[38] P.V. Spade, *Five Texts on the Medieval Problem of Universals* (Indianapolis: Hackett 1994); Edward P. Warren, *Porphyry the Phoenician: Isagoge*. (Toronto: Pontifical Institute 1975).

[39] Jonathan Barnes, *Porphyry's Introduction* (Oxford: Clarendon Press 2003).

[40] Eric R. Dodds *Proclus: The Elements of Theology*. (Oxford: Clarendon Press 1963), 3.

tone, which in Platonic literature is often most audible where the matter is most abstruse.

Translation of other works by Proclus has been slower. The American scholar Glen Morrow gave the *Commentary on Euclid* to English readers for the first time in 1970, but after his death in 1973, another 14 years elapsed before his version of the *Commentary on the Parmenides*, completed by John Dillon, left the press.[41] Those who attempt the more ponderous works that have yet to be translated will no doubt be as sorely exercised as Dillon[42] (1987: xlv-xlvi) by the want of an English word to supply an equivalent for the same Greek word in all cases, and by the difficulty of choosing between the higher and the lower case in rendering words for intellect and soul.[43]

Mediaeval Experiments

Rigour and exactitude are the sole ornaments of prose for a mediaeval theologian, and it follows that he will seldom be read with pleasure, or translated with any sense of profit, except by those who incline to his philosophy. Mere bulk may deter a publisher even where the mere eminence of an author gives him a claim upon translators, so that to this day many excellent works by Ockham and Duns Scotus cannot be read in the language of their own countrymen. So far it is a handful of minor authors who have been edited and had the 'sense coaxed out' of them[44] in the series *Auctores Britannici Medii Aevi,* printed on behalf of the British Academy by the Oxford University Press in America. Cambridge University's

---

[41] Glen Morrow, *Proclus: Commentary on Euclid's Elements* (Princeton: Princeton University Press) 1970. Reprinted 1992

[42] Glen Morrow and JohnDillon *Proclus: Commentary on the Parmenides* (Princeton: Princeton University Press 1987 xlv-xlvi

[43] As evidence of the continuing neglect of later Neoplatonism, readers may consult J. P. Warren (ed.), *The Routledge Companion to Ancient Philosophy* (London: Routledge 2014), which allots eight chapters to Plato, nine to Aristotle and one to Plotinus, while stampeding Syrianus, Proclus and Damascius into a single chapter and all the Aristotelian commentators into another. That the latter should appear at all is of course an advance on all previous volumes of this kind and a tardy vindication of the project of translating the Aristotelian commentators, which, according to Richard Sorabji. was opposed by Harold Cherniss. For further information on this enterprise see below.

[44] Alexander Broadie, *Robert Kilwardby O.P., On Time and Imagination*, vol. 2: *Introduction and Translation* (New York: Oxford University Press for the British Academy 1992), vii.

series of texts in the history of political science can accommodate Marsilius of Padua and John of Salisbury,[45] but the only scholastics to have found a place in series that were first conceived as libraries of world literature are Anselm and Aquinas. Penguin shuns the dogmatic works of Anselm, but his prayers and meditations, in the clear and sometimes musical prose of Benedicta Ward[46], join *the Imitation of God* and the *Cloud of Unknowing* as spiritual classics. In the old Everyman series (more hospitable to philosophy than its rivals), a volume dedicated to Aquinas mingles poems and hymns with extracts from the *Summae* and the Aristotelian commentaries. Once literature had come to be defined as that which is read in universities, it was possible for a more representative body of Anselm's writings to be published by Oxford World's Classics; the same publisher, declining to compete with the Dominican translation of the entire *Summa Theologiae*, has issued a selection from Aquinas in which lesser works predominate, some translated for the first time.

In translating Anselm, Brian Davies and Gillian Evans[47] – one distinguished as a philosopher, the other as a historian of theology – adhere closely to his constructions and are generally able to substitute the same English term for the same term in the Latin. There is no accommodation to modern idiom, except where (as is customary) a long cascade of clauses is broken down into two or three crisp sentences. Timothy McDermott, on the other hand, accelerates the magisterial rhythms of Aquinas. The first proposition of the treatise *On Being and Essence* runs, in the literal translation of George Leckie: "[O]ne should know, as the Philosopher says in the fifth of the *Metaphysics*, that being by itself is said to be taken[48] in two modes"[49] (1937: 3). MacDermott writes: "Note then that Aristotle says that there

---

[45] Cary J. Nederman, *John of Salisbury: Policraticus* (Cambridge: CUP, Texts in the History of Political Thought 1991); Cary J. Nederman, *Marsiglio of Padua, Defensio Minor and De Translatione Imperii* (Cambridge: CUP, Texts in the History of Political Thought 1993); Annabel Brent, *Marsilius of Padua: The Defender of the Peace* (Cambridge: CUP, Texts in the History of Political Thought 2005).
[46] Benedicta Ward, *The Prayers and Meditations of St Anselm.* (Harmondsworth: Penguin Classics 1973).
[47] Brian Davies and Gillian Evans *Anselm of Canterbury: The Major Works.* (Oxford: Oxford University Press, World's Classics 1998).
[48] For an exact translation, 'said to be taken' should read 'predicated'.
[49] George, G. Leckie, *Aquinas: Concerning Being and Essence* (New York and London: Appleton-Century-Crofts 1937), 3.

are two proper uses of the term being"[50] (1993: 91-2). These volumes in the World's Classics series mark the extremes of freedom and fidelity in the translation of a homogeneous dialect, in which there are no ambiguities or ornaments that resist conversion into an alien tongue.

The waning of Latin in the twentieth century stole the light from Eriugena and Nicholas of Cusa, the morning and evening stars of mediaeval thought. Eriugena's garrulous *Periphyseon* was abridged in the translation of the mediaevalist I.P. Sheldon-Williams, whose labours have now been eked out to the dimensions of the original by J.J. O'Meara, a specialist in the Platonism of late antiquity.[51] It is characteristic of the modern age that the second version puts the necessities of the scholar above the convenience of the ordinary reader. Nicholas of Cusa was also a thinker of some stature, and his claim to be a philosopher has been cemented by the addition of his *Catholic Concordance* to a series of texts in the history of political thought, published by Cambridge University Press.[52] On the other hand, Lawrence Bond's translation of his masterpiece, *On Learned Ignorance*, as a "classic of western spirituality"[53] camouflages the density of its arguments, which draw upon technical and abstruse traditions spanning almost a millennium of Christian metaphysics. There is no inaccuracy to complain of, only the fact that mediaeval philosophy must so often be represented as something else before can enter a popular format.

Translator's Renaissance

More and Erasmus were the two great wits of the renaissance. Sinuous eloquence was for both a lubricant to unconventional thoughts, and no reduction of their gilded sentences to plain English can be called an exact translation. The elasticity of English prose in the sixteenth century enabled the first translator of More's *Utopia*, Ralph Robinson, to innovate with dignity, though he is apt to become circuitous where the Latin is outstandingly

---

[50] Timothy McDermot, *Aquinas: Selected Philosophical Writings.* (Oxford: Oxford University Press, World's Classics 1993), 91-92.
[51] I.P. Sheldon_Williams, *Erigena: Periphyseon*, 4vols (Dublin: Dublin Institute for Advanced Studies 1968); J.J. O'Meara, *Eriugena: Periphyseon* (Montreal: Éditions Bellarmin 1987).
[52] P.E. Sigmund, *Nicholas of Cusa: The Catholic Concordance.* (Cambridge: CUP, Texts in the History of Political Thought 1991).
[53] Lawrence Bond, *Nicholas of Cusa: Selected Works* (New York: Paulist Press, Classics of Western Spirituality 1997).

dense or subtle.[54] This is the translation that the old Everyman Library and the World's Classics offer to modern readers, though it might be feared that the reader at whom they aim will find it scarcely more perspicuous than the Latin. Paul Turner, writing for Penguin Classics,[55] adopts a commonplace vocabulary and a terse, rectilinear syntax: the result, except for a peppering of clichés, is not ugly or unfaithful to the sense, but robs the work of graces which to More would not have seemed wholly superficial. A scholarly translation has now appeared as a Cambridge Text in the *History of Political Thought* (Logan and Adams, 2002).[56] The prose of Erasmus is more Ciceronian, his vocabulary wider, the structure of his *Praise of Folly* infinitely devious. Betty Radice, for Penguin Classics, retains the pedantic humour of the original, but couples it with a demotic brusqueness not so characteristic of Erasmus: "I certainly don't envy the 'mighty Son of Cronus' his she-goat nurse"[57]. Other translators of the modern era write less jauntily than Radice, though Adams, unlike Dolan, still allows himself an occasional contraction. Both, in their translation of the sentence quoted above, disarm Erasmus of his comic pedantry by turning the Son of Cronus into Jupiter or Jove.[58].

Marsilio Ficino was, by contrast, an exemplar in all his writings of the clear, harmonious Latin that served scholars in his time as a crib for Greek. Latin was a vernacular both for him and for his intended audience, and it remained true up to later twentieth century that the majority of those who desired to read him had no need of any mediating language. Sears Jayne, revising his scholarly and literal translation of *On Love*, was unable to name an English predecessor (1985).[59] The common reader thus owes no small debt to Michael Allen, whose editions of the commentaries on the *Phaedrus* (1981), *Sophist* (1989), and *Republic VIII* (1994) are all

---

[54] Ralph Robinson, (1551) reprinted in Everyman's Library (London Dent 1910) and in the World's Classics in *Three Early Modern Utopias* (London: Dent 1999)
[55] Paul Turner, *Thomas More: Utopia*. (Harmondsworth: Penguin Classics 1965).
[56] G.M. Logan and Robert M. Adams, R.M. (*More: Utopia* (Cambridge: CUP, Texts in the History of Political Thought, 1995 and 2002).
[57] Betty Radice *Erasmus: The Praise of Folly* (Harmondsworth: Penguin Classics, 1971 and 1991), 17.
[58] J.P. Dolan, *The Essential Erasmus* (New York: New American Library, Mentor Classics 1964), 104, has "Jupiter" where R.M. Adams *Erasmus: The Praise of Folly and other Writings*. (New York: Norton 1989), 11 has "Jove". .
[59] Sears Jayne, *Marsilio Ficino: Commentary on Plato's Symposium on Love* (Dallas: Spring Publications), superseding his earlier translation for University of Missouri Press (Columbia, Missouri 1944).

accompanied on facing pages by an English version.[60] The longest of his translations is a complement to James Hankins' edition of the *Platonic Theology* (2001-2006).[61] All are equally close in sense and texture to the original; indeed, since Ficino's syntax is Italian rather than classical and the majority of his words have English cognates, it is not unusual for the rendering of a whole sentence to be perfectly homologous with the Latin. Thus, on p. 83 of *The Phaedran Charioteer*, we read in Latin *animum future poetae sic affectum esse, ut sit quasi tener atque mollis, praterea ut sit intactus*. On p. 82 this passes word by word into English: "the soul of the future poet must be so affected as to become almost tender and soft and untouched too". At times we might complain that the result is more of a calque than a translation: if one cannot make anything of the Latin on p. 125 of the same book – *Intellectus igitur intelligibilis est et maxime unum et universaliter universum* – one is unlikely to make more of Allen's English, 'So the intelligible intellect that is immediately born from it is one in the highest degree and universally the universe.' No doubt, in the spirit that once prevailed among Biblical translators, he thinks it better to leave the sense obscure than to pre-empt the interpretation of a moot text.

Concluding observations

A translator shirks his task when he transliterates, though a word of debatable meaning may be retained to pre-empt a choice between imperfect substitutes, as Richard Janko retains the term *catharsis* in translating the *Poetics* of Aristotle.[62] It is almost as grave a delinquency if he fills the page with terms that are merely calques on the Greek original, or adopts an unnatural and perplexing syntax in pursuit of a Latin construction. Mere paraphrase, on the other hand, is a crime akin to treason in the rendering of a philosophical text, where it should be possible to say of every word that it was chosen because no other would have expressed the thought so well. The difficulties multiply wherever a great exponent of ideas is also a literary artist: his genius will seduce many and

---

[60] Michael J.B. Allen, *Marsilo Ficino and the Phaedran Charioteer: Introduction, Texts, Translations.* (Berkeley: University of California Press 1981); *Icastes: Marsilo Ficon's Interpretation of Plato's Sophist.* (Berkeley: University of California Press 1989); *Nuptial Arithmetic. Marsilio Ficino's Commentary on the Fatal Number in Book VIII of Plato's Republic* (Berkeley: University of California Press 1994).

[61] Michael J.B. Allen, *Marsilio Ficino: Platonic Theology*, 6 vols. Text edited by James Hankins (Cambridge, Mass.: Harvard University Press 2001-2006).

[62] Richard Janko, *Aristotle: Poetics I* (Indianapolis: Hackett 1997), 7.

subdue them all, with the consequence that the most polished and felicitous translation of Boethius or Plato cannot hold the field as long as the most obsequious crib to an Aristotelian commentary, which "in affecting the ancients writes no language". Above we have seen instances of both, and we must remember that both are counterfeits. Translation is always a hedge between the reader and the original; the most literal and the most liberal ministrations differ only as pruning differs from topiary.

Bibliography

Includes only works quoted in the chapter or cited by title without full bibliographical particulars.

Arnold, Matthew (1990), 'Marcus Aurelius", in *Essays in Criticism* (London: Dent, Everyman's Library), 207-230. First published 1862, then in *Essays in Criticism*, 1865.
O'Daly, Gerard (1991), *The Poetry of Boethius*. (London: Duckworth).
Saunders, Trevor (1975), "The Penguinification of Plato", *Greece and Rome* 1975, 19-28.

ANSELM OF CANTERBURY

Brian Davies and Gillian Evans (1998), *Anselm of Canterbury: The Major Works*. (Oxford: Oxford University Press, World's Classics).
Ward, Benedicta (1973), *The Prayers and Meditations of St Anselm*. (Harmondsworth: Penguin Classics)

APULEIUS

Bridges, Robert (1885), *Eros and Psyche* (London:
Woodward, Geo. Ratcliffe (1912), *Cupid and Psyche, from the Latin of Apuleius*. (London: Herbert and Daniel)
Graves, Robert (1950), *Apuleius: The Golden Ass* (Harmondsworth: Penguin Classics)

THOMAS AQUINAS

Leckie, George, G. (1937), *Aquinas: Concerning Being and Essence* (New York and London: Appleton-Century-Crofts).
Gilby, Thomas (1963), ed., *St Thomas Aquinas: Summa Theologiae*. (London).
T. McDermott (1993), *Aquinas: Selected Philosophical Writings*. (Oxford: Oxford University Press, World's Classics).

ARISTOTLE

Warrington, John (1956), *Aristotle: Metaphysics* (London: Dent, Everyman's Library)
Janko, Richard (1997), *Aristotle: Poetics I* (Indianapolis: Hackett)

Aristotelian commentators, translated by various hands, ed. Richard Sorabji. (London and Ithaca, NY: Duckworth and Cornell University Press, 1987-).
Sorabji, Richard (2004), ed., *The Philosophy of the Commentators 200-600 A.D.* Vol 1: *Psychology (with Ethics and Religion).* Vol 2: *Physics.* Vol 3: *Logic and Metaphysics.* (London: Duckworth 2004).

BOETHIUS

Chaucer, Geoffrey (d. 1400), ed. R, Morris (1868), Chaucer's Translation of Boethius' De Consolatione Philosophiae (Oxford: Oxford University Press).
Watts, V.E. (1969), *Boethius, The Consolation of Philosophy.* (Harmondsworth: Penguin Classics)
Tester, J.K. (1973), Boethius: *De Consolatione Philosophiae*, with the *Tractates*, translated by various hands (Cambridge, Mass.: Harvard Universaity Press, Loeb Library)
Walsh, P.G. (2000), *Boethius, The Consolation of Philosophy.* (Oxford: OUP, World's Classics)
Renihan, S. (2001), *Boethius: On the Consolation of Philosophy* (Indianapolis: Hackett)

CICERO

Griffin, Miriam (1991), *Cicero: On Duties* (Cambridge: Cambridge University Press, texts in the History of Political Thought)
Walsh, P.G. (2001), *Cicero: On Obligations.* (Oxford: OUP, World's Classics).

ERASMUS

Dolan, J.P. (1964), *The Essential Erasmus* (New York: New American Library, Mentor Classics)
Radice, B. (1991), *Erasmus: The Praise of Folly* (Harmondsworth: Penguin Classics, initially published 1971).
Adams, R.M. (1989), *Erasmus: The Praise of Folly and other Writings.* (New York: Norton).

ERI(U)GENA

Sheldon_Williams, I.P. (1968), *Erigena: Periphyseon*, ed. and trans., 4vols (Dublin: Dublin Institute for Advanced Studies)
O'Meara, J.J. (1987), *Eriugena: Periphyseon* (Montreal: Éditions Bellarmin)

FICINO

Jayne, Sears (1985), *Marsilio Ficino: Commentary on Plato's Symposium on Love* (Dallas: Spring Publications), superseding his earlier translation (1944) for University of Missouri Press (Columbia, Missouri).
Allen, Michael J.B. (1981), *Marsilo Ficino and the Phaedran Charioteer: Introduction, Texts, Translations*. (Berkeley: University of California Press)
Allen, Michael J.B. (1989), *Icastes: Marsilo Ficon's Interpretation of Plato's Sophist*. (Berkeley: University of California Press)
Allen, Michael J. B. (1994), *Nuptial Arithmetic. Marsilio Ficino's Commentary on the Fatal Number in Book VIII of Plato's Republic* (Berkeley: University of California Press).
Allen, Michael J.B. (2001-2006). *Marsilio Ficino: Platonic Theology*, 6 vols. Text edited by James Hankins (Cambridge, Mass.: Harvard University Press).

GREEK PHILOSOPHY

Barnes, J. (1987), *Early Greek Philosophy* (Harmondsworth: Penguin Classics).
Dillon, John and Gergel, Tania (2003), *The Greek Sophists* (Harmondsworth: Penguin Classics).
Turner, Paul (1961), *Lucian: Satirical Sketches* (Harmondsworth: Penguin Classics).
Warner, Rex (1971*), Plutarch: Moral Essays* (Harmondsworth: Penguin Classics).

LUCRETIUS

Leonard, William Ellery (1916). *Lucretius: On the Nature of Things*. (New York: Dutton). Reprinted in Everyman Library from 1921.

Rouse, W.H.D. (1975), *Lucretius*, revised by Martin Ferguson-Smith (Cambridge, Mass.: Harvard University Press, Loeb Classical Library, initially published 1924)
Latham, R.E. (1951), *Lucretius: On the Nature of the Universe,* revised by J. Godwin. (Harmondsworth: Penguin Classics). Revised in 1994.
Ferguson-Smith, Martin (1969), *Lucretius: On the Nature of Things.* (Indianapolis: Hackett)
Esolin, Anthony (1995), *Lucretius: On the Nature of Things* (Baltimore: Johns Hopkins Press)

MARCUS AURELIUS

Long, George (1990), *The Meditations of Marcus Aurelius Antoninus* (Chicago: University of Chicago Press). First published 1862.
Haines, C.R. (1916), *Marcus Aurelius: Meditations* (Cambridge, Mass.: Harvard Universaity Press, Loeb Classical Library). Revised 1930.
Staniforth, Maxwell (2004), *Marcus Aurelius: Meditations* (Harmondsworth: Penguin Classics, initially published 1964).
Hammond, Martin (2006), *Marcus Aurelius: Meditations*, with introduction by Diskin Clay (Harmondsworth: Penguin Classics).
Hays, Gregory (2004), *Marcus Aurelius: Meditations.* (London: Phoeinix Books).

MEDIAEVAL PHILOSOPHERS

Broadie, Alexander (1992), *Robert Kilwardby O.P., On Time and Imagination*, vol. 2: *Introduction and Translation* (New York: Oxford University Press for the British Academy).
Nederman, Cary J. (1991), *John of Salisbury: Policraticus* (Cambridge: CUP, Texts in the History of Political Thought).
Nederman, Cary J. (1993), *Marsiglio of Padua, Defensio Minor and De Translatione Imperii* (Cambridge: CUP, Texts in the History of Political Thought).
Brent, Annabel (2005), *Marsilius of Padua: The Defender of the Peace* (Cambridge: CUP, Texts in the History of Political Thought).

THOMAS MORE

Robinson, Ralph (1551), reprinted Everyman's Library (1910), World's Classics in *Three Early Modern Utopias* (1999).
Turner, Paul (2003), Thomas More: Utopia. (Harmondsworth: Penguin Classics, initially published 1965).
Logan, G.M. and Adams, R.M. (2002), *More: Utopia* (Cambridge: CUP, Texts in the History of Political Thought, initially published 1995).

NICHOLAS OF CUSA

Bond, Lawrence (1997), *Nicholas of Cusa: Selected Works* (New York: Paulist Press, Classics of Western Spirituality).
Sigmund, P.E. (1991), *Nicholas of Cusa: The Catholic Concordance.* (Cambridge: CUP, Texts in the History of Political Thought).

PLATO

P. Shorey (1930), *Plato: Republic*, 2 vols. (Cambridge, Mass.: Harvard University Press, Loeb Classical Library).
F.M. Cornford (1935), *Plato's Theory of Knowledge.* (London: Routledge and Kegan Paul).
F.M. Cornford (1937), *Plato's Cosmology.* (London: Routledge and Kegan Paul).
F.M. Cornford (1939), *Plato and Parmenides.* (London: Routledge and Kegan Paul)
J.B. Skemp (1952), *Plato: Statesman.* (London: Routledge and Kegan Paul).
P.M. Hackforth (1952), *Plato: Phaedrus.* (Cambridge: Cambridge University Press).

PLOTINUS

Taylor, Thomas (1929), *Select Works of Plotinus*, ed. G.R.S. Mead (London: Bohn). First published 1817.
Mackenna, Stephen (1990), *Plotinus: The Six Enneads* (Chicago: University of Chcicago Press). Translation initially published in stages from 1917 to 1930, then revised by B.S. Page (London: Faber, 1956).
Armstrong, A.H. (1966-1984), *Plotinus, Enneads*, 7 vols. (Cambridge, Mass.: Harvard University Press, Loeb Classical Library).

PORPHYRY

Warren, Edward P. (1975), *Porphyry the Phoenician: Isagoge*. (Tornto: Pontifical Institute).
Spade, P.V. (1994), *Five Texts on the Medieval Problem of Universals* (Indianapolis).
Barnes, Jonathan (2003), *Porphyry's Introduction* (Oxford: Clarendon Press).

PROCLUS

Dodds, E.R. (1963), *Proclus: The Elements of Theology*. (Oxford: Clarendon Press).
Morrow, Glen (1970), Proclus: *Commentary on Euclid's Elements* (Princeton: Princeton University Press). Reprinted 1992.
Morrow, Glen. and Dillon, John (1987), *Proclus: Commentary on the Parmenides* (Princeton: Princeton University Press). Reprinted 1992.

Mark Edwards
Christ Church,
University of Oxford, UK

CHAPTER EIGHT

THE NEOPLATONIC DEBATE ON EVIL IN LATE ANTIQUITY

CHRISTOPH HORN

One of the most important contributions to philosophy brought up by late antique Neoplatonism is its theory of evil. It inspired a number of later positions – especially the theodicies of Christian and Islamic authors – since it presents evil as a mere *sterêsis* or *privatio boni*, i.e. as something inferior, defective and un-substantial. This suits well a picture of the world as an ideal divine order organized by a benevolent creator. Neoplatonists try to avoid both a description of the sensible world as thoroughly bad and a dualistic interpretation of the creator as an evil demiurge. Apparently, the adversaries attacked by Plotinus who first developed such a Neoplatonic theory of evil (*kakon, kakia*) are dualistic Gnostics. As is well known, Plotinus wrote an entire treatise against Gnosticism (*Ennead* II.9 [33]) in which he both defended the relative goodness of the world of our experience and the monistic idea that each entity, even the lowest, has its origin in a single, absolute, transcendent principle which he called 'the One' or 'the Good'. Additionally, he composed a complete essay devoted to the topic of evil: *Ennead* I.8 [51]. Proclus later shared both this goal of Plotinus and his basic assumptions; he also dedicated a treatise to the topic: *De malorum subsistentia*. Nevertheless, he arrived at a view that considerably differs from that of his Neoplatonic predecessor.

To better understand the debate under consideration, it is useful to introduce a distinction employed in early modernity by Leibniz in his *Theodicée*: namely that between physical evil (*malum physicum*), metaphysical evil (*malum metaphysicum*), and moral evil (*malum morale*). The first signifies the type of natural evil humans have to face in the sensible world such as diseases, aggressive animals, or disasters such as floods or earthquakes. The second means the defectiveness of all things that are not perfect, i.e. which are not like God. The third is the evil willingly caused by men such as murder, robbery, or theft. Clearly, God or the demiurge of the cosmos is responsible for the first two sorts of evil; but is that a reason to blame him? Not necessarily, if a world-order containing these two sorts of evil constitutes a good universe altogether, maybe even the best possible (as Leibniz would have said). Should we, however, consider God as the origin of the third type of evil, the moral one? No, since one can plausibly argue that moral wrongdoing falls under the responsibility of humans. The difficulty here is that, according to the monism mentioned above, also human freedom to commit moral evil is given to us by God or the First Principle. Now, how can these difficulties be resolved and integrated into a comprehensive metaphysical picture? This exactly is what Plotinus and Proclus tried to achieve.

I. Plotinus' conception of matter as evil

The highly original position formulated by Plotinus rests upon the idea that matter (*hulê*) is evil. Moreover, he claims that matter is the 'evil-in-itself' (I.8 [51] 3,35-40; 8,13; 13,7-14) and that it is the 'substance of evil' (I.8 [51] 3,38). But not every kind of matter does fit this description; there is also an 'intelligible matter' which is not something inferior at all (II.4 [12]). The lower instantiation of matter is, according to Plotinus, a 'non-being' (II.4 [12] 16,3; II.5 [25] 4; III.6 [26] 7,1-19). In this respect, Plotinus is strikingly different from the doctrine of evil which we find in Middle-Platonism (cf. Numenius, fr. 52 des Places).

Plotinus justifies his theory by the following line of argument: Being evil basically means being defective (i.e. to exist in the sense of a Leibnizian *malum metaphysicum*). Although each derived entity is imperfect and unlike God, there are highly different degrees of their defectiveness, more precisely according to ontological rank of an entity. The final entity in the process of *top down*-derivation is matter. There exists nothing that is inferior to it and more defective, since matter is an entity devoid of any sort of form. If that is correct, then matter *must be* evil and the evil. It even must be the principle of evil, namely in the sense that every phenomenon in the world that can be described as having its evil aspect from matter and insofar as matter is involved (I.8 [51] 3,35-40; 8,13; 13,7-14). At the same time, the idea that matter is non-being does not mean that it is non-existent in the sense of a *nihil negativum*, but in two further senses: (a) in that of *nihil privativum* (*sterêsis*) and (b) in that of ‚being different from being' (like in Plato's *Sophist*) (II.4 [12] 16,3; II.5 [25] 4; III.6 [26] 7,1-19). The decisive passage in the treatise on evil runs as follows (*Ennead* I.8 [51] 3):

If, then, these are what really exists and what is beyond existence, then evil cannot be included in what really exists or in what is beyond existence; for these are good. So it remains that if evil exists, it must be among non-existent things, as a sort of form of non-existences, and pertain to one of the things that are mingled with non-being or somehow share in non-being. Non-being here does not mean absolute non-being but only something other than being; not non-being in the same way as the movement and rest which affect being, but like an image of being or something still more non-existent. The whole world of sense is non-existent in this way, and also all sense-experience and whatever is posterior or incidental to this, or its principle, or one of the elements which go to make up the whole which is of this non-existent kind. (transl. A.H. Armstrong)

Following Plotinus, matter is not an everlasting entity, let alone a second principle of reality. It is a product of a derivational process (the ultimate one), brought about by the penultimate level of reality, the lower souls (III.9 [13] 3,7-16). There must be something like matter (i.e. something completely deprived of any excellence) to end up the *top down*-derivation process. Otherwise, this process would be a *progressus ad infinitum* which were unacceptable. Each higher entity producing an inferior one is simply fulfilling its necessity when it produces a lower entity. This holds true also in the case of the lowest entity: the production of matter is not something bad even if what is generated, i.e. matter, is absolutely bad. Matter, by the way, is thereby not a direct product of the First Principle, but only an indirect and final one. And we should keep in mind that it is not an independent second principle as opposed to the first.

Additionally, Plotinus emphasizes that matter is devoid of any form and in this sense something 'unmeasured' and infinite (*Ennead* I.8 [51] 3):

At this point one might be able to arrive at some conception of evil as a kind of unmeasuredness in relation to measure, and unboundedness in relation to limit, and formlessness in relation to formative principle, and perpetual neediness in relation to what is self-sufficient; always undefined, nowhere stable, subject to every sort of influence, insatiate, complete poverty: and all this is not accidental to it but in a sort of way its essence; whatever part of it you see, it is all this; and everything which participates in it and is made like it becomes evil, though not essential evil. What sort of entity, then, is it, in which all this is present, not as something different from itself but as itself? For if evil occurs accidentally in something else, it must be something itself first, even if it is not a substance. Just as there is absolute good and good as a quality, so there must be absolute evil and the evil derived from it which inheres in something else. What then is unmeasuredness, if it is not in what is unmeasured? [But what about "measure which is not in that which is measured?"] But just as there is measure which is not in that which is measured, so there is unmeasuredness which is not in the unmeasured. If it is in something else, it is either in something unmeasured – and then this something will have no need of unmeasuredness if it is unmeasured itself – or in something measured; but it is not possible for that which is measured to have unmeasuredness in the respect in which it is measured. So there must be something which is unbounded in itself and absolutely formless and has all the other attributes which we mentioned before as characterizing the nature of evil; and if there is anything of the same sort posterior to this, it either has an admixture of this or is of the same sort because it directs its attention towards it, or because it is productive of something of this kind. So that which underlies figures and forms and shapes and measures and limits, decked out with an adornment which belongs to something else, having no good of its own, only a shadow in comparison with real being, is the substance of evil (if there really can be a substance of evil); this is what our argument discovers to be the primal evil, absolute evil. (transl. A.H. Armstrong)

This remarkable text seems to follow a famous paradigm: that of Parmenides who, in this poem, develops a list of characteristics (*sêmata*) to describe the ontological essence of being (*DK* 28B8.1-21). Plotinus attributes to matter the terms 'unmeasuredness' (*ametrian*), borderlessness (*apeiron*), being formless (*aneideon*) and being permanently indigent (*aei endees*); matter is 'always indeterminate' (*aei ahoriston*), 'never stable' (*oudamê hestôs*), 'open for all sorts of impact' (*pampathes*), 'insatiable' (*akorêton*) and 'complete poverty' (*penia panteles*). Nevertheless, Plotinus does not share the conviction of the Gnostics that the sensible world is bad. On the contrary, he believes that it is as good as it can be (II.9[33]4,22-32) given the *top down*-derivation which is based on the idea of an increasing decline in excellence.

Moral evil (a state of a wicked person) must be, according to Plotinus, distinguished from evil in the sense above (the *malum physicum* and the *malum metaphysicum*). The *malum morale* comes up in a soul which turns to matter. Only by the voluntary turn of the soul towards matter its wicked character can be explained, namely by getting involved in material things and by being thus deprived. The process of the soul's turning towards the lower world and especially towards matter is described by Plotinus in an interesting passage (*Ennead* III.9 [13] 3,7-16):

> But the [universal] Soul is always above, where it is natural for it to be: that which comes next to it is the All [the physical universe] both the immediately neighboring part and that which is beneath the sun. The partial soul, then, is illuminated when it goes towards that which is before it – for then it meets reality – but when it goes towards what comes after it, it goes

towards non-existence. But it does this, when it goes towards itself, for, wishing to be directed towards itself it makes an image of itself, the non-existent, as if walking on emptiness and becoming more indefinite; and the indefinite image of this is every way dark: for it is altogether without reason and unintelligent and stands far removed from reality. Up to the time between it is in its own world, but when it looks at the image again, as it were directing its attention to it a second time, it forms it and goes into it rejoicing. (transl. A.H. Armstrong)

Maybe the text shows a certain confusion about the ultimate origin of moral evil. At least, there seems to occur a serious shortcoming within the Plotinian account since he clearly says that only a soul already affected by matter is so weak that it turns to matter; but at the same time, he believes that it is matter that weakens the soul. Proclus, as we shall see in a moment, will attack this point made by Plotinus.

Since (according to what we said above) matter is not only potentiality (in the Aristotelian sense of a *hupokeimenon*), but also ‚different from being' (in the Platonic sense of matter as *chôra* spelled out in the *Timaeus*), it is not only mere plasticity, but has an active faculty to deprive and reduce whatever comes into contact with it. Matter is not primarily described as inert and passive, but as rather unstable and fugitive. In an extremely impressive metaphysical text, Plotinus describes the ontological nature of matter as follows (*Ennead* VI.6[34]3):

> But how can this infinite really exist as infinite? For what really exists and is, is already determined by number. But before we consider that, if there is really multiplicity in the real beings, how is multiplicity evil? Now [multiplicity there is not evil] because the multiplicity is unified and not allowed to be altogether multiplicity, being a one-multiple. And because of this it is less than the One because it has multiplicity, and in so far as it is compared with the One, it is worse; and since it does not have the nature of that One, but has gone out from it, it has been diminished, but it keeps its majesty by the one in it, and it turned back its multiplicity to one and there it stayed. But how about infinity? For if it exists in the real beings it has already been limited, or if it has not been limited, it is not in the real beings, but perhaps in the things which come to be, as also in time.[2] Now even if it is limited, it is by this very fact infinite [or unlimited]; for it is not limit but the unlimited which is limited [or bounded]; for there is certainly nothing else between limit and unlimited which receives the nature of boundary. This infinity, certainly, in itself runs away from the idea of limit, but is caught by being surrounded externally. But it does not run away from one place to another: for it does not even have any place; but when it is caught, place comes into existence. Therefore, one cannot assume that what is called its movement is movement in place nor does any other one of what are called forms of movement belong to it of itself; so that it would not be in motion. But

on the other hand, it does not stand still either: for where could it, when "where" came to be afterwards? But the movement of infinity itself seems to mean that it does not stay still. Is it then in a state of being up above in the same place, or swinging to and from? Certainly not: for both are judged in relation to the same place, what is up there and does not swing towards the same place and that which swings. In what way, then, could one conceive infinity? By separating its form in one's reasoning. What, then, will one conceive? One will conceive it as the opposites and at the same time not the opposites: for one will conceive it as great and small – for it becomes both- and at rest and moving- for it does really become these. But it is obvious that before becoming them it is neither definitely: otherwise, you have limited [or defined] it. If then it is infinite, and infinitely and indefinitely infinite, it could be imagined as either. And when you come up close to it and do not throw any limit over it like a net you will have it slipping away from you and will not find it any one thing: for [if you did] you would have defined it. But if you approach any of it as one, it will appear many; and if you say that it is many, you will be wrong again: for if each [part] of it is not one, all of them cannot be many. And this nature of it according to one and another of your imaginations is movement, and, according as imagination has arrived at it, rest. And the impossibility of seeing it by itself is movement from intellect and slipping away; but that it cannot run away but is held fast from outside and all round and is not able to go on, this would be its rest: so that one may not say that it is only in motion. (transl. A.H. Armstrong)

Plotinus believes that there are no real hylomorphic compounds or hybrids (this point is directed against Aristotle; and in a sense, he might therefore be seen as the first Cartesian). According to Plotinus, matter resembles the state of ‚a prisoner in golden chains' or a ‚decorated corpse' (*nekron kekosmêmenon*: II.4 [12] 5,18). Plotinus characterizes this aspect of matter as follows (*Ennead* VI.7 [38] 28,1-12):

> Now we must look at what follows from the discussion. For if everywhere what comes as a good is form, and one single form is the good for matter, would matter wish, if it had the power of wishing, to become only form? But if so, it will wish to perish; but everything seeks what will be good for itself. But perhaps it will not seek to be matter, but to be, and in possessing this to let its evil go. But how can evil have a desire of the good? But we did not assume that matter was desirous, but our argument framed a hypothesis by giving it perception – if it was possible to give it and still keep it as matter; but we assumed that when form came upon it, like a good dream, it came to be in a fairer order. (transl. A.H. Armstrong)

In this passage by Plotinus, matter is characterized by its self-destructive, self-annihilating tendency to strive for a form (VI.7 [38] 28,1-12). It is not easy to see how this might be reconciled with the idea that it is basically fugitive and unseizable. But doubtlessly, Plotinus emphasizes both aspects.

The theory of evil developed by Plotinus can be misunderstood in different ways. Sometimes, his doctrine has been seen as being close to Gnosticism regarding its denial of the material world and the characteristic ethical escapism (see e.g. Jonas 1971). But Plotinus emphasizes that the inferior world is as good as it can be and that we should 'flee' from it simply in the sense of an ascent towards the better reality (II.9 [33] 4,22-32). Furthermore, a potential misunderstanding results from the interpretation that, according to Plotinus, matter is completely non-existent (this reading has been advanced by Pistorius 1952). As D. O'Brien (1999) rightly pointed out, the non-existence of matter should be understood following the Platonic *Sophist*. The meaning of 'non-existence' in the Plotinian theory of evil is that of a contrast with the substantiality of higher reality (cf. I.8 [51] 10). Another false reading is based upon the thesis that matter in Plotinus' *Enneads* can be seen as a second principle that causes opposite effects to those generated by the One (we find a version of that reading in Schwyzer 1973: 275-278). But on a closer reading, Plotinus can be shown to severely stick to anti-dualism; the entire reality, including matter, is said to be a derivation from the First Principle (III.9 [13] 3,7-16).

A further mistaken reading is based on the idea that, following Plotinus, the human souls are unavoidably contaminated as soon as they come into contact with matter. If this were correct, then Plotinus could not defend the concept of human responsibility for the *malum morale*. Plotinus, however, clearly describes the 'fall' of certain individual souls as the result of a freely chosen, intense turn towards matter which then, consequently, corrupts these souls. Human souls become morally bad if and only if they consciously chose to prefer the material to the spiritual world (on this point, see the interpretation of O'Brien 1993 against that of K. Corrigan 1986). On the one hand, one can plausibly show that matter, in Plotinus' eyes, is a derivational product, caused by souls that are incarnated in plants (III.4 [15] 1).

On the other hand, scholarship has supported the view that souls become morally bad only if they voluntarily turn towards matter. This implies that it is wrong to think that, for Plotinus, the origin of matter goes back to a bad act of the soul (as Rist 1961 claimed).

II. Proclus' rejection of the Plotinian account and his alternative theory of evil as a *parhupostasis*

Proclus, on the one hand, shares the Plotinian convictions that there is (a) no second principle at work to create the universe (especially not a malicious one), that (b) the sensible world is good (against the Gnostics) and that (c) matter is the ultimate entity being in a state of inferiority which cannot be further reduced or diminished. On the other hand, he rejects the Plotinian idea of an intelligible matter. Concerning the question of evil, however, Proclus turns quite fundamentally against Plotinus' solution and rejects it in several respects.

One initial consideration taken by Proclus concerns the question in which we can assume a certain reality of the non-being as Plotinus does. He answers this question in *De malorum subsistentia* 8-9:

> 8. [...] Indeed, the same holds for being itself and the nature of being: in the higher realm being is really being and merely being, but in the last things, being is somehow mixed with non-being. For take that which in one respect is, but in another is not, that which at times is, but is not for countless times, that which is this but is not all the other things: how could one say that it is, rather than it is not, when it is completely filled with non-being? And non-being itself, too [is twofold]: on the one hand, that which absolutely does not exist – it is beyond the lowest nature, whose being is accidental – as it is unable to exist either in itself or even accidentally, for that which does not exist at all does not in some respect exist, in another not. On the other hand, [there is] non-being that is together with being, whether you call it privation of being or 'otherness'. The former [i.e. absolute non-being] is in all respects non-being, whereas the latter [i.e. relative non-being] is in the higher realm 'not less than being', as the Eleatic Stranger asserts, but when it is present among the things that sometimes are and sometimes are not, it is weaker than being, but nonetheless even then it is somehow dominated by being. 9. Hence, if someone were to ask whether non-being is or is not, our answer would be that what absolutely does not exist and has no share whatever in being has absolutely no being; however, we would concede to the questioner that what somehow is not, should be counted among beings. (transl. Opsomer and Steel)

Non-being, following the quoted passage, should be understood in two different ways, namely in the sense of absolute non-existence and in the sense of 'otherness' – as developed by the Eleatic Stranger in Plato's *Sophist*. Something beneath the lowest entity, something completely formless, cannot exist, not even as an accidental being. A relative non-being is accidentally defective. A solution to the problem of evil is impossible as long as one mixes up these two meanings. Apparently, this is directed against Plotinus:

> The same reasoning, then, holds for evil, since this is twofold too: on the one hand, that which is exclusively evil; on the other hand, that which is not, but is mixed with the good. We will rank the former beyond that which absolutely does not exist, inasmuch as the good is beyond being, and the latter among beings, for, because of the mediation of the good, it can no longer remain deprived of being and because of its being it cannot remain deprived of the good. Indeed, it is both being and good. And that which is in all respects evil, being a falling off and, as it were, a departure from the first good, is of course also deprived of being: for how could it have an entrance into beings if it could not participate in the good? But that which is not in all respects evil, is on the one hand ‚contrary' to some good, though not to the good in general; on the other hand, it is ordered and made good because of the pre-eminence of the wholes that are good. Andi t is evil for those things which it opposes, but depends on other things [i.e. the wholes] as something good. For it is not right that evil oppose the wholes, but all things ought to follow in accordance with justice or not exist at all. (transl. Opsomer and Steel)

For Proclus, there cannot exist something absolutely bad since that would be, at the same time, something completely non-existent. But nothing completely non-existent can be real. There can only be bad entities that are, simultaneously, good in some respect.

Form this standpoint, Proclus criticizes Plotinus in several points. First, he asks why and how evil can exist if the world is governed by divine providence. Additionally, he rejects the idea that there exists one single cause of evil. In Proclus' *De malorum subsistentia* we read (47,1-2):

> By no means we should posit one cause that is of itself the cause of evils. For if there is one cause of good things, there are many causes, and not one cause alone, of evils. (transl. Opsomer and Steel)

Hence, matter cannot be the evil-in-itself. Furthermore, according to Proclus, matter cannot be absolutely bad since it is derived from the One, the First Principle. The fact that this derivational process is an indirect one, is, for Proclus, irrelevant here. As an ultimate product of the highest reality, even matter must be a good entity, at least at some degree. In the background, Proclus is defending a principle of resemblance which he believes is valid between the cause and that which is caused. According to Proclus, Plotinus commits a mistake when he describes matter as an evil. What his predecessor is entitled to claim is only that matter is the least good entity in the universe. Describing it as intrinsically bad amounts to a secret introduction of a counter-principle to the One.

Instead, we should see the production of evil as a sort of involuntary byproduct (*De malorum subsistentia* 50):

> In order to exist in a proper sense, an effect must result from a cause which proceeds according to its nature towards a goal that is intended. [...] Whenever an effect is produced that was not intended or is not related by nature or *per se* to the agent, it is said to exist besides (*para*) the intended effect, parasitically upon it, as it were. (transl. Opsomer and Steel)

Proclus introduces here the concept of a *byproduct* (*parhupostasis*) and founds his theory of evil on it. As Steel and Opsomer explain Proclus point: „He argues that evil does not have an existence of its own, but only a derivative or parasitic existence (*par-hypostasis*, sc. on the good). Evils are shortcomings and mistakes; as a failure is never intended *qua* failure by an agent, but is an unfortunate by-effect of his action, so is evil *qua* evil is never produced by a cause. Therefore, Proclus continues, it is better to call its mode of existence a *parhupostasis*, rather than a *hupostasis*, a term that belongs to those beings "that proceed from causes towards a goal." *Parhupostasis* or 'parasitic existence,' on the contrary, is the mode of existence of "beings that neither appear through causes in accordance with nature nor result in a definite end."

Proclus further explains this thought in the following lines (*De malorum subsistentia* 50,3-9. 29-31):

> Evils are not the outcome of goal-directed processes, but happen *per accidens*, as incidental by-products which fall outside the intention of the agents. [...] Therefore, it is appropriate to call such generation a parasitic existence (*parhupostasis*), in that it is without end and unintended, uncaused in a way (*anaition pôs*) and indefinite. (transl. Opsomer and Steel)

The *parhupostasis* theory of evil seems to have considerable advantages to the *hulê* model of Plotinus.

There are still two Proclian objections left. First, according to Proclus, Plotinus is wrong when he identifies the weakness (*astheneia*) of the soul with its moral badness (*kakia*). A soul is morally bad if and only if it willingly or consciously turns to the inferior reality (instead of striving upwards towards the intelligible, divine reality). Proclus consequently blames Plotinus for having neglected moral responsibility which must be based on the idea of a free will. If Plotinus were right, "where would be the soul's self-motion and its ability to choose?" as he puts it (33,23). Secondly, Proclus rejects the Plotinian idea that matter has to be understood rather in the non-Aristotelian sense of actively depriving every form which gets into contact with it. Plotinus, according to Proclus leaves no (sufficient) room for (a) the potentiality/plasticity of matter and (b) for the strive of matter to ameliorate itself and to ultimately ‚return' to its cause.

III. Concluding remarks

The Plotinian solution had an enormous impact on the history of thought, despite the criticism advanced by Proclus. We find, e.g. in Augustine (who of course lived before Proclus' times) a well-developed Neoplatonic view of evil as non-being, quite close to the position of Plotinus. In the *De libero arbitrio*, Augustine claims that the concept of 'nothingness' is far from being meaningless. On the contrary, he says that "all defectiveness comes from nothingness" (*omnis autem defectus ex nihilo est*: II.54). He further develops this idea especially in the Confessions where he identifies the source of all evil as something 'formless close to nothingness' (*informe prope nihil*: 12.6,6). The radical innovation brought up by him, however, consists in his idea of an absolute free choice.

Augustine's innovative idea of an uncaused spontaneous will as the ultimate source of moral evil is best explained in a passage from the *De civitate dei* (XII.6):

> If the further question is asked 'What was the efficient cause of their evil will?' then the answer must be: there is none. For what is it which makes the will bad, when it is the will itself which makes the action bad? And consequently the bad will is the cause of the bad action, but nothing is the efficient cause of the bad will. [...] For if two men, alike in physical and moral constitution, see the same corporal beauty, and one of them is excited by the sight to desire an illicit enjoyment while the other steadfastly maintains a modest restraint of his will, what do we suppose brings it about, that there is an evil will in the one and not in the other? What produces it in the man in whom it exists? Not the bodily beauty, for that was presented equally to the gaze of both, and yet did not produce in both an evil will. Did the flesh of the one cause the desire as he looked? But why did not the flesh of the other? Or was it the disposition? But why not the disposition of both? For we are supposing that both were of a like temperament of body and soul. Must we, then, say that the one was tempted by a secret suggestion of the evil spirit? As if it was not by his own will that he consented to this suggestion and to any inducement whatever! This consent, then, this evil will which he presented to the evil suasive influence,— what was the cause of it, we ask? For, not to delay on such a difficulty as

this, if both are tempted equally and one yields and consents to the temptation while the other remains unmoved by it, what other account can we give of the matter than this, that the one is willing, the other unwilling, to fall away from chastity? And what causes this but their own wills, in cases at least such as we are supposing, where the temperament is identical? The same beauty was equally obvious to the eyes of both; the same secret temptation pressed on both with equal violence. However minutely we examine the case, therefore, we can discern nothing which caused the will of the one to be evil.

The remarkable point of this text is: in order to explain the fall of angels (or that of humans), we should not look at causes like pride (*superbia*) or arrogance (*arrogantia*). It is by their radical free choice that they go astray. This idea, found neither in Plotinus nor in Proclus (who at least criticizes his fellow-Platonist for this lack) seems to be the most important contribution of Christian authors to the Neoplatonic theory of evil.

Bibliography

J.-M. Narbonne: *Plotinus in Dialogue with the Gnostics*, Leiden 2011.
D. O'Brien: *Plotinus on the Origin of Matter*, Naples 1991.
D. O'Brien: „La matière chez Plotin: son origine, sa nature", in: *Phronesis* 44 (1999), 45-71.
K. Corrigan: *Plotinus' Theory of Matter-Evil and the Question of Substance: Plato, Aristotle, and Alexander of Aphrodisias* (II.4, II.5, III.6, I.8), Leiden 1996.
H. Jonas: "The Soul in Gnosticism and Plotinus", in: *Le néoplatonisme*. Royaumont. 9-13 juin 1969, Paris 1971, 45-53.
D.J. O'Meara: "Evil in Plotinus (Enn. I, 8)," in D.J. O'Meara, *The Structure of Being and the Search for the Good*, Aldershot 1998, §IX.
D. J. O'Meara: "Notes on the Aporetics of the One in Greek Neoplatonism", dans *Pensées de l' "UN" dans l'histoire de la philosophie, études en hommage au professeur Werner Beierwaltes*, édité par Jean-Marc Narbonne et Alfons Reckermann, Collection Zêtêsis, Paris / Québec, Vrin / Presses de l'Université Laval, 2004, 98-107.
D. J. O'Meara: „The Metaphysics of Evil in Plotinus: Problems and Solutions ", in *Agonistes. Essays in Honour of Denis O'Brien*, J. Dillon & M. Dixsaut (eds), Burlington, Ashgate, 2005.
J. Opsomer: „Proclus vs Plotinus on Matter (De mal. subs. 30-7)", *Phronesis* 46, 2 (2001), 154-188.
J. Opsomer: „Some problems with Plotinus? Theory of matter/evil: An ancient debate continued", *Quaestio* (7), 2007, 165-189.
P.V. Pistorius: *Plotinus and Neoplatonism*, Cambridge 1952.
J.M. Rist: „Plotinus on Matter and Evil", in: *Phronesis* 6 (1961), 154-166.
Ch. Schäfer: *Unde malum? Die Frage nach dem Woher des Bösen bei Plotin, Augustinus und Dionysius vom Areopag*, Würzburg 2002.
Ch. Schäfer: *Matter in Plotinus's Normative Ontology*, in: *Phronesis* 49 (2004), 266-294.
H.-R. Schwyzer: Zu Plotins Deutung der sogenannten platonischen Materie, in: Zetesis. FS Emile de Strijke, Antwerpen 1973, 266–280.

Christoph Horn
Institute of Philosophy
University of Bonn, Germany